Kathy McAfee was educated first at Vassar College, where she graduated with a BA degree, Magna Cum Laude, and subsequently at Princeton. In 1973 she co-founded City Life/*Vida Urbana* – a bilingual community-based organization in Boston, Massachusetts, with programs addressing issues of inner-city health, housing, employment and discrimination. For several years she held a succession of related posts – first as Project Director of Urban Planning Aid, then working as an advocate for community groups with the Massachusetts Attorney General's Office, and finally as a researcher with the Urban Analysis Group.

In 1983 she joined the staff of Oxfam America where from 1985 to 1989 she was a senior member of its Policy Research and Advocacy Unit. As Oxfam America's Development Education Officer, she has written extensively on international debt, the impoverishment of the Third World and the alternative development models and processes emerging in many parts of the global South.

D1598213

Storm Signals

Structural Adjustment and Development Alternatives in the Caribbean

Kathy McAfee

South End Press   in association with   **Oxfam America**

Storm Signals was first published in the United States of
America by South End Press, Institute for Social and Cultural
Change, 116 St Botolph St, Boston, Massachusetts, MA 02115,
USA, and in the Rest of the World by Zed Books Ltd,
57 Caledonian Road, London N1 9BU, UK, in association with
Oxfam America, 115 Broadway, Boston, Massachusetts, MA 02116,
USA, in 1991.

Cover designed by Sophie Buchet.
Cover photograph by Kathy McAfee
Typeset by EMS Photosetters, Thorpe Bay, Essex.
Printed and bound in the United Kingdom
by Biddles Ltd, Guildford and King's Lynn.

Library of Congress Cataloging-in-Publication Data

McAfee, Kathy.
    Storm signals : structural adjustment and
    development alternatives in the Caribbean/Kathy
    McAfee.
        p.   cm.
    ISBN 0-89608-420-5 : $15.00
    ISBN 0-89608-421-3 : $40.00
    1. Caribbean Area – Economic policy.
    2. Caribbean Area – Economic conditions
    – 1945–   I. Title.
    HC151.M38   1991
    338.729–dc20   91-683
                                                CIP

To my father, Glenn K. McAfee

Contents

Acknowledgements

More people than I can possibly thank by name have made this book possible. What began as a modest research project grew into the present work, thanks in large part to the help I received from literally hundreds of people in the Caribbean.

Development workers and grassroots activists were exceedingly generous in sharing information, insights, and introductions. Many of them, particularly the staff of the organizations listed in chapter 1, took on the project in part as their own. They helped to shape it into something we all hope will be of use to popular organizations in the global South and advocates of development with justice everywhere.

It was they who reminded me of the work's value when, on occasion, my spirits drooped. But such times were rare; over and over again I was inspired by their clarity of purpose and caught by their contagious enthusiasm for their countries and cultures.

While some officials of regional institutions and governments asked, for understandable reasons, to be interviewed off the record, many others put forward frank and thoughtful critiques of the policies of their own governments and those of their powerful Northern neighbour.

Not only development workers and officials, but also farmers and fishers, market vendors and shopkeepers, school teachers and seamstresses rewarded my interest in their lives with wisdom and wit. Those who invited me into their homes and communities invariably met with grace my nosy requests for everything from family histories, crop prices, and political views to recipes and dance steps. It was this, even more than the Caribbean's great natural beauty, that made my experience there unforgettable.

Oxfam America supported me during most of the writing of this book and helped make the direct participation of our Caribbean partner organizations possible. I am grateful to my colleagues at Oxfam America's headquarters in Boston for this and for their considerable patience, and to friends at Oxfam UK&I, Inter Pares and Oxfam Canada, and The Development GAP in Washington for their assistance and encouragement. Special appreciation goes to the female members, leaders and staff of virtually every organization I worked with for their understanding of the particular challenges that confront every working woman — which is to say every woman.

If it were not for my previous experiences as an anti-war activist and community organizer, I doubt I could have come nearly as close to an understanding of Caribbean peoples' struggles; for this I must especially thank the members of City Life/Vida Urbana in Boston, Massachusetts. Finally, I owe deep personal debts to Steve Fahrer, to my son, Sam McAfee, and to my parents, Glenn and Marion McAfee.

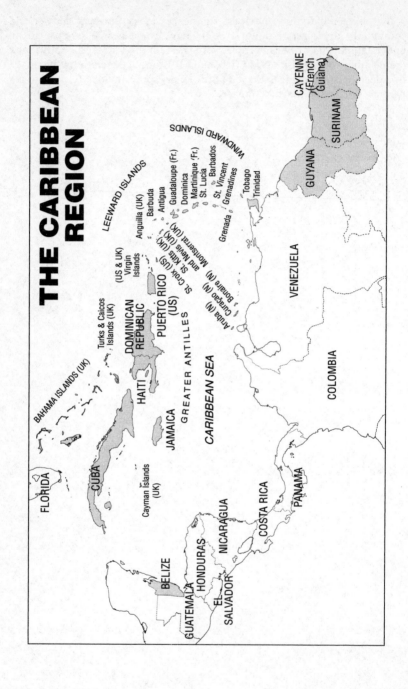

THE CARIBBEAN REGION

Part I:
The Deepening Crisis

1. Whose Caribbean

Look at an island, say, like Montserrat, or the others. If their governments could be persuaded to sell land for retirement homes for wealthy Americans, the place could be another Monte Carlo! The ones [Montserrat citizens] who stay would have higher incomes. But they don't want to do it. They regard the land as some sort of birthright.

A World Bank former senior economist for Jamaica

In the 500 years since the entrepreneur explorer Christopher Columbus stepped ashore in the Caribbean, human society and its environment have changed more rapidly than in the preceding five millennia of civilization. The age we think of as beginning with Columbus' voyage has seen unprecedented plunder and destruction, and also undreamed-of achievement. As a result, for better or worse, the world has become one.

It is a world in which the fate of five billion can be shifted by the decisions of a few thousand who control incalculable resources. At the moment when most of us on the planet are coming to realize that our futures are inextricably linked, the guiding principle adhered to by most of that handful of powerful people, and upheld as a precept for all humanity, is not that of mutual responsibility, but rather the pursuit of private gain in the unfettered free market.

Among the consequences of that principle, applied on the global scale, are hunger for many millions, privation and increasing marginalization for the majority, and the lack of rational connection between the distribution and use of the earth's resources and the knowable needs of present and future generations. In few places can the effects of this maldistribution of power and wealth be seen more clearly today than in the lands that Columbus first sighted, those of the Caribbean.

Many in Europe and North America will see 1992 as the 500th anniversary of a new age which culminated in the ascendancy of their nations. The same year will have a quite different meaning for most in the Caribbean. Consolidation of the European common market in 1992 will threaten the preferential trade agreements which have brought a partial and precarious prosperity to a number of Caribbean nations. At the same time, the likely acceleration of the effort by the United States to establish a US-dominated free trade zone encompassing all the Americas will pose an even greater challenge.

Will the Caribbean be further absorbed, as a source of even cheaper labor and natural resources, into the North American economic sphere? Or will Caribbean nations move toward greater unity among themselves and with their Latin American neighbors? The latter course offers the only hope for ending the pillage of the region by outsiders and for developing its resources for the Caribbean people's own needs. To whom will tomorrow's Caribbean belong?

The Caribbean Crucible

The 28 nations and territories of the Caribbean form a sweeping arc, stretching from Belize in Central America and the Bahamas east of Florida to the Greater Antilles (Jamaica, Cuba, Haiti and the Dominican Republic, and Puerto Rico), through the smaller Leeward and Windward island chains, through Trinidad and Tobago, to Guyana, Surinam, and Cayenne (French Guiana) on the northern Coast of South America. The region is home to 35 million people.[1]

The Caribbean is also the vacation playground of eight million visitors yearly, mainly from North America and Europe. Tourists are attracted by the promise of a brief escape to a tropical paradise. They come by air or on cruise ships, and congregate at beachfront nightclubs, casinos and secluded luxury resorts. There, waiters and waitresses, maids, guides and entertainers cater to the tourists' needs and desires. Visitors rarely have the opportunity to understand who these smiling Caribbean workers really are and what compels them to work at survival-level wages for strangers from abroad.

The minority of visitors who venture beyond the tourist enclaves are struck by the richness and beauty of the land, at least where deforestation or strip mining has not scarred the horizon. Brilliant birds and fragrant flowers abound. Where the soil has not been lost to erosion or overcultivation, the earth yields a bounty of fruits, spices, coffee, cocoa, coconuts, sugar cane, essential oils and an impressive variety of root crops, legumes and other vegetables. Few of those who consume Caribbean crops exported to Europe and North America are aware that many of the farmers who produce them themselves go hungry.

Hidden to casual visitors, other wealth lies beneath the soil: rich deposits of nickel, bauxite and gold in the Greater Antilles, Guyana and Suriname; oil and natural gas in Trinidad and Barbados. The vast rivers of Guyana and the volcanic mountains of the Windward Islands are potentially great sources of hydroelectric and geothermal energy. Yet in much of the region, rural households still lack electricity, and many Caribbeans cannot afford to ride a bus to work because of the high cost of imported fuel. Unemployment ranges from 20 to 50 per cent of the male workforce, and is even higher in some countries among women and youth. Available jobs often pays wages too low to support a family. Women who assemble electronic goods for export, or who labor on agricultural estates, typically earn the equivalent of less than five US dollars a day.

Most Caribbean countries lack unemployment benefits, and there are few government programs to help families meet the costs of housing and health care. Most households depend on the work, both paid and unpaid, of several adults, and often of children as well. Many families could not survive but for the money sent home by relatives who have emigrated.

The vibrant culture of the Caribbean echoes worldwide through its music. The sinuous rhythms of salsa, evolved from rhumba and its Spanish and African roots in Cuba and Puerto Rico, and the driving electric pulse of modern merengue, from the Dominican Republic, and cadence and zouk, from the Creole-speaking islands, can be heard on the streets of every major city in Europe and North America. Jamaican reggae and dub styles have influenced music around the globe. Yet to achieve success, most Caribbean musicians must leave the region and settle in the United States, Canada or Europe. Eastern Caribbean calypso and soca merge African rhythms and poetic traditions with Afro-American jazz and pop styles. Modern electronics enhance both traditional and ingenious newer local technology, such as steel drums fashioned from recycled oil barrels. The result is a music that expresses the joy of living, but also the deepening anger of people burdened by increasing hardship and discontent.

The Exodus North

While North Americans dream of a vacation or even retirement in the Caribbean, the idea foremost in the minds of many Caribbeans, especially young adults, is how to get away. 'I love my home of Bequia. I think it must be the most beautiful island in the world,' said a 16-year-old girl from the Grenadine islands. 'But I've made it as far as St Vincent, and as soon as I get the money, somehow, I'm heading straight for New York. There's no future here for me.' Said a banana farmer from the hills of Dominica: 'Banana prices are OK this year, so you can make it if you work like a donkey, but if prices go down or another hurricane hits, we'll all be scruntin' [barely getting by]. I'll have to leave my family and go to Canada again, and hope I can make enough money to send a little home.'

Despite their potential for prosperity, the economies of the Caribbean, as they are currently structured, cannot support their own populations. Consequently, the major export of the region today is *people*. An estimated 20 per cent of those born in the Caribbean live in the United States, while many others have migrated to Canada, Europe, or Central and South America. There are nearly as many Puerto Ricans in the United States (2.3 million) as on the island itself (3.2 million). Approximately one in three people born in the Windward Islands lives somewhere else.

The mass exodus continues despite tightened immigration restrictions in Britain and North America. So great is the desperation of many would-be emigrants that they risk their lives to escape destitution. Every year, thousands seeking clandestine entry into the United States perish when overloaded wooden fishing boats capsize in the dangerous Mona passage between the Dominican Republic and Puerto Rico, in the Guadeloupe Channel and in the Atlantic ocean between Haiti and the Florida coast.

The majority of Caribbean people who find employment abroad work as nurses' aides, cleaners, cooks, or in other low-paying service industry jobs, either because they have had little formal education or because they are denied access to better jobs because of racial discrimination. Seasonal migrants from Jamaica and Haiti are imported as virtual indentured laborers to harvest sugar cane and fruit in the southeastern United States, where they endure horrendous conditions in overcrowded labor camps.

Also among those who emigrate are skilled workers and professionals who cannot find jobs in the Caribbean in the areas for which they have been trained. A great many, if not the majority, of the Caribbean's most talented scholars, teachers and artists today work far from their homelands. Although sorely needed at home, many thousands of Caribbean carpenters, nurses, mechanics, accountants, technicians and administrators serve businesses and institutions in the industrialized countries. Their departure contributes to the brain drain that deprives the Caribbean of the talents of its best-educated daughters and sons. Meanwhile, the majority of the region's youth who complete secondary school at about age 15 find no means locally to continue their education and no place in the region's understaffed and underfunded universities.

The unemployed who cannot emigrate seek whatever seasonal or part-time work they can find: hauling wood to make charcoal, packing bananas, cutting sugar cane, clearing brush from roadsides or the villas of the wealthy, or selling candy, fruit and other goods on the street. Meanwhile, dire poverty and the lack of other options are causing growing numbers of Caribbean youth to resort to theft and other crimes. The use of hard drugs and the incidence of violent crime in many Caribbean countries have reached a scale unheard of only a decade ago.

The Structural Adjustment Ultimatum

While there are few paying jobs, there is much work that needs to be done: roads are badly in need of repair; in many villages there are no schools, health clinics or libraries; most houses in rural areas lack piped water and sanitation facilities; deforested lands need replanting; children of working mothers need day care; and farmers need the means to get their produce to markets. Many who had to leave school for economic reasons remain eager to learn to read and acquire practical and marketable skills.

Programs to address these needs are, however, being reduced, not expanded. Caribbean governments are cutting their expenditures on health, education, agricultural extension and other badly needed public services. Teachers, nurses, mechanics and technicians are being laid off by the thousand. These belt-tightening measures are part of the effort by Caribbean governments to apply the medicine of 'structural adjustment' prescribed for them by international lending agencies and governments of the industrialized countries.

During the 1980s, most Caribbean countries have experienced a dramatically worsening economic and social crisis. This crisis is reflected in the region's rising external debt, which reached US$21 billion, a staggering burden on the area's relatively small economies. While the world's biggest debtor, the United States, continues to drift on a rising tide of red ink, Caribbean countries are being told they must stop 'living beyond their means', or they will be allowed to sink.

This message is being conveyed by a powerful consortium of industrial country governments and multilateral agencies, led by the World Bank and the International Monetary Fund (IMF), and including the US Agency for International Development (USAID) and the Interamerican Development Bank (IDB). Currently, this consortium is pressing 22 Caribbean governments to adopt far-reaching economic and social policy changes. These changes, similar to those being imposed on many other indebted nations in Asia, Africa and Latin America, are packaged in the form of 'sectoral' or 'structural adjustment programs'. Countries which fail to implement the proposed adjustments are threatened with the cut-off or drastic reduction of loans, credit to buy essential imports and even food aid.

Adjustment programs are designed to ensure that indebted countries earn more foreign exchange and that the money they earn is used to repay their loans and to promote private investment. But the actual effect of structural adjustment is to deepen the dependency, poverty and debt of Caribbean countries. Structural adjustment programs are tailor-made by the World Bank, USAID and other creditors for each country, but all have a common thrust: to transfer more funds from impoverished debtor nations into the coffers of the Northern governments, commercial banks and multilateral lending agencies to which they are officially indebted.

Most Caribbean governments have been doing just that. The region is paying out more than it receives in total financial resources. In addition, higher debt service payments and more public spending on investment incentives result in even higher government deficits. This adds to the sea of public debt that already threatens to drown the foundering economies of the Caribbean. In response, the World Bank, the United States and other creditors are directing Caribbean governments to lighten their fiscal load by throwing overboard more of the public sector programs that have maintained basic services in health, education and small-farm agriculture. Adjustment also entails lower real wages, higher food prices and increased taxation of the majority. 'We ourselves, and our capacity to produce, are the collateral used by our heads of government who traipse to the World Bank and IMF for loans, against our knowledge,' observes noted Jamaican artist and scholar Rex Nettleford.[2]

Thus, structural adjustment programs are making it even harder for Caribbean people to survive in their own countries. In Jamaica, the first major test case for structural adjustment in the region, the policies implemented by the Manley and Seaga governments after 1977 were accompanied by decreased food production, increased malnutrition, a sharp decline in the number of students completing basic education and a serious deterioration in health services. The sponsors of structural adjustment, however, are more concerned with the credit ratings and export statistics of Caribbean countries than with the living conditions of the region's citizens.

Caribbean Solutions to Caribbean Problems

While crisis and 'adjustment' take their toll, Caribbean grassroots and non-governmental organizations (NGOs) are working to resist poverty-creating policies and to formulate an alternative, Caribbean-centered approach to development. Few believe that any single or simple economic model or blueprint can or should shape the region's future. Most agree, however, that workable solutions to the area's development challenges must be *Caribbean* solutions.

Caribbean development workers and organizations are not asking the United States or any other foreign governments or international agencies to develop the Caribbean. Rather, like many development leaders and grassroots groups in Asia, Africa and Latin America, they are asking Northern governments, banks and multilateral lenders *to change those of their policies that hinder development* by Caribbean people and nations on their own behalf.

For more than a decade, Oxfam America has been supporting the efforts of Caribbean organizations to devise and test new, more self-reliant approaches to development. Oxfam America and its sister agencies are building new relationships with NGOs and grassroots organizations in the global South (Asia, Africa, Latin America and the Caribbean). In this process, Caribbean organizations are not merely recipients of charity or vehicles for dissemination of resources and ideas from the North. Increasingly they are determining the nature, uses, terms and goals of external non-governmental aid.

Because of their direct involvement with the region's poor, NGOs have taken the lead in analysing the Caribbean's development dilemmas, identifying alternative options and proposing policy changes. Earlene Horne, General Secretary of the National Farmers Union of St Vincent and the Grenadines, is herself a farmer and a mother of eight. According to Horne:

> Most non-developed countries have had to look at the IMF and the World Bank as their saviours. But before they get a loan they have to pass the IMF test, cut back services, and 'put their house in order' even if the whole country has to go hungry to do it. We have to find a better way . . . I believe we in the farmers' organizations and unions and women's associations can do that.

As in other countries, women in the Caribbean are especially hard-hit by structural adjustment austerity. Women have been at the forefront of the resistance to lowered living standards and exploitative working conditions, and are among those advancing the most profound critique of structural adjustment. In addition, a woman's perspective on development alternatives is often a particularly holistic one, taking into account social and psychological as well as economic factors, and encompassing community as well as individual goals.

Projects carried out by Caribbean NGOs serve as a testing-ground and, at their best, embody or prefigure elements of an alternative model of development. Among the most effective projects are those that help farmers and working people to organize themselves, devise their own solutions to local problems and identify problems that cannot be solved at the local level. Says Earlene Horne: 'We NGOs in development have been building consciousness and skills, and bringing people into groups to figure out how to change things . . . We are analysing what it is we need to do ourselves and also what the government must do.'

Some of the projects carried out by Oxfam America's Caribbean partners may seem mundane and even insignificant in contrast to USAID's $200–300 million Caribbean budgets, the multi-million dollar schemes of the World Bank, and other mega-projects that promise a quick fix to the problems of the Caribbean. The programs supported by Oxfam America and its sister agencies, however, differ from World Bank and USAID schemes in a fundamental way: they are projects conceived and carried out by Caribbean people, using Caribbean skills and resources to meet Caribbean needs. They include:

- farmers organizing to maintain food crop production for local and regional needs, in the face of policies which offer loans, marketing help and other incentives only for export crops;
- producers' and workers' cooperatives developing practical technologies and marketing systems for foods and other goods processed from local crops and raw materials;
- young adults struggling to acquire literacy and economic skills so that they and their families can survive in a system that makes no room for them;
- women fighting for economic survival and success, equality and respect in the face of laws and customs that restrict their rights and devalue their labor, and in spite of media images that assault their dignity;
- teachers and animators working to strengthen leadership skills and build community awareness and pride among the residents of poor rural villages and urban neighborhoods;
- grassroots theatre groups, poets and musicians striving to rescue and renew traditional arts and values and to counteract the effects of commercialism and the seductive fantasy world of US satellite television; and
- regional organizations that link NGOs and grassroots groups in different countries in sharing experiences, planning programs and conveying views from the region to policy-makers in the North.

The models and methods of these projects vary, but most share the view that for the Caribbean to prosper:

- its resources must be developed and employed first and foremost to meet the needs of the region's own population;
- it is essential that Caribbean people, not foreign companies, governments or aid agencies, control the development process; and,
- if development is to benefit all Caribbean people and not only an élite, those

who have been impoverished and marginalized must be centrally involved in creating and applying a new development model.

Partnership for analysis and action

In preparing this book, the author was able to draw upon the insights and experiences of Caribbean NGOs, particularly in the Eastern Caribbean and Jamaica. This was made possible by support from Oxfam America, the direct assistance of the Caribbean People's Development Agency (CARIPEDA), and of researchers trained by the Caribbean Association for Feminist Research and Action. Atherton Martin, a policy analyst and development advocate from Dominica, provided valuable guidance during his tenure at The Development Group for Alternative Policies (The Development GAP) in Washington DC.

A process of interactive research with Caribbean NGOs was an essential complement to the author's own research for this study. During the first phase, the author made available to local NGOs and grassroots groups documentation of USAID, World Bank, and IMF programs and loan and grant conditionalities. (Such documents, although in theory available to the public in the United States and elsewhere, are rarely made accessible to the people they are supposedly designed to help.) Then, in a series of workshops in different Caribbean countries, NGO participants presented their own views and identified areas for further research.

In the second phase of the study, researchers identified by the NGOs investigated the actual impact of selected USAID projects and particular structural adjustment policies on affected populations and communities. The draft manuscript was then prepared, and later reviewed by representatives of 20 Caribbean NGOs, who met for this purpose in Grenada in March of 1989 under the auspices of CARIPEDA and Oxfam America. The participating NGOs were: Caribbean Peoples' Development Agency (CARIPEDA); Caribbean Conference of Churches (CCC); Women and Development (WAND); Caribbean Association for Feminist Research and Action (CAFRA); Windward Islands Farmers Association (WINFA); Eastern Caribbean Popular Theatre Organization (ECPTO); Projects Promotion (St Vincent and the Grenadines); Small Projects Assistance Team (SPAT, Dominica); Development Alternatives (Dominica); Association for Rural Transformation (ART, Grenada); Grenada Community Development Agency (GRENCODA); Association of Development Agencies (ADA, Jamaica); Projects for People (Jamaica); Folk Research Centre (St Lucia); Action Committee of Women Against Free Trade Zones (Trinidad and Tobago); Belize Agency for Rural Development (BARD); Grenada Cane Farmers Association; GRENSAVE (Grenada); Grenada Food and Nutrition Corporation; the Caribbean branch of the Canadian University Service Organization (CUSO); InterPares (Canada); The Development GAP (USA); and Oxfam America.[3]

The process of writing the book thus both built upon and also added to the ongoing critical analysis of development problems and alternatives by Caribbean organizations. The book is also a response to the call by Caribbean and other Southern peoples for Oxfam America and other Northern agencies to work more actively to educate their own constituencies and to mobilize their supporters to press for the transformation of our governments' trade and development policies.

Creation of a development alternative or, more likely, a spectrum of alternatives, is an active, ongoing process that is far from complete. It cannot be complete almost by definition, since the model (or models) must evolve through education, debate, practical experimentation and evaluation, in which the Caribbean's poor and working people must be the central actors.

Nor can the transition to more genuine development be an entirely harmonious and amicable process. Foreign banks and corporations and members of the Caribbean's governing and economic elites derive benefits from existing, poverty-creating structures. Multilateral aid and lending agencies have an institutional stake in maintaining their present, powerful role. Creation of a more equitable and sustainable economic system cannot occur without some degree of conflict and confrontation. Moreover, future political events and economic trends in the world, especially in Latin America, will affect Caribbean development options by erecting new constraints or opening new possibilities.

The elements of an alternative development strategy sketched in these pages are glimpses of a work-in-progress. Its completion depends primarily on the peoples of the Caribbean, but its chances of success can be enhanced if North American and European citizens work to alter those policies originating in our own nations that impede Caribbean development.

Whose Caribbean?

It is hard to avoid the conclusion that from the point of view of the powerful international lending agencies and foreign governments the Caribbean does not really belong to the Caribbean people. If millions more are forced to leave their homelands, or to remain there only to serve the wants of the world's wealthy for exotic foods, low-priced electronics and vacation retreats, that is not a problem that concerns the World Bank: 'There is no doubt,' remarked the Bank's senior economist for Jamaica, 'that emigration is an essential part of any development strategy for the region.' Through the lenses of the World Bank and other creditors, Caribbean countries appear not as the homes of people with their own needs and ideas, not as societies with their own histories and destinies, but rather as the potential source of so many tons of bauxite, so many board-feet of timber, so many shiploads of fruits or so many million worth of gadgets and garments for export.

Whose Caribbean is it? For nearly 500 years, Caribbean people have resisted conquest and invasion, enslavement and economic exploitation, the rending of families and communities and the imposition of foreign values. They have nurtured and drawn strength from their rich and unique cultural heritage and their strong ties to the land.

The challenge they face today is immense. It threatens the sovereignty not just of any one country but of the region as a whole. But Caribbean people are not ready to concede. Throughout the region and among its diaspora, daughters and sons of the Caribbean are working to regain their sovereignty and to reclaim and develop the region's resources for the benefit of its people. The movement for genuine development in the Caribbean has many aspects and actors: farmers' organizations and workers' unions, women's associations and community cooperatives, clergy and Christian-based groups, teachers, scholars, activists and artists. Their struggles, the obstacles they face and their visions of the future are the subject of this book.

Notes

1. The Caribbean region includes the independent nations of Antigua/Barbuda (independent in 1981), Barbados (1966), Belize (1981) on the Atlantic coast of Central America, Cuba (1898), the Dominican Republic (1844), Dominica (1978), Grenada (1974), Haiti (1804), Jamaica (1962), St Kitts/Nevis (1983), St Lucia (1979), St Vincent and the Grenadines (1979), and Trinidad and Tobago (1962); the US territories of Puerto Rico and the US Virgin Islands; the French island departments of Martinique and Guadeloupe; the British crown colonies and dependencies of Anguilla, the Bahamas, Bermuda, the Cayman Islands, Montserrat, the Turks and Caicos and the British Virgin Islands; the Netherlands Antilles, a partially self-governing Dutch colony; and on the South American mainland, the independent nations of Guyana (1966) and Suriname (1975) and French-governed Cayenne (French Guiana).

2. Author interview, November 1989, Mona, Jamaica.

3. Among the other Caribbean NGOs that contributed to the research for this book are the regional Caribbean Network for Integrated Rural Development (CNIRD); Projecto Caribeno para Justicia y Paz (Puerto Rico); National Association for Mass Education (NAME, St Vincent); National Farmers Union (St Vincent); Rural Transformation Collective (St Vincent); Caribbean Natural Resources Institute (CANARI); the Oil Workers Trade Union (OTWU, Trinidad and Tobago); the Haitian Association of Voluntary Agencies (HAVA); Movement for Cultural Awareness (Dominica); Association for Caribbean Transformation (ACT); Sistren (Jamaica); and Social Action Centre (Jamaica).

In addition, a series of three public forums organized by The Development GAP for the US Congress in the Caribbean between 1987 and 1989 provided a particularly significant opportunity for the perspectives of the region's NGOs and other Caribbean organizations on US–Caribbean economic relations to be widely heard. The author also gathered pertinent background information from the work of Peggy Antrobus of Women and Development (WAND), Crispin Gregoire of Development Alternatives (Dominica), Joan French of the NGO-sponsored Caribbean Policy Unit and scholars associated with Policy Alternatives for the Caribbean and Central America (PACCA, Washington).

2. Unnatural Disaster

A development assault has been launched upon our countries, conceived in the North and — as the events of the last 10 years have shown — *for* the North. We've seen countries that were self-sufficient in food and resources become net importers.

We've seen the use of reports and consultants to hide the impact of that development assault on the poor, used to justify structural adjustment. We've seen efforts to manipulate NGOs into bandaging the wounds from the World Bank machete. But the percentages don't show the pain; the figures don't show the faces.'

Atherton Martin, policy analyst from Dominica

The social and economic crisis facing the 28 countries and territories of the Caribbean threatens to sweep the region under a tidal wave of debt, depression and foreign economic control. This crisis, which had been building since the end of World War II, has intensified during the 1980s.

A Haemorrhage of Dollars

One telling fact denotes the depth of the economic crisis: in 1987, the Caribbean as a whole paid out US$207 million more to the foreign governments, banks and multilateral agencies that are 'aiding' the region than it received from all of them combined in the same year.[1] This net outflow of funds was mainly in the form of interest and principal payments on the region's foreign debt, which totalled US$20.9 billion in 1988. The removal of funds from the Caribbean would have been even greater had not a major portion of official debt bills been repeatedly postponed; Jamaica's debt payments, for example, have been rescheduled every year since 1979. The consequence is accumulation of arrears and even higher bills to be paid in the future.

Many in the Caribbean, as in other impoverished former colonies, dispute the validity of the debts on the books of lending agencies, commercial banks, and governments. These debts, they rightly point out, were taken on under pressure from the lenders themselves, and have been raised by inflated interest rates to levels far beyond the debtors' ability to pay. In addition, some add, if one takes into account the huge transfers of wealth from debtor to lender nations in the form of low-priced exports, the debts on the books have already been paid many times over.

The Caribbean nations with the largest debts are Cuba, Jamaica, the Dominican Republic, Guyana, and Trinidad and Tobago, which together are liable for 88 per cent of the region's total external debt, including arrears. Just three countries — Jamaica, the Dominican Republic, and Trinidad and Tobago — paid out a combined total of US$1.3 billion more in debt repayments and interest charges in only three years (1986–88) than they received in loans and grants during the same period.[2] In June 1990, the Caribbean country with the most severely depressed economy, Guyana, paid off back debt bills of US$237 million by taking on more than US$276 million in new debt, which it has slim prospects of paying back except by surrendering its patrimony in bauxite, gold and agricultural land to its foreign creditors.

Even though Caribbean countries have been paying out more in debt bills than they receive in new lending, the region's total debt continues to increase as interest charges accumulate and the rescheduling of unpayable debts adds to future charges. Even while private bank lending declined and IMF lending slowed, total Caribbean external debt grew by 125 per cent from 1980 to 1988. The Caribbean's debt service ratio (its yearly debt bills as a percentage of its annual export earnings) has more than doubled during the same period, meaning that Caribbean countries have been paying out a growing proportion of their declining or stagnating incomes.

While the total foreign debt of Caribbean countries is not nearly as large as the massive debt bill of Latin America excluding the Caribbean, which totalled US$368 billion in 1988, the burden of debt on Caribbean economics is as great or greater than that of Latin America. The debt of Caribbean countries as a percentage of the region's combined gross national product (GNP) is 79 per cent, compared to 44.2 per cent for Latin America. Caribbean countries owe US$752 for every Caribbean child, woman and man, although the per capita debt of Latin America is greater — US$982 for each Latin American citizen — than that of the Caribbean.

A relatively high proportion of the Caribbean external debt, 23.7 per cent in 1989, is owed to multilateral lending institutions, mainly the IMF, World Bank and IDB. Unlike private banks and foreign governments, the multilaterals rarely agree to reschedule payments or sell debt IOUs at discounts, and almost never consent to forego principal or interest payments. Although interest rates charged by the multilaterals are lower for some categories of loans than those of private banks, countries that cannot meet multilateral debt bills often have to turn to high-cost commercial lenders or make drastic economic sacrifices to meet rigid multilateral repayment schedules.

Caribbean countries' debts to foreign governments comprise 40.5 per cent of the region's total, in contrast to 11.5 per cent for the rest of Latin America.[3] While some governments, such as Canada, have agreed to forgive the clearly unrepayable loans of Caribbean debtor nations, the region's largest bilateral creditor, the United States, has not.[4] The remaining portion of Caribbean countries' debts is owed to banks and other private creditors. (In the rest of Latin America, the portion of total debt owed to private sources is much greater, 70.7 per cent.)

At least as significant as debt payments but harder to measure, is the removal of resources from the region by other means. The statistics above do not account for the outflow of capital in the form of profits repatriated by foreign corporations or in the form of legal and illegal capital flight (the transfer of funds abroad by individuals and companies). Nor do they include the most significant means of resource removal from the Caribbean and other countries of the South: the under-valuation of agricultural and mineral commodity exports and the exploitation of low-paid workers in Caribbean agriculture and manufacturing.

A special vulnerability

A very large percentage of what Caribbean countries produce is exported, rather than used locally, while a high proportion of what Caribbean societies consume is imported from abroad. Economists describe such countries as 'extremely open'. Jamaica, for example, exported 58 per cent of its gross domestic product (GDP) and imported goods costing the equivalent of 67.8 per cent of its GDP in 1985.[5] The Windward Islands of Dominica, Grenada, St Lucia, and St Vincent and the Grenadines export nearly two-thirds of what they produce and import goods costing the equivalent of about four-fifths of their GDPs. (A country's GDP is the combined final sales value of all income-earning goods and services produced in the country in a given year.)

When countries have little or no control over the prices of what they buy and sell, such openness makes them especially vulnerable to sudden losses of income when the world market prices of their exported commodities drop. In addition, decisions by the trading partners of small, open economies to increase or decrease their purchases of particular commodities can have a devastating impact on the exporting countries. In May of 1982, the United States slashed the amount of Caribbean sugar permitted under the quota system to enter the United States. The quota reduction was a result of the Reagan administration's effort to keep the support of a small but influential group of US Republican Party allies, mainly sugar growers in the southern United States. This politically motivated move reduced the value of Caribbean sugar exports to the United States by three-quarters.

Furthermore, when the demand for Caribbean commodity exports declines in response to economic recession in the countries that purchase them, the effects of this vulnerability are multiplied. A small decrease in the growth rate of the US economy results in the loss of millions worth of export earnings in the Caribbean Basin countries. The extreme vulnerability of Caribbean economies is made worse by the fact that they are relatively undiversified. This is true of many formerly colonized nations in the global South, but is particularly characteristic of most Caribbean and many African countries. Each produces one or a few main export commodities and each depends on one or a few main trading partners, from which it imports consumer goods and also goods needed to produce its export crops, mainly fertilizers, as well as machinery and raw materials for the small manufacturing sectors.

Under these circumstances, Caribbean countries cannot easily increase their earnings by shifting to the production of different exports for which world demand is greater or prices higher. When export earnings fall and outside loans, grants and investments decline, as has been happening since the mid-1980s, they must greatly curtail their imports. The effect of the reduced ability to purchase imports on such undiversified economies is an immediate decrease in domestic consumption and in the living standards of the poor majority, as well as impaired production of food and other goods for domestic needs and for export. The economic policies being pressed on Caribbean nations are increasing rather than reducing the defenselessness of Caribbean economies in the face of changing economic conditions and political alignments in the North.

The Costs of Indebtedness

The structures of production and trade that have drained material and human resources from the Caribbean have also created extremes of wealth and poverty and a disjuncture between the needs of the Caribbean people and how the region's resources are used. It was evident in the post-independence period of the 1960s and 1970s, before the intervention of the IMF, World Bank, and USAID, that this pattern could not be sustained without terrible human and environmental costs. But the direct involvement of these agencies has reinforced the region's impoverishing economic and social structures, deepened its dependency and established the conditions for further economic and social deterioration. Among the consequences are declining living standards and decaying social services, decreasing food self-sufficiency, and degradation of the environment.

Declining living standards and decaying social services
The social damage caused by fiscal austerity, deflationary adjustment and the shift of resources to export promotion can perhaps best be seen in Jamaica, which has experienced the longest-term and most extensive economic intervention by the multilateral lending agencies and, in the 1980s, the US government. A thoroughgoing study by the Working Group on Debt of the Association of Caribbean Economists (ACE) found that as a result of Jamaica's adjustment effort, which began with the country's first IMF agreement in 1977:

> real expenditure on social services was cut by 41 percent over the ten-year period, 1975/6–1985/6. The share of government expenditure devoted to debt service climbed from 21 percent in 1980/81 to 44 percent in 1986/7 . . . Real spending on education per Jamaican below 15 years of age fell by 40 percent between 1981/2 and 1985/6, most of this being concentrated in the two fiscal years following the 1984 IMF agreement. The impact on the quality of the educational services provided has been quite dramatic. One indicator is the rate of passes in high school leaving exams (CGE O level and CXC) which fell from 62 percent in 1980 to 34 percent in 1985.
>   Total real spending on health was cut by 35 percent between 1982/3 and 1985/6 alone . . . Low-cost housing is another item which fell casualty to adjustment programmes. Capital expenditure on housing in 1985/6 had fallen to some 11 percent only of the level of 1982/3 . . . The costs of

purchasing the least-cost basket of minimum food requirements for a five-person household, as determined by the Jamaican Ministry of Heath, increased by 429 percent over the six-year period June 1979 to July 1985.[6]

The Dominican Republic has undergone the Caribbean's second most extensive adjustment process. There, as elsewhere in the region, economic crisis rooted in structures of dependency has been exacerbated by rising import costs and declining export earnings. The crisis came to a head in the late 1970s. According to the ACE Working Group:

> By 1983 it became necessary to make the first IMF agreement . . . By February of 1984, the real value of the minimum wage had declined to just 42 percent of the level in January 1980. . . . Real per capita expenditure declined as follows: 31 percent on education in 1981–1985; 27 percent on health and social assistance in 1981–1986; 33 percent on housing, potable water, and municipal services during 1980–1985, and 45 percent on urban transport and communication in 1981–1984 . . . Infant malnutrition, grade III, in one of the principal hospitals in Santo Domingo increased from 14 percent to 30.8 percent for admitted infants between 1977 and 1986; and from 3.9 percent to 10 percent for infant out-patients. Maternal mortality in a major maternal hospital in Santo Domingo grew from 15 to 22 per 100,000 between 1981 and 1985.

Haiti, the Caribbean's poorest nation, has received funds from the IMF and other multilateral lenders since the 1970s. These loans, which have been extended with ever more stringent austerity and privatization requirements, brought Haiti's debt to US$957 million in 1987. As debt levels rose, the country's economy deteriorated. Agriculture, investment, imports, exports and consumption all fell further during the late 1980s, while consumer prices, government deficits and balance of payments deficits rose. Loans and structural adjustment have not alleviated the country's horrendous poverty, reported by the World Bank in 1990 as 70 per cent in the cities and 80 per cent in rural areas. Haiti's infant mortality rate has remained one of the world's highest, 114 per 1000 live births.

High petroleum prices in the 1970s helped to postpone economic crisis in Trinidad and Tobago, the region's only producer of substantial amounts of oil and natural gas, but economic decline set in with a vengeance in the 1980s. Between 1983 and 1988, the country's per capita income had dropped by 50 per cent while unemployment doubled. Trinidad and Tobago's external debt reached US$2.4 billion in the same year, equivalent to 57 per cent of the country's GDP, according to the World Bank. The annual debt bill was equal to a quarter of the country's export earnings.

In a desperate effort to cope with the debt burden, the Trinidad government undertook a series of IMF loans, beginning in November 1988, and increased the country's debt to more than US$3 billion. In conjunction, the government of A.N.R. Robinson imposed a series of austerity measures: it devalued currency for the second time in three years, imposed a 15 per cent value added tax (VAT) on most goods and services, and gave government workers a 10 per cent salary cut while letting others go at a time when the official unemployment rate was already 23 per cent. These measures soon led to food shortages, price increases and labor strikes. Some university students had to forgo graduation because they could not afford the new charge imposed by the government for graduation papers. Social tensions exploded in the arson and looting which accompanied the July 1990 hostage-taking of the Cabinet by members of the Jamaat el Muslimeem religious minority.

The worsening social effects of economic crisis and the adjustment response can also be seen among the member nations of the Organization of Eastern Caribbean States (OECS), even though these seven small countries have high average annual per capita incomes relative to those in the larger Caribbean countries. OECS country per capita incomes range from US$5,990 in Barbados to US$1,100 in St Vincent and the Grenadines, in contrast to US$1,080 in Jamaica, US$680 in the Dominican Republic, US$410 in Guyana and US$360 in Haiti. This puts the OECS countries in the middle-income range according to World Bank classification methods, but here, as in many other countries where wealth is distributed very unequally, per capita income statistics disguise the extreme poverty of a large sector of the population.

The OECS countries are especially dependent on foreign grants and loans, and during the past decade have become more so. According to World Bank figures for 1977–88, external debt levels increased from US$19.8 million to US$266.9 million in Antigua; US$5.2 million to US$26.4 million in St Kitts/Nevis, US$10.6 million to US$64.1 million in Dominica; US$8.0 million to US$48.4 million in St Lucia; US$4.7 million to US$46.0 million in St Vincent and the Grenadines; and US$9.2 million to US$80.1 million in Grenada. This rapid influx of loan money has not been translated into better living standards for most of the islands' populations.

In the area of education, for example, a World Bank 1990 survey reports that, 'The quality of education is low.' Fifty per cent or more of takers fail common entrance or 11+ exams in the OECS countries; these rates reflect the lack of secondary-school places, says the Bank. 'CXC examination . . . results show that many students are not successful in attaining their educational goals, a sign of wastage in the system.' In St Vincent and the Grenadines in 1986, 'only 12% of those writing obtained a pass in the C.G.E. "O" level in mathematics and only 27% in English . . . Enrollments in tertiary programs in all countries are often under 2% [of total school enrollments].'

The Bank study notes that, 'In general, public education expenditures have not kept pace with the total current government expenditure on nominal GDP.' This is hardly surprising in light of the strong pressure to reduce public spending placed upon all the OECS countries by the foreign governments that supply them with grants and loans, as well as by the multilateral creditors. This applies to countries such as St Vincent and the Grenadines, which have undertaken austerity programs in the absence of formal IMF and World Bank requirements to do so. In the OECS country which has followed adjustment strictures most fully and formally, Dominica, even primary-school enrollment declined during the 1980s.

Decreasing food self-sufficiency

Export-centered policies create disincentives for Caribbean food self-reliance at every point in the system of food production and distribution. Farmers can get loans more easily for export crops than for traditional staple foods. Available packages of fertilizers and pesticides are geared to export crops. Decisions about where farm roads and irrigation facilities are built are determined by the goal of maximizing export earnings. Many agricultural extension personnel have more knowledge of and interest in exports than in the production of food for local subsistence and sale. The problem is compounded because the farmers who grow mainly non-export crops are more often poor and because a relatively high proportion are women, who often face gender discrimination.

When farmers do produce food for local or regional sale, frequently they cannot earn enough to recover their costs. Farmers in Dominica who grow root crops and vegetables must compete for trucks and drivers with the more profitable cargo of bananas. Communities that once raised sheep, goats and cattle have planted most of their former pasture land in bananas and eat expensive frozen chicken, when they can afford meat at all. A village that was renowned before the banana boom for the high quality of the dasheen (a root crop) it grew produced almost none for sale for years until most of its banana crop was destroyed by Hurricane Hugo in 1989. Root crops, including dasheen, yams, tannias, eddoes and cassava, known as ground provisions, are the main staple of traditional diets in most of the rural Caribbean.

Women in Grenada who were encouraged to grow cabbages and carrots found the markets flooded because of lack of planning for staggered planting and varied crops. Shoppers in urban areas of Barbados and Trinidad find that the root crops and fruit from nearby islands are becoming more scarce and expensive. At rural stores in St Vincent, villagers can buy imported macaroni and canned beef but not locally grown staples such as tannias or pigeon peas.

Tons of citrus and other fruits go to waste in the Windward Islands because of lack of facilities for processing them. Imported soda and fruit-flavored beverages are sold from every store and on street corners in town, while local juices are often hard to find, and a fruit-juice processing plant in Dominica operates at 30 per cent of its capacity. According to a village schoolteacher in Grenada:

> One night I woke up and heard a loud noise going boom-boom-boom-boom. At first I thought it was another invasion. Then I realized it was just a strong wind knocking all the ripe grapefruits onto the galvanized [roofs]. It's a shame that most of that fruit would have gone to waste anyway.

Facilities for efficient transport, storage, processing and packaging of food for local and regional sale simply do not exist on a significant scale. Feasibility studies and the results of field tests for producing and processing more local foods and for alternative uses for existing crops gather dust on the shelf. Putting them into practice is not a priority of most Caribbean governments nor of the foreign agencies that influence their policies.

As a consequence, per capita food production for domestic use is declining in all but a few Caribbean countries, while many Caribbean citizens suffer from malnutrition. A survey by the Group of Experts who examined Caribbean Common Market (CARICOM) economies reported that 44 per cent of the region's population consumed less than the minimum dietary requirement for protein, and that 56 per cent had an insufficient intake of calories.[7] (CARICOM is a regional federation that includes the majority of Caribbean countries as members or observers.) Since then, the region's trade deficits have continued to grow, in no small part because of increasing imports of relatively expensive foreign food. The needless drain of resources from the Caribbean is symbolized by the fact that Geest Industries, the company that carries Windward Islands bananas weekly to England, makes more profit on the farm inputs, food and other goods it brings back to the islands in its fleet than it gains from the bananas it transports from the Caribbean.

Degradation of the environment
The process that keeps wealth flowing from South to North violates the natural environment while it undermines people's ability to earn a livelihood. In the Caribbean and elsewhere, the growing separation of those who control the process of production in industry and agriculture, those who do the labor and those who consume the final products results in a lack of incentives to carry out farming and manufacturing in a way that is sustainable and safe.

Investors who come to the Caribbean to take advantage of subsidies and tax holidays are not likely to be concerned about the long-term effects on the land and water they use, since typically they expect to move their operations elsewhere when the incentives expire. A major reason why multinational oil companies such as Hess and Shell chose to locate their refining and transshipment depots in the Caribbean was the relative lack of controls to prevent pollution. The predictable result has been the fouling of beaches and harbors and the depletion of fish and shellfish stocks.

In recent years, governments, international agencies and agribusiness corporations have promoted the increased use of imported agricultural technology to boost exports. The aerial spraying of toxic chemicals on banana plots, for example, also blankets nearby subsistence crops, vegetation, livestock and people, kills animals, seeps into village water supplies and is rarely monitored adequately. In Puerto Rico, which (along with Cuba) is the most industrialized and developed Caribbean country, poorly regulated mining and manufacturing has poisoned shores and inland water sources and reduced underground fresh water supplies to dangerously low levels. Another ominous trend in the Caribbean and in other parts of the South is pressure on indebted governments to accept payment for the dumping of toxic wastes from industrialized countries. Only an angry public outcry prevented the cash-strapped government of Guyana from accepting, in exchange for dollars, a shipment of several thousand tons of toxic waste from the United States in 1988.

The pressure to increase production of bananas and other export crops, combined with the lack of income alternatives, compels farmers to adopt agricultural practices that undermine the long-term productivity of the land and health of the people. Cultivation of steep hillsides and watersheds causes erosion and the loss of fertile soil. Increasing application of chemical fertilizers, herbicides and insecticides without careful planning also degrades the soil, and creates dangerous hazards for present and future generations.

Plans now under discussion would speed the extraction of timber from the region's few remaining virgin forests and divert waterways to produce power mainly for export industries. Utilization of forest and water resources should be part of any comprehensive plan for regional development. But the current situation, in which the need for quick cash drives most development decisions, virtually ensures that these resources will not be developed in the best long-term interests of the Caribbean people.

Consumers in the United States, Canada and Europe do not witness the human and environmental damage that results from the process of producing the Caribbean-grown or manufactured goods they buy. Meanwhile, the Caribbean workers and farmers who are affected directly by pollution and dangerous working conditions have little power to challenge damaging practices which are endorsed or overlooked by their own governments and encouraged in the name of export efficiency.

Exporting More, Earning Less

While 15 Caribbean countries exported more commodities in 1986 than they did in 1980, all but five earned less because of the drop in world market prices for their exports.[8] The prices of most Caribbean commodity exports continued to fall during the years 1987–90, while the gap between most Caribbean countries' expenditures on imports and their earnings from exports widened. With very few exceptions, Caribbean countries suffered substantial trade losses during the past decade. In addition, World Bank figures show that of 15 Caribbean countries studied, all but three showed negative estimated payments balances on current accounts in 1988. In 1987, the combined balance of payments deficits of the 15 countries added up to US$1.6 billion. This is a tremendous loss relative to the size of Caribbean economies; only eight countries in the region have an annual GDP of greater than US$1 billion.[9]

In trade between the Caribbean and the United States, the Caribbean has become the loser. The region's net surplus in its trade with the United States from 1983 to 1986 was transformed into a trade deficit by 1987–88. The value of total US imports from the Caribbean had already fallen by US$800 million between 1980 and 1983. From 1983 to 1986, in spite of the promised trade benefits of the Caribbean Basin Initiative, US imports from the Caribbean dropped an additional 30 per cent. Despite special USAID-funded programs to promote US private investment in the Eastern Caribbean, the region's share of total imports to the United States from foreign countries fell from 1.05 per cent to 0.73 per cent in the same period, the World Bank reports.

The global competitiveness of Caribbean exports also declined in relation to exports from the rest of the global South (Asia, Africa and Latin America). The volume of trade between the Caribbean and the rest of the world dropped by 2.6 per cent between 1980 and 1986, while the total value of Caribbean exports fell by 0.1 per cent.[10] The main reasons for the decline in the value of Caribbean exports relative to those of the rest of the global South are:

- World market prices have fallen for nearly all non-manufactured exports from the Caribbean.
- Slow growth of the world economy has lowered demand for primary products from the Caribbean and other countries of the South. Consumers worldwide cannot afford as much coffee, chocolate and other tropical products; many stagnating industries are using less oil and minerals.
- Synthetic or Northern-grown substitutes have increasingly replaced traditional exports from the South, such as corn syrup and aspartame ('Nutrasweet') in place of Caribbean sugar.
- Other countries of the global South are also increasing their exports in response to their own debt crises and to pressure from USAID, the World Bank, the IMF and other creditors; many of these exports compete directly with exports from the Caribbean.
- It remains relatively costly, primarily for reasons of geography, to produce export commodities in much of the Caribbean, particularly the small, rugged English-speaking Eastern Caribbean islands.
- Increased protectionism on the part of Northern countries has resulted in quotas and other barriers which restrict Caribbean imports. Because of lower quotas, US imports of Caribbean sugar fell from 5 million tons in 1981 to about 1 million tons in 1987.

The region's continuing and worsening earnings gap (income from exports and tourism minus the costs of imports), along with the decline in per capita food production, is deepening the indebtedness and dependency of Caribbean economies. Of the goods imported, at ever higher cost, by Caribbean countries, a growing proportion consists of finished consumer goods and processed and packaged food. In Jamaica, for example:

In 1989 the share of raw materials in total imports had fallen to 48 percent compared to 69 percent in 1980; the share of capital goods had increased from 24 to 31 percent; while the share of consumer goods had increased from 11 percent to 21 percent, in a total import bill that had grown by 56 percent. Consumer good imports have been the most rapidly growing component of the import bill.[11]

In other words, Jamaica is not only importing more and paying more for what it imports; it is also meeting fewer of its own people's needs by domestic production and processing of food and consumer goods.

Three Prescriptions for Growth

'I don't think anybody has the answers for the Caribbean, least of all the World Bank,' confided a Bank official in the summer of 1990, when asked why his agency planned further reductions in its financing in the Caribbean. 'Don't shoot me — I'm only the messenger,' a senior USAID official reportedly told Caribbean representatives when he announced yet another major cut in US assistance to the region earlier the same year. The IMF had no need to announce funding cuts; during the period 1984–88, the agency had already collected US$854.6 million more from the Caribbean than it loaned to the region in the same period; the trend has continued.[12]

Foreign assistance to Caribbean countries (excluding Cuba and the region's remaining colonies) reached a peak of US$1.6 billion in 1982 and then fell for the next six years at an annual rate averaging 14 per cent. A special 1990 World Bank report on the Caribbean regional economy forecasts an ever steeper decline in future foreign assistance, both grants and loans, including World Bank financing. At the brink of a new development decade, the officials in charge of external aid and policy directives for the Caribbean appeared empty-handed and bereft of hope. Their response to the region's crisis is a demand for more of the same austerity, privatization, export promotion and other free market policies that failed in the 1980s, but with less economic aid to ease the pain.

During the 1980s, Caribbean economies became weaker and the majority of Caribbean citizens became poorer; real per capita income in most Caribbean countries was lower in 1988 than in 1980.[13] USAID's own budget request for 1991 reports that:

> Widespread malnutrition, illiteracy, deficient educational and training opportunities, poor health conditions, and inadequate housing threaten to erode the foundations of the region's fragile democratic institutions and limit prospects for economic growth over the long term.

In their official reports, the World Bank and USAID present cautiously optimistic forecasts for Caribbean economic recovery. They could hardly do otherwise. It is the World Bank and the United States, along with the IMF, that today claim the right to set the conditions under which Caribbean countries struggle to reverse their development decline. They have more power than Caribbean governments to determine the context and direct the details of internal economic and social policies within the region.

From year to year, the emphasis of World Bank and AID policies for the Caribbean has shifted slightly. For a while, agricultural diversification was vaunted as the region's best hope for achieving economic growth. Then the low-wage export industry was seen as the region's salvation. As the 1990s began, tourism topped the list. What has not changed is the insistence by these agencies that Caribbean countries must 'adjust' to forces outside of Caribbean control, by adapting, developing or discarding their own material and human resources in response to the fickle and fleeting demands of more powerful economies to the North.

Most Caribbean governments have attempted to implement US and World Bank prescriptions. But on the whole, the results have been disastrous. A close reading of the World Bank's own reports reveals that the Caribbean economic crisis has not only intensified under Bank, USAID and IMF stewardship in the 1980s, but may be approaching catastrophe just when aid from these same agencies is rapidly being withdrawn.

Caribbean citizens, few of whom have access to World Bank reports, do not need highly-paid economists to tell them the region is in crisis. The symptoms affect almost everyone, the poor most directly. Women in public hospitals give birth unattended because health budget cuts have created a severe nursing shortage. More and more bright children are failing secondary-school entrance exams because cuts in education spending have denied them a chance to learn, and even many who qualify cannot get a place in high school.

While growing numbers of young women work in garment assembly sweatshops for less than the cost of supporting themselves and a single child, overall unemployment rates continue to climb. Signs of economic depression are everywhere: young men in clean but tattered clothes hawk food and trinkets for pennies or beg for work at urban intersections. At night, many must sleep on the floor of a friend's one-room shack or on the street. Increased food prices and health care costs are reflected in rising rates of malnutrition among children, low infant birth weights and high maternal mortality, especially in Jamaica, the Dominican Republic, Haiti and Guyana. Emigrants pour out of the region, many of them risking their lives to find employment abroad at sub-poverty wages.

Can the Caribbean's downward economic spiral be reversed? The sponsors of structural adjustment have proposed three main strategies which, they contend, in the context of structural adjustment could turn the region's economies around. However, none of the three — more agro-exports, increased low-wage manufacturing and expanded tourism — nor all three combined, is likely, in light of current trends, to save the region.

Bleak forecast for agricultural exports

The almost certain prospect in the realm of agricultural exports, still the largest source of income for most countries in the area, is further loss of the region's limited competitive advantage. Sugar remains the Caribbean's most important agricultural export; it is about nine times more significant as a source of foreign exchange to Caribbean countries than to the rest of the global South.[14] Reinstatement of protectionist policies by the United States in 1982 cut the region's sugar exports to the US by more than 80 per cent, an economic blow from which the area has not recovered. World sugar prices may increase slightly, the World Bank predicts, and the US government is under pressure to reduce its quota barriers to sugar imports. But even if the US does accept a bit of its own free trade medicine, countries such as Brazil which produce sugar more cheaply are more likely to benefit than Caribbean sugar exporters. Nor can the current preferences granted by the Caribbean's largest sugar market, the European Community (EC), be counted upon in the 1990s.

Jamaica, Belize, Surinam and, especially, the English-speaking Windward Islands are heavily dependent on the market preference granted them by Britain for their banana exports. Free trade may soon end this arrangement. After tariff barriers among European nations are dismantled in 1992, there will be little to prevent Germany, France or other European countries from selling the bananas they import from Africa and Latin America to the United Kingdom. Most Caribbean-grown bananas cannot compete with fruit produced more cheaply in these regions. Already competition from these sources has resulted in lower earnings for Caribbean banana exports.

The free trade outlook is also poor for all the other most important Caribbean agricultural exports. An excess supply of cocoa on world markets is likely to mean lost earnings for the Dominican Republic, Haiti, Grenada, Dominica, and St Vincent and the Grenadines. The collapse of the International Coffee Agreement in 1989 has hurt exports and earnings from Jamaica, Haiti and the Dominican Republic, as these countries are displaced by more efficient larger-scale exporters of coffee.

Grenada's windfall in nutmeg and mace export earnings, achieved as a result of a protectionist cartel agreement with Indonesia, may soon be wiped out as other exporters, such as Sri Lanka and Brazil, skirt the cartel to reap the benefits of the temporary price boom. The Caribbean has long been underpriced and outcompeted in world copra (dried coconut) markets by the Philippines and other low-cost producers. The non-traditional extra-regional agricultural exports touted by USAID and some World Bank spokespeople can at best become a minor source of income for the region, as Chapter 4 will explain.

Earnings for the Caribbean's most significant non-agricultural exports, bauxite (produced in the Dominican Republic, Jamaica, Guyana and Surinam, and formerly in Haiti) and alumina (produced in Jamaica and Surinam, and formerly in Guyana), recovered somewhat in the late 1980s from their 1985 low point. The export value of the region's bauxite and alumina exports had reached US$858.9 million by 1988, according to a World Bank estimate, but was not expected to return to anything close to its nominal 1980 export value of US$1.3 billion. Moreover, the proportion of bauxite earnings that accrue to Caribbean exporting countries will continue to decline, and foreign corporations will take a growing share, as a consequence of privatization and the reduced amount of Caribbean-mined bauxite that is refined into alumina in the region.

Low-wage export industry: miracle or mirage?

'Free trade policies have been proven to increase exports and employment in the Caribbean,' pronounces the World Bank. As evidence, Bank experts cite what they interpret as the benefits of export processing zones (EPZs) and, sometimes, free trade zones (FTZs), where garments and other goods are assembled for export. (Bank documents refer to these zones as 'simulated free trade regimes'.) The Bank notes that in the region's most successful EPZ host country, the Dominican Republic, the number of export processing factories rose from 70 in 1980 to 330 in 1990. According to the Bank, 'The EPZs have provided one-fifth of the urban jobs created since 1980, and now account for about half of all manufacturing employment . . . EPZ exports have replaced sugar as the largest foreign exchange generator'.[15]

The economic benefits of EPZs are more dubious than the Bank's enthusiasm suggests. The net costs to host-country economies, in the form of subsidies and forgone taxes, may well exceed their gains, especially given the extremely low wages paid and the scant value added in export assembly. Nor is it clear that the new jobs in export factories exceed the number of jobs lost as a consequence of the related diversion of resources from the public sector and agriculture, and from the demise of local producers in the face of EPZ competition for credit, labor, infrastructure, and energy, and in some cases, markets. There is strong reason to doubt that investment in export manufacturing will continue at the pace it followed in some Caribbean countries in the 1980s, or that the trend might extend throughout the region. Even if the Caribbean were to become the export manufacturers' paradise that EPZ advocates suggest it can be, the labor conditions and social consequences involved can hardly be considered a desirable form of development.

The endorsement by the World Bank and USAID of the EPZ job-creation panacea is determined more by ideology than practical reality. Under the best-case scenario for export manufacturing investment increases in the Caribbean, only a small proportion of the region's need for employment would be met. A May 1990 study sponsored by a US Congressional commission notes that, '$1 million (in 1982 dollars) of investment would create about 28 jobs in Caribbean island countries'. The study's author, economist Stuart K. Tucker, also observes that the Caribbean has not been and is not likely to become the site of substantial US private investment, and that the investment that has occurred has brought few new jobs. According to the study, for countries in the Caribbean Basin other than Costa Rica:

> the [potential] new jobs represent less than 20 percent of the expected labor force growth, even with a manufactured export growth rate of 13 percent per year. At the more achievable 9 percent annual growth rate (the 'Medium' scenario), the jobs represent less than 10 percent of the new entrants to the work force for the Dominican Republic and less than five percent for the other countries.[16]

'The region's workers will sink further into poverty,' if current trends continue, Tucker predicts. He recommends reduction of US protectionist barriers to Caribbean exports and increased production of food and manufactured goods in the Caribbean for domestic consumption. The former runs counter to the current climate in the United States — 'the threat of future US trade restrictions hangs like a black cloud over investment decisions', Tucker states — while the latter is precisely the opposite of the IMF, World Bank and USAID push for more export-oriented economic policies region-wide.

The tourism trap

What of the World Bank's other prescription for Caribbean development — increased export of its 'tourism product'? Both the Bank and USAID have warned in the past that tourism is a risky and limited basis for economic growth for most of the Caribbean; vulnerability to hurricanes is only one reason why tourism is unreliable as a growth strategy. The case of Antigua illustrates another.

Antigua/Barbuda had the most noticeable Caribbean tourism boom in the 1980s. It also accumulated the region's largest per capita debt, US$3,030 per Antiguan citizen, and a debt-service burden so high it alarms even the World Bank. This is hardly surprising, since an estimated 80 cents or more of every dollar earned by Antigua's tourism industry accrues not to Antiguans but to foreign companies and investors who own airlines, hotels, supply services and cruise ships. Without taking note of this dilemma, the Bank advises Caribbean countries blithely, in general, to increase their public investment in tourism infrastructure and promotion. At the same time, it sharply warns the government of Antigua to 'cease from further direct investment in tourism . . . constrain imports and consumption . . . generate a surplus on its recurrent obligations through increases in tax receipts and reductions in expenditures', and seek to reschedule its debts.[17]

Among the independent Caribbean countries which had economies largely based on tourism, only the Bahamas has achieved the status of being 'creditworthy for private market funding' in the eyes of the World Bank. The Bahamas' proximity to the United States gives it some particular, if dubious, advantages. Its tourism industry has been lubricated by cash and investments connected to gambling, offshore banking, the drug trade and related money-laundering. The other Caribbean country which has experienced relative prosperity based substantially on tourism, Barbados, has 'priced itself out of the international tourist market' by providing workers in tourism with 'too high' an average wage, a World Bank official observed in 1988.[18]

By 1990, the World Bank was pointing to the Dominican Republic as a more promising model for tourism-based growth because of its 'more competitive tourism product'. That cheaper product, of course, is based on extremely low wages in the country's tourism industry, made possible by the abject poverty of the majority of the Dominican Republic's population. The country is the third poorest in the region, after Haiti and Guyana, with a per capita GNP of only US$680. In 1984, in the wake of IMF-required currency devaluation, real wages were only 42 per cent of what they had been at the beginning of 1980.

The World Bank pays no heed whatsoever to the damaging effects of tourism on communities and social values, a matter which greatly concerns many Caribbean citizens and NGOs. Some Bank officials, however, are worried about the potential threat to tourism earnings caused by the rapid increase in pollution in the region:

> Environmental problems could also become a deterrent to future tourism. Marine pollution, beach pollution, land degradation, beach mining, inadequate sewerage facilities, together with household, industrial, and municipal waste, lack of or deterioration of forest cover, and improper siting of beach front facilities are major environmental problems affecting Caribbean countries. Oil spills could damage tourism activity.[19]

The Bank's report makes no reference to the fact that IMF and World Bank-required austerity has greatly reduced the ability of Caribbean countries to cope with these very problems. Nor does it allude to a major environmental problem that affects a far greater number of Caribbeans: the damage to food production for subsistence and regional trade caused by soil erosion, reduced fertility and toxic residues resulting from overcultivation and the heavy use of agro-chemicals in the expansion and modernization of export-crop farming promoted by the Bank and other creditors.

As bad as the economic setbacks suffered by the Caribbean in the 1980s were, things are likely to get worse. Much of the losses likely in the 1990s will come about as the inevitable result of the underlying economic principle most ardently championed by the World Bank and the US government: the expansion of global free trade. This principle, as we shall see, is more often violated than respected by the world's wealthy nations, even while they attempt to press it upon poorer countries. Policies imposed in the name of free trade and market-led development are wreaking further havoc on the economies of the Caribbean and much of the global South, while blocking all exit routes from the debt trap. But in the light of the post-independence crisis, the structures of oppression and the mechanisms of exploitation are more starkly revealed. With the aid of this sharpened insight, those who desire a better life for the region's impoverished majority have begun to lay the foundations of an alternative, Caribbean-led model of development.

Notes

1. This figure from World Bank sources does not include Cuba or the region's French, Dutch, British and US colonies.

2. Norman Girvan, Ennio Rodriguez, Mario Arana Sevilla and Miguel Ceara Hatton, *The Debt Problem of Small Peripheral Economies: Case Studies from the*

Caribbean and Central America. Association of Caribbean Economists (ACE), 1990.

3. Ibid.

4. The US Enterprise for the Americas Initiative proposed by US President Bush in 1990 would write off a portion of the outstanding debts of Caribbean and Latin American countries to the US government, but with stringent conditions that would include tightened schedules for repayment of their other foreign debts.

5. IMF, *International Financial Statistics*, Vol. XLI, No. 6, June 1988.

6. Girvan *et al.*, *The Debt Problem of Small Peripheral Economies*.

7. A 1981 study by the CARICOM Group of Experts, cited in Clive Thomas, *The Poor and the Powerless*, Latin America Bureau/Monthly Review Press, New York and London, 1988.

8. World Bank, *Caribbean Exports: Preferential Markets and Performance*, May 1988.

9. World Bank, *Caribbean Countries — Balance of Payments Current Account, 1978–88*.

10. World Bank, *Caribbean Exports*, May 1988.

11. Girvan *et al.*, *The Debt Problem in Small Peripheral Economies*.

12. Calculated from the World Bank, *Net Transfers to Caribbean Countries, 1978–88*.

13. Statement by the CARICOM Secretariat to the Caribbean Group for Cooperation in Economic Development (CGCED), June 1988.

14. World Bank, *Caribbean Exports: Preferential Markets and Performance*, May 1988.

15. World Bank, *The Caribbean Region*, April 1990.

16. Stuart K. Tucker, *The Potential of Trade Expansion as a Generator of Added Employment in the Caribbean Basin*, US Commission for the Study of International Migration and Cooperative Economic Development, Washington DC, May 1990.

17. World Bank, *The Caribbean Region*, April 1990.

18. Author inverview, June 1988.

19. Ibid.

Part II
US Aid and Free Trade

3. The Failure of the Caribbean Basin Initiative

> The CBI was misconceived and oversold. It was a quick fix worked out by the big boys in the private sector. We couldn't persuade them that the private sector here isn't the big boys only. They failed to understand the Caribbean and the Caribbean people.
> William G. Demas, former president, Caribbean Development Bank

During the 1980s, the Caribbean region became the object of heightened attention and involvement by the United States. Washington enacted a set of new aid and trade policies and revived old practices, including direct military intervention, to strengthen US influence in the region. The Caribbean provides a particularly well-defined example of the policy agenda which the US has thrust upon low-income countries throughout the world under the banners of privatization and market-led economic development. These are also a direct precedent for the Western hemispheric free trade zone proposal unveiled by the US government in 1990 in the form of the Enterprise for the Americas Initiative.

Central to the recent US role in the Caribbean has been an enlarged military presence. The Caribbean is a focal point in the effort to strengthen and link US forces from the North Atlantic to Central America. Military involvement by the United States in the Caribbean is not new, but US military strategists are concerned with more than projecting US power in the country's backyard. US officials view the greater Caribbean region as crucial to maintaining the United States as the dominant military power worldwide: 'National security, and not immigration or economic concerns, has been the driving force behind US efforts to foster economic development in the Caribbean Basin,' noted a 1990 US congressional study.[1] US policies in the region must be viewed with that understanding in mind.

Unrest in the US Backyard

The economy of the United States entered a new stage during the 1970s. The *de facto* devaluation of the US dollar by President Richard Nixon in 1971, negative trade balances, surging public debt, declining real wages and stalled economic growth were among the signs that the US would no longer enjoy uncontested dominance of the global economy. Although the US economy and overseas investments continued to expand, US corporations faced growing competition in domestic and foreign markets from Europe, Japan and some of the newly industrializing countries (NICs) of the South.

The 1970s also marked a turning point for many nations of the South, including those of the Caribbean. Steep oil price increases in 1973 and 1979, combined with a dramatic drop in the world market prices of many of the crops and minerals exported from Asia, Africa and Latin America, led to severe financial crises throughout the South, especially in non-oil-exporting nations. Falling prices for sugar, cocoa, coffee, bauxite and other major exports of the Caribbean and Central America dealt a severe economic blow to nearly all the countries of the region. (The Caribbean's only substantial oil exporter, Trinidad and Tobago, benefited through most of the 1970s from increased petroleum earnings, but many of the country's gains were wiped out when oil prices fell in the 1980s.)

During this same period came the crest of another wave of social unrest in Central America and the Caribbean. The struggles of organized peasants and farm workers for access to land, better wages and an end to military repression gained momentum in El Salvador, Guatemala and Nicaragua. In the Caribbean, the 1970s saw a resurgence of 'regional nationalism', calls for political nonalignment and a more equitable New International Economic Order (NIEO), and the renewed growth of socialist-oriented parties and movements.

During the 1970s and early 1980s, Washington officials became alarmed about trends in the Caribbean. Their concern was not so much the region's economic crisis but rather the movements which had arisen in response to that crisis. Pre-eminent among them was the government of democratic socialist Michael Manley, whose People's National Party (PNP) won office in Jamaica in 1972, a time when unemployment ran at at least 24 per cent and the incomes of most Jamaicans were at sub-poverty levels and falling.[2] Manley's government did not carry out a socialist program, but did espouse the goal of creating a more egalitarian society by means of a 'third path', neither socialist nor capitalist. His PNP government also attempted to retain for Jamaica a larger share of the profits from bauxite mining by North American companies, and to maintain friendly relations with Jamaica's socialist neighbor, Cuba.

In response, the Ford and Carter administrations applied US economic and political muscle to weaken the PNP government, further undermining the Jamaican economy and setting the stage for Manley's 1980 electoral loss to US protégé Edward Seaga. The incoming Reagan administration then moved quickly, in 1981, to boost aid to Jamaica in the hope of creating a private enterprise showcase.

At the other end of the island chain, the March 1979 revolution in Grenada provoked a more extreme US response. The revolution was led by the New Jewel Movement, which held power until the US-led invasion in October 1983. The New Jewel Movement arose in reaction to economic decline and the erratic despotism of Prime Minister Eric Gairy. It was also part of a larger movement in the Eastern Caribbean of new parties and popular organizations, encouraged by the Jamaican quest for political and economic independence and inspired by the Black Power and pan-African movements.

The revolutionary government stressed the needs of the poor, Caribbean pride and the right of Grenada, as a sovereign state, to pursue relations with both Western and Eastern-bloc countries. It developed successful and popular programs in literacy, education, health and construction, with help from Western Europe and Cuba. The United States cut off all domestic aid to Grenada, and blocked loans and funds to Grenada from other sources.

US policymakers were even more disturbed when, four months later, the Sandinista-led revolution in Nicaragua overthrew the closest US ally in Central America, dictator Anastasio Somoza. Although the Sandinistas did nationalize some lands and enterprises, Nicaragua's economy remained largely in private hands, just as Grenada's did. Leaders of both new governments felt they could not afford to sever political and economic ties to the United States. Both, however, sought to counterbalance economic dependence on the United States (and, in the case of Grenada, on Britain) by drawing closer to Western Europe and Latin America and making new alliances with Eastern-bloc nations, including Cuba. Both Nicaragua and Grenada also adopted broad social reforms to address the needs of their nations' poor majorities.

The US response
The United States again reacted with hostility. Rather than recognizing the ongoing impoverishment that fueled these movements for change, the US government interpreted them as an escalation of the East–West conflict. Instead of seeing the potential benefits to the United States of more equitable, prosperous and stable economies in the Caribbean and Central America, the Carter and Reagan administrations viewed the new governments as threats.

A set of options for US action against this perceived danger was explored in a series of studies, including the 1980 Committee of Santa Fe Report, the Report of the National Bipartisan Commission on Central America (the *Kissinger Report*) and the related Central America Initiative, developed as an aid proposal in 1984 and revised in 1986. The strategies which emerged from these commissions were an updated version of the US Monroe Doctrine that declared the right and necessity of active US dominance in the hemisphere.

The military aspect of the modernized doctrine called for reassertion of US power, using proxy forces for 'low-intensity conflict' (Guatemala, El Salvador, Nicaragua, Peru, Colombia) and avoiding US troop involvement except when quick victory could be assured (Grenada in 1983, Panama in 1989). Politically, the strategy allowed for support of traditional repressive oligarchies where necessary, but preferred incorporation of more modern and 'moderate' sectors of the region's elite into ruling structures. Elections, engineered or heavily influenced by the United States, helped create an image of democracy.

Beginning in the early 1980s, 'In Jamaica, St. Lucia, St. Vincent, Antigua, and Dominica, the U.S. openly and successfully supported conservative neocolonial political forces, thus creating a favorable environment for its regional military buildup (and, eventually, for invading Grenada),' writes Jorge Rodriguez Beruff of the University of Puerto Rico.[3]

In October 1980, the US Army Office for Operations and Plans ordered a study to analyse 'emerging nationalism, Cuban activism, and expanding Soviet interest in the region . . .' and to 'emphasize the development of military alternatives designed to reduce the occurrence of destabilizing events . . .'. The report was released in October 1981, four months before the US Caribbean Basin Initiative (CBI) was announced. It recommended that the US military work more closely with 'regional military establishments' to increase 'their self-confidence in handling both external and internal threats', and that the US military:

> Establish a network of military-to-military relationships that can: (1) gain for the United States an understanding of the current position and future direction of various Caribbean militaries and leadership elites; (2) foster increased access to decisional elites in order to enhance U.S. influence; and (3) serve as a bridge between regional military elites. . . .[4]

Economically, US strategy first emphasized direct aid to governments for emergency stabilization. US economic aid to Caribbean Basin countries tripled, from US$238 million in 1980 to US$736 million in 1983.[5] The US economic strategy evolved to focus, after 1985, on economic austerity, structural adjustment, privatization and free trade to promote greater US access to the region's markets and resources.[6] The US military goals have been pursued with some success, and the political aims achieved in part. But the stability of pro-US elected governments is threatened by the failure of the strategy's economic component to reverse the region's decline.

In 1983, the US government launched a special package of new regulations governing US trade with Central America and the Caribbean under the Caribbean Economic Recovery Act, more commonly known as the CBI. The CBI established the framework for the export of Reaganomics to the Caribbean. It has helped to set the tone for parallel policies applied by the US worldwide. In its first seven years, however, the CBI failed utterly to deliver its highly publicized promises of improved trade earnings and employment in the Caribbean. In the words of one official with long experience in USAID's Eastern Caribbean program, 'The effect of the CBI has been the opposite of what was intended.'[7] Prior to the CBI, the Caribbean had enjoyed a trade surplus in its commerce with the United States. But by 1989, Caribbean CBI-eligible nations imported US$6.8 billion worth of US goods and sold only US$4.7 billion worth of Caribbean products to the United States.[8] Since the CBI's inception, unemployment has increased and Caribbean trade deficits have grown. At the same time, the CBI has been a short-term political success for the Reagan and Bush administrations. A closer look at how the CBI has failed economically sheds light on the underlying structural causes of poverty and instability in the Caribbean and on the real goals of US Caribbean policy.

Securing the US's 'Third Border'

By 1981, the first year of the Reagan administration, State Department officials had begun sounding the alarm about the 'state of danger in the Caribbean

Basin'. In a statement characteristic of US official pronouncements at the time, Assistant Secretary of State for Interamerican Affairs Thomas O. Enders told the Senate Subcommittee on Western Hemispheric Affairs that US interests in the region, particularly the Panama Canal and control of sea lanes and oil supply routes, were at risk as a result of 'a new Cuban strategy' aimed at 'the destruction of existing governments in the region'.[9]

It was in the context of this supposed 'state of danger' that President Ronald Reagan announced the US CBI in February 1982. At the core of the CBI package as presented to Congress were two related economic goals: (1) the promotion of Caribbean exports to the United States by means of new trade legislation; and (2) the increase of US investment in CBI target countries by means of aid programs and policy changes to make such investment more profitable. Legislation to implement these goals was enacted in 1983. In the view of the program's designers, increasing US investment in the region was one means of pursuing US geopolitical interests. They expected that market-driven economic growth would result from CBI policies and eventually seep down to the poor, and thus defuse the region's social crisis. In reality, the CBI and its accompanying aid policies represented the abandonment of the flagging US effort to address directly the needs of the region's impoverished majority.

CBI planners also thought that increased US investment in the Caribbean and Central America, especially in the Eastern Caribbean where the US presence was not strong, would help justify the expanding US military operations there. The location of more US businesses and personnel in the Caribbean could lend legitimacy, perhaps even more than the presence of American medical students in Grenada had done, to direct US military intervention should it become necessary again. Closer economic ties between individual Caribbean states and the US would be an added incentive for Caribbean political leaders to cooperate with the US in other policy areas.

An additional aim of the CBI and the related USAID policies was to enable US companies to take greater advantage of sources of low-wage labor close to the US mainland. This, CBI backers thought, might help US-owned firms to regain some of the competitive advantage they were losing to other exporters, especially Asian nations. Some observers pointed out that the model of 'industrialization by invitation' had already failed to produce prosperity in Caribbean countries. That model has been drawn in large part from the experience of Puerto Rico.

> Although it has never been publicly stated, the underlying model of the CBI is Puerto Rico's 'Operation Bootstrap' — that is, an export-oriented industrial development fostered by a strong injection of US investment . . . . Most certainly, the problems currently faced by the Puerto Rican economy, which are the direct consequences of development policies adopted under Operation Bootstrap, would discourage the island's neighbors from embracing the CBI.[10]

The CBI: Less Than Appearances

The CBI as enacted by Congress had two major components: 'emergency' aid funds for some of the governments in the region — 27 countries in Central America and the Caribbean were listed as potentially eligible — and a new set of trade regulations affecting the export of certain of the region's products to the United States.[11] The aid component of the CBI consisted of US$350 million in supplementary economic support funds to be distributed through USAID to governments in the region in 1984. El Salvador received the largest amount, 21 per cent. The remainder of the funds was divided among selected countries in the Caribbean and Central America, with the Eastern Caribbean receiving a total of US$10 million.[12] For most CBI recipient countries, this extra, one-time dose of aid was not significant in comparison to the size of their debts and deficits, but it increased the total of US economic assistance to the basin countries to US$958 million in 1984.

The second major component of the CBI, the Caribbean Basin Economic Recovery Act (CBERA), empowered the US president to grant duty-free entry into the United States of certain eligible exports from CBI beneficiary countries for a period of 12 years. The rationale for this was that it would stimulate exports to the United States and yield a rise in export earnings. In addition, it was thought, US corporations would initiate or expand operations in the region's export industries, creating new jobs for Caribbeans and Central Americans. According to the logic of the bill's promoters, by opening the door to US markets, the new CBERA trade laws would allow the 'magic of the marketplace' to solve the region's economic problems. But the potential impact of the CBI trade legislation on the economies of the Caribbean, even under the best of market conditions, was minimal, for the following reasons.

Most of the Caribbean exports granted duty-free entrance into the United States by the CBI had already been exempted from duties by previous trade laws:[13] Estimates by economists of the proportion of Caribbean exports which became eligible for duty-free status as a result of the CBI range from only 7 to 10 per cent of the region's exports to the United States.[14]

Important Caribbean exports were specifically excluded from CBI duty-free status because they might compete with similar goods produced in the United States: These include petroleum and petroleum derivatives, clothing and textiles, and shoes and other leather goods. Oil and oil products have been the Caribbean's leading export to the United States in recent decades. The clothing industry, primarily the assembly of garments from cloth or cut pieces manufactured elsewhere, is the Caribbean's fastest-growing export industry. Thus, the greatest potential increases in trade revenue for the Caribbean were eliminated from the start.

To the extent that Caribbean exports might increase as a result of the CBI, the

main beneficiaries would be US rather than Caribbean exporters: Of the 12 leading products which became duty-free through the CBI, seven are produced mainly by US companies.[15] In addition, Caribbean exports are defined in such a way by the CBERA that as little as 35 per cent of the eligible products' value need come from work done or materials originating in the region (or as little as 20 per cent if 15 per cent of the parts or materials used come from the United States). This makes it possible for US companies to cut costs by using low-paid workers in one or more Caribbean or Central American countries to assemble components made outside the area, then bring the goods duty-free into the US as CBI-eligible Caribbean Basin exports.

The losses to the Caribbean resulting from new protectionist policies adopted by the US far outweigh the small potential gains from the CBI: 'Reductions in US sugar quotas since 1982 have resulted in greater losses to Caribbean countries than they have gained from 807 and CBI-specific trade preferences.'[16] In addition, complex and sometimes contradictory regulations of the US Department of Agriculture, the US Bureau of Customs and other agencies effectively exclude many Caribbean products not barred by tariffs and quotas.

The CBI increases the economic and political fragmentation of the Caribbean: Instead of negotiating the terms of the CBI with the countries of the region as a group, the United States required separate bargaining for CBI eligibility between the US and each country in the region. This process bypassed and weakened regional institutions and ignored the ongoing efforts by Caribbean nations to build a framework for development through regional cooperation.[17] Thus, the CBI has promoted competition among Caribbean countries for trade benefits and fostered bilateral relations of economic dependency between Caribbean countries and the US.

A country's eligibility for CBI benefits is based on political criteria: The CBERA explicitly excluded Cuba and Nicaragua from CBI eligibility. Initially, its politically discriminatory criteria also excluded other governments not favored by the Reagan administration, including the Maurice Bishop government in Grenada (which was displaced by the time the CBI trade rules took effect) and the People's National Congress (PNC) government of Guyana. The CBI trade legislation also contains a list of political conditions which, if not met, would automatically exclude any country from the CBI. The bill states that a country becomes ineligible if it is 'Communist', if it is deemed by the US to have placed 'unfair' restrictions on the economic activities of US corporations or citizens, if it nationalizes or levies 'excessive' taxes on firms owned 50 per cent or more by US citizens, or if it grants trade preferences to products of any developed country which compete with US exports.

Once a country attains CBI eligibility, the CBI continues to limit its economic options and political sovereignty: Under the CBI, the US president has the power to grant or to withdraw the duty-free status of any of the region's CBI-eligible exports, on a product-by-product or a nation-by-nation basis. This is a potential deterrent to any Caribbean or Central American country that might want to adopt policies not pleasing to the United States, a deterrent that becomes more powerful to any country that increases its exports to the United States and becomes more dependent on earnings from them as a result of taking advantage of the CBI.

Tightening the Noose

The CBERA's detailed list of requirements for CBI eligibility relates not only to the trade and foreign investment policies but also to the internal economic policies of the affected countries. To remain CBI-eligible, a country must provide 'reasonable access' for US companies to its own 'markets and basic commodity resources . . .' and must refrain from protecting its own industries or promoting its own exports in a way deemed by the US to 'distort international trade'. Another requirement for countries requesting CBI status is 'the degree to which such country is undertaking self-help measures to promote its own economic development', as determined by the US president. The vague and broad wording of this stipulation makes countries desiring CBI eligibility vulnerable to subjective and ideologically determined judgments by the US executive.

Overall, the CBI adds to the mechanisms by which the United States promotes and protects the activities of US-based corporations in the region. These mechanisms already included the Latin American Agricultural Development (LAAD), a government-financed consortium of agribusiness companies, the Overseas Private Investment Corporation (OPIC), which insures US investment abroad, the Export/Import Bank (Eximbank), which finances the overseas trade of US companies, and the services of US government departments, including Commerce and Agriculture which promote US foreign investments. To help carry out CBI goals, a new, private investment promotion agency, the Caribbean/Central America Action, under the leadership of David Rockefeller, was added to these government-sponsored programs. Also in conjunction with the CBI, an arsenal of projects to subsidize and promote US investments in the region, described in Chapter 4, was added to the Caribbean program of USAID.

Together, these regulations and institutions place the power to determine the flow of trade and finance between the United States and the Caribbean firmly in the control of the US executive, with significant input from private US corporations. At the same time that the CBI promotes subsidies, government guarantees and other incentives to US businesses, it restricts the degree to which its beneficiary countries may use similar mechanisms to protect their own economic interests. Caribbean governments have little influence over the goals and requirements of the CBI and how those requirements are interpreted; Caribbean regional institutions and grassroots organizations have even less. CBI II, enacted by the US Congress in 1990, contained no substantial changes other than a provision for the year-by-year automatic extension of the legislation.

The Results

Despite the promotion of the CBI as a mini-Marshall Plan for the Caribbean and Central America, and as the Reagan era equivalent of the 1960s Alliance for Progress, the CBI as an economic policy to aid the region has failed. In terms of its stated goal of increasing Caribbean exports to the United States, that failure has been stark. The value of Caribbean exports to the US plunged by US$1.5 billion between 1983 and 1986. This decline was even greater than the revenue losses that occurred during the pre-CBI recessionary period of 1980–83, when the value of Caribbean exports to the US fell by US$815 million. At the same time, other exporters to the US have gained at the expense of exporters based in CBI-eligible countries; CBI countries' share of the US market fell from 3.4–1.7 per cent in the same period.[18]

The value of exports to the United States of those few Caribbean products which became eligible for duty-free status under the CBI did increase, from US$116 million in 1983 to US$276 million in 1986. But these products represent only 11 per cent of the total of Caribbean exports to the US in that year.[19] There was also a slight increase, enthusiastically publicized by USAID and CBI supporters, in Caribbean exports of exotic fruits and winter vegetables. However, the value of these new agricultural exports was only one-twelfth of the value of the region's five main traditional agro-exports (coffee, cocoa, sugar, tobacco and bananas) in 1986 and has not increased substantially since then.

Caribbean exports of textiles, sporting goods, pharmaceuticals, electronics, chemicals and coffee to the United States have increased during the 1980s, but these gains have been far outweighed by the decline of earnings from oil, bauxite, sugar and other traditional exports. This overall loss of income is not mainly because Caribbean countries have become less efficient exporters; in fact, they have exported more goods at lower prices. The volume of Caribbean non-fuel exports grew by an average rate of 4.4 per cent from 1980 to 1986, but because during the same period the world market prices of these exported commodities fell, the net result was a 0.1 per cent decline in the income from non-oil exports, and an even greater decline in the oil export earnings of the countries in question.[20]

Reflecting a decline in the export competitiveness of Caribbean countries, the market share of exports to the United States, Canada and Europe from the Caribbean was 20 per cent lower in 1986 than it had been in 1980. According to a 1988 World Bank study, the loss of the market share of Caribbean exports was most severe in the United States. 'Ironically,' comments the Bank, 'a part of the world which in theory was to gain a strong impetus from major exporting nations has lost, not gained, a market share in these markets.' The Bank estimates that this decline cost Caribbean countries US$1.7 billion. These facts add to the evidence that a development strategy based on manufacturing for export in competition with Asian and other nations will not succeed for the Caribbean.

The category of Caribbean exports to the United States (and to the world) which has grown the most since 1980 is clothing and textiles, which make up more than one-third of the region's manufactured exports to the US. Between 1980 and 1986, these exports grew at an average annual rate of 18.3 per cent. Clothing and textiles, however, are not eligible for CBI duty-free status.[21] It is not the CBI, but rather other benefits which have influenced non-Caribbean corporations to set up clothing manufacturing operations in the Dominican Republic, Haiti, Jamaica, Barbados and the OECS states. The most important incentive is low wages. The workers, most of whom are women, could hardly afford to buy the clothes they cut and stitch for 60 cents an hour or less, even if the garments were for sale locally.

The other major economic goal of the CBI, the increase of job-creating foreign investments in the region, has also not been met. Direct US investment in the island nations of the Caribbean dropped from US$1,849 million in 1983 to US$1,714 million in 1985, during the first two years of the CBI.[22] In contrast, direct US investments worldwide increased by 9 per cent during the same period.[23] This trend of declining US investment in the CBI target region has continued in subsequent years. A 1985 study by the US Department of Commerce claimed that between January 1984 and May 1985, 285 new investment initiatives resulted from the CBI, creating a total of 35,891 new jobs. A subsequent investigation by the US Government Accounting Office found that the Commerce Department's methods were unreliable and that its claims of employment creation as a result of the CBI were greatly exaggerated.[24] The director of a Caribbean loan project, funded by USAID to promote small enterprises, described AID's fixation on generating statistics to indicate progress in job creation:

> US AID requires . . . certain key indicators, mainly the impact on jobs. A small farmer may get a loan through this office and then hire two or three workers for a few days or a few weeks. Is this 'six new jobs'? That's how we are to report it. If there are no reports, then there's no more money [from AID].[25]

Further evidence that the CBI and related US policies have helped US corporations more than the people of Central America and the Caribbean is the fact that US companies have been able to expand their sales to CBI countries while CBI-country sales to the US have faltered: US imports from CBI countries fell from US$8.5 billion in 1983 to US$6.6 billion in 1989; US exports to CBI countries rose from US$4.9 billion to US$8.3 billion over the same period.[26] This setback to the Caribbean is the predictable outcome of the CBERA stipulations that CBI countries make their markets and resources 'accessible' to US firms and that they refrain from protecting their own industries and from regulating US investment in their territories.

Large US-owned and other transnational firms, by virtue of their size, access to financing and control of marketing channels, were already in a better position before the CBI to compete in Caribbean and world markets than were Caribbean companies and Caribbean farmers. The conditions contained in the CBI legislation and related US aid requirements and trade policies have strengthened further their advantage over Caribbean exporters. At the same time as the United States has been requiring Caribbean governments to dismantle barriers to US products, it has been erecting more and higher barriers against sugar and other Caribbean exports to the United States.

Thus, the United States government has made good its promise to the US business community, reported in the December 1984 issue of *AID Update*: 'Given our strong track position throughout the Caribbean Basin, US companies can expect to fill a large part of the region's rising demand for exports.' The goal of aiding the US economy by promoting sales of domestic exports to the Caribbean was always a central, if unwritten, aspect of the CBI. But given the policy's failure to aid Caribbean economies as well, it is unlikely that the US exporters will continue to find growing markets in the region. Impoverished farmers, exploited workers and debt-strapped governments do not make good customers.

The view from the South: the CBI in the Windwards
By 1988, Eastern Caribbean government officials were nearly unanimous in concluding that the CBI had failed to have any significant positive impact on their countries' economies. Dominica's Prime Minister Eugenia Charles, who was enthusiastic about the CBI when it was first announced, stated in 1987: 'We never really expected results from the CBI . . . We got some citrus juice and some essential oils into the US market, but not much.' Because of tight US regulations, she complained that, 'We can't even go *through* Miami' to ship fruit to other countries. 'The CBI hasn't delivered,' stated Dominica Economic Planning Ministry official Irwin Larogue. The country's Chief of Economic Planning, Cary Harris, said, 'There's no use in the US giving us money without giving us access to US markets.'[27]

The head of St Vincent's National Development Corporation remarked that, 'We can't even get our best-quality mangoes into the US market.'[28] In Grenada, 'The expectations [raised by the CBI and the US presence] haven't been met at all,' according to Chasley Bishop, director of the country's AID-supported National Development Foundation. 'Nothing has happened here. There's been no real development . . . The Government of Grenada has let the US off the hook.'[29]

CBI Success — for the US

The outcome of CBI has confirmed the predictions made by many Caribbean observers that the program would aid the US more than the Caribbean. But to the extent that the CBI was intended not as an aid program but as a way to enhance US influence and economic interests it can be judged a success. In response to the expectations of increased US investments and market access, most Caribbean governments made significant concessions to US and other foreign businesses. They gave up substantial tax revenues and relinquished many of their rights to regulate foreign corporate activities. They shifted resources away from farming and manufacturing for Caribbean markets and away from vital public services. They provided factory buildings, utilities and other services to foreign investors at rates below their actual costs, incurring debts that have yet to be paid.

In return, they have received publicity and promises. In the coming decade, their concessions are likely to bring about results even more damaging to the majority of Caribbeans than the current neglect of regional development needs and the weakening of national sovereignty that has accompanied the CBI. In the opinion of Emilio Pantojas-Garcia:

> The CBI has begun to pave the way for a new role in the international division of labor of the region, as an appendix of the new US agro-industries and as a low-wage area for labor-intensive industries producing for international markets. . . . That was the whole point of the CBI, and measured along these lines, it begins to bear fruit.[30]

The United States has achieved political as well as economic goals through the CBI, at least in the short term. According to a senior official in the second PNP government in Jamaica, the CBI 'seeks to steer official policy in the beneficiary countries in the direction of support for foreign investment and towards an accommodating foreign policy posture towards the US government'. As a result of CBI promises, he points out, 'Major social classes came to perceive their interests as dependent on greater access to the US market and to US aid . . . The economic nationalist inclinations of the 1970s were effectively blunted.' The CBI has enabled the United States to weaken movements for greater political and economic independence in the Caribbean without making significant trade concessions of its own and at a very small cost in aid funds. Such success, however, can only be temporary.

The US invasion of Grenada in 1983 also achieved at least one of its political objectives: the discouraging of similar experiments in the Caribbean. There is little likelihood that any party similar to the New Jewel Movement might achieve power in the region in the near future. However, the conditions which gave rise to the revolution in Grenada — poverty, unemployment, the disruption of families and communities by economic stress, and political turmoil and corruption — have grown worse throughout most of the region in the years since the Grenada revolution's demise. Strikes, attempted *coups d'état*, and protests against rising prices and government austerity policies, in Jamaica, the Dominican Republic, Guyana, Haiti and Trinidad, are visible signs of the discontent which simmers beneath the surface among farmers, workers, the urban poor and, increasingly, the middle classes. Even among the region's governing élites, long-held assumptions about the goals of national development and the means to achieve it are being shattered by the deepening economic crisis and growing political unrest.

Free Trade for the Americas?

In the coming decade, challenges to US global economic dominance are likely to stimulate even more direct US intervention in its traditional spheres of influence in the Caribbean and Latin America. Even before the fall of the Berlin Wall, the consolidation of the EC, added to continuing West German and Japanese export success, presaged a restructuring of worldwide economic power at the expense of the United States. US capital may remain a front-running contender in the race for new opportunities in the emerging market economies of Eastern Europe and Asia. However, the opening of Eastern Europe's infrastructure, markets and, especially, its low-cost labor present new advantages to the EC, particularly to Germany. In this context, US business will seek to enhance its exploitative advantage of economic dominance, backed by military power, closer to home.

The announcement of a US Enterprise for the Americas Initiative by President George Bush on 27 June 1990 was one step in this direction. Bush cheered the trend in 'Latin America and the Caribbean [where] nations are turning away from the statist economic policies that stifle growth and are now looking to the power of the free market to help the hemisphere realize its untapped potential for progress'. He called for a 'hemisphere-wide free trade zone . . . stretching from the Port of Anchorage to Tierra del Fuego'. The high-flown rhetoric was accompanied by three vaguely sketched US offers for trade concessions, private investment promotion, and conversion of limited amounts of debt to the United States by means of debt-for-equity and debt-for-nature swaps and forgiveness of debts incurred by Latin American countries that purchase US food aid. In calling for the dismantling of 'overrestrictive' trade barriers within the Americas, Bush hinted that the United States might negotiate reductions of its own barriers against the import of 'certain products of special interest' to its neighbors to the south, but made no specific commitments.

Bush's proposed investment fund would total only US$300 million, the equivalent of only three-quarters of 1 per cent of the total foreign debt of Latin America and the Caribbean, and only 2.5 per cent of the region's debt to the United States. Even that amount would depend on grants from Europe and Japan to match the meagre US offer of US$100 million. Disbursal of the proposed fund, to be administered by the IDB, would be conditional on adoption by recipient countries of IMF and World Bank-type structural adjustment programs and on agreements to ensure their payment of debts to commercial banks.[31]

The guiding principles of the Enterprise for the Americas Initiative are not new. They have already been applied to the Caribbean and Central America in the form of the trade provisos of the CBI and the investment promotion schemes and structural adjustment conditionalities of USAID. Where these programs have had any impact at all, it has been primarily to the detriment of Caribbean economies and the advantage of US exporters and investors. As Edward Cumberbatch of the Caribbean Council of Churches said:

> If the CBI did work, it would work to the disadvantage of our Caribbean communities. By sending cheaper food products from here to the US, and by encouraging capital outflow from profits made here, it could only make the rich richer and the poor poorer.

Those concerned with the potential of the Enterprise Initiative and other free trade policies would be well-advised to heed the consequences of similar schemes as applied to the Caribbean in the 1980s and before. Jamaican development activists Horace Levy and Joan Ross-Frankson note that:

> History has already warned us about U.S. President Bush's proposal to create a Free Trade Zone comprising North, South, and Central America and the Caribbean. 'Privatisation' courtesy of structural adjustment builds on decades of transnationalisation of the region through giant U.S. corporations. Bush's 'new' proposal is as unlikely to bring benefits to the region's people as did those policies or the CBI.[31]

Notes

1. Nellis Crigler and Steven Lande, *Trade Policy Measures as a Means to Reduce Immigration in the 1990s: An Update.* Commission for the Study of International Migration and Cooperative Economic Development, US Congress, April 1990.

2. Clive Thomas, *The Poor and the Powerless*, Latin America Bureau/Monthly Review Press, New York and London, 1988.

3. Jorge Rodriguez Beruff, 'United States Policy and Regional Militarization', Projecto Caribeno para Justicia y Paz, Rio Piedras, Puerto Rico, June 1988.

4. Strategic Studies Institute, US Army War College, 'The Role of the US Military: Caribbean Basin', October 1981, quoted by Rodriguez Beruff, *United States Policy*.

5. USAID *Congressional Presentations* for fiscal years 1983 and 1984. US economic aid to the Caribbean Basin countries was US$1.5 billion in 1990; US military aid was US$110 million. US economic aid to the region for fiscal 1992 was projected at US$925 million, and military aid at US$124 million.

6. Emilio Pantojas Garcia, 'Restoring Hegemony: The Complementarity between the Security, Economic, and Political Aspects of US Policy in the Caribbean in the 1980s', in *Peace and Development in the Caribbean*, Figueroa, Green and Rodriguez Beruff (eds), Macmillan, London, 1990.

7. Author interview, February 1988.

8. US Department of Commerce, June 1990.

9. US Department of State Policy Paper, 14 December, 1981. After his tenure as a US official, Enders stated that the CBI had been largely his own idea. Its main purpose, and the reason for the State Department and White House support for the

plan, was to draw attention away from the Nicaraguan revolution and from the growing controversy about US support of militarism and the lack of human rights in Central America, and especially in El Salvador. (Interview with researcher Dara Menashi, 7 September, 1988.)

10. Emilio Pantojas Garcia, 'The US Caribbean Basin Initiative and the Puerto Rican Experience: Some Parallels and Lessons', *Latin America Perspectives*, Fall 1985.

11. A third component proposed by President Reagan was a 10 per cent tax credit for US corporations investing in designated beneficiary countries. This measure was reduced by Congress to a tax credit for expenses incurred by US companies for business conventions held in the region.

12. Ibid.

13. The relevant regulations are the Generalized System of Preferences (GSP) and sections 806.30 and 807.00 of the Special Tariff Provisions.

14. Emilio Pantojas Garcia, 'The CBI and Economic Restructuring in the Caribbean and Central America', a report prepared for the Projecto Caribeno para Justicia y Paz, Rio Piedras, Puerto Rico, 1987; Richard Newfarmer, 'Economic Policy Toward the Caribbean Basin: The Balance Sheet', *Journal of Interamerican Studies and World Affairs*, Vol. 27, No. 1, February 1985; US International Trade Commission, *First Report on the CBI*, Washington DC, 1986.

15. Newfarmer, *Economic Policy*.

16. World Bank, *Caribbean Exports: Preferential Markets and Performance*, May 1988.

17. One important body bypassed by the CBI is CARICOM, the regional federation that includes the majority of Caribbean countries. CARICOM promotes coordination in regional development, a division of labor in trade and production among member nations to prevent destructive forms of competition and to make up for the member countries' small size.

18. Emilio Pantojas-Garcia, 'The CBI and Economic Restructuring', World Bank, *Caribbean Exports*.

19. Calculated from figures presented in the World Bank's *Caribbean Exports: Preferential Markets and Performance*, May 1988. According to the World Bank, more than 90 per cent of the Caribbean exports to the US given duty-free status under the CBI consist of only seven items: beef and veal, rum, tobacco, certain pharmaceuticals, ethanol, steels, iron ware and bars, and electrical capacitors.

20. World Bank, *Caribbean Exports*.

21. Some clothing items cut and sewn in have since been made eligible for CBI benefits, but only if they use US-made cloth. Other textiles containing US-made components were already exempt from US duties.

22. These data do not include investment in the Bahamas, and the British Cayman Islands, the British Virgin Islands and Montserrat, where US investment did increase. Increased investment in these small territories was largely in the form of off-shore banks and other financing operations used to launder drug profits and to avoid US taxation and regulation of the transfer of corporate funds.

23. US Department of Commerce, International Trade Commission, *International Direct Investment, Global Trends and the US Role*, Vol. II, Washington DC.

24. US General Accounting Office, *The Need for More Reliable Data on Business Activities and Effectiveness of the Caribbean Basin Initiative*, August 1986.

25. Author interview, November 1987.

26. US Department of Commerce, CBI Office.

27. Author interviews, December 1987.

28. Author interviews, November 1987.

29. Author interview, November 1987.

30. Emilio Pantojas-Garcia, *The CBI and Economic Restructuring*, pp. 19–20.

31. Portions of the Bush proposal were adopted in amended form by the US Congress in March 1991, with additional provisions left pending.

32. Joan Ross-Frankson and Horace Levy, 'Networking on the Debt', *For Your Information*, newsletter of the Association of Development Agencies (ADA), August 1990, Kingston, Jamaica.

4. USAID in the Caribbean: Do As We Say . . .

> AID and American business are natural partners.
> Donald Woods, administrator of AID under Ronald Reagan

> The strings attached to US aid are the strings that are strangling the Caribbean.
> Jacqueline King, Caribbean Conference of Churches

The USAID is the main channel through which the US government sends non-military assistance to foreign countries. The rapid expansion and reshaping of AID programs in the Caribbean since 1980 make those programs a particularly useful indicator of changing US foreign assistance priorities.

US Foreign Assistance: Strategic Spending

The foreign aid programs of the US government are determined primarily by the economic and geopolitical priorities of the White House, the Pentagon and Congress. Spending decisions are shaped and justified mainly in accordance with US security interests. Consequently, the overwhelming majority of US foreign assistance dollars go to a small number of governments considered strategic allies of the United States. Hunger and poverty are not major criteria in the distribution of the aid funds. In 1989, just two countries, Israel and Egypt, received 48 per cent of the total US economic and military assistance to foreign governments and regions. Ten other countries each received more than US$150 million. Together, these 12 out of the 133 countries that received US foreign aid, got 77 per cent of the total. Of the 12 recipients of more than US$150 million, only 3 are considered 'low-income countries'.[1]

US non-military assistance, almost all of which is administered by USAID, is divided into three major categories: food aid, development assistance and economic support funds (ESF). ESF and direct military aid, which is distributed through other channels, together comprise US 'security assistance'. ESF grants are often an indirect form of military aid. In some countries, such as El Salvador, they are used to help governments allied with the United States cover non-military expenses, with the result that more money is available to them for military weapons, training, and salaries.

Most US government food aid is channeled through AID under the PL 480, or 'food for peace', program. PL 480 food aid accounted for 1.4 per cent of total US bilateral foreign aid in 1989. More than half of this food falls under Title I of PL 480; it is not given to the hungry but is sold to foreign governments, which usually resell the food. The government of Jamaica, for example, received about US$30–$40 million in US food aid annually in the late 1980s, reselling most of it to help finance its debts. US food aid is a means of supporting US allies financially, of obtaining policy changes desired by the United States and of enlarging foreign markets for US commercial food exports. According to the AID administrator under US President Reagan, Alan Woods, 'Of the 50 largest buyers of U.S. farm goods, 34 are countries that have received food aid from the United States.'[2]

US development assistance, too, serves a variety of purposes, not all of them related to economic development or the reduction of poverty. In Guatemala, for example, USAID development assistance funds have been used to support the displacement and resettlement of civilians by military force.[3]

USAID's budget grew from about US$2 billion in 1961, the year it was established, to a peak of US$7.2 billion in 1987. It has declined gradually since then. In 1988, the United States ranked 18th among all nations in terms of the proportion of its total budget spent on foreign aid. Japan has surpassed the US as the source of the largest total amount of aid funds worldwide.

AID Discovers the Caribbean

Under the Reagan administration, which took office in 1981, AID spending in the Caribbean soared; before the 1980s, the United States had spent relatively little there. USAID's Caribbean budget averaged US$66 million between 1962 and 1982. Total US development assistance, food aid and ESF in the Caribbean jumped to US$302 million in 1983 and US$359 million in 1984, the year following the Grenada invasion, and then began to decline. (AID spent US$209 million in the region, including Belize, in 1990.)[4] While financing from other foreign governments and multilateral agencies fell by about 60 per cent from 1982 to 1988, the higher US spending in the region helped to make up the difference.

In 1983, the recipient of the third largest per capita amount of US foreign aid funds in the world was Jamaica. The Eastern Caribbean, which before 1980 received scant attention and only token funding from USAID, became the focus of an expanded AID program fashioned to reflect the political priorities of the Reagan administration. In 1984, USAID spent US$440 for every citizen of Grenada, making that small nation the recipient of the second largest amount, after Israel, of US aid funds per capita in the world that year.[5]

The goals and results of US economic assistance to the Caribbean might dismay US citizens who believe US development aid money is spent to assist the hungry and the poor and to win friendship and respect for the United States. While some of the Caribbean projects of USAID do attempt to address the needs of the poor, AID's program in the region has become increasingly subordinate to the White House political agenda. AID funds in the Caribbean have been used to reward those governments which support the United States in international forums. Grenada twice sided with the United States in 1985 and 1986 in the United Nations (UN) as part of a small minority of nations voting in opposition to anti-apartheid sanctions against South Africa.

Dominica, which became a virtual US client state in the 1980s, was one of the first two countries, and the only one in the Caribbean and Latin America, to express support of the US invasion of Panama in 1989, and the only country to side with the United States and Israel in a major 151–3 UN vote for a political settlement of the Palestine–Israel conflict. The blatantly political use of aid funds has added to widespread skepticism in the region about the United States' expressed interest in promoting democracy and the economic well-being of the Caribbean. Even influential members of the region's governing parties and business elites express resentment of what they perceive as Washington's arrogant and heavy-handed approach.

The main AID recipient countries in the Caribbean are Jamaica, the Dominican Republic, Haiti and Belize, which in 1989 received US$120.1 million, US$50.1 million, US$30.6 million and US$7.6 million respectively. During the years 1984–87, AID expenditures per capita were: Belize, US$79; Jamaica, US$51; the Dominican Republic, US$15.46; and Haiti, US$11.70. The high per capita Belize budget reflects the US goal of building a back-up base in western Central America to supplement its strongholds in Honduras in the center and Panama at the far eastern end of the isthmus. High AID spending in Jamaica in the 1980s was part of the US effort to bolster the government of conservative Edward Seaga. Haiti and the Dominican Republic, although their peoples' incomes are among the lowest in the Caribbean, received much less. Guyana, the second poorest country (after Haiti) in the greater Caribbean, got almost nothing until 1986, when it began receiving US food aid and, along with it, pressure to undergo economic structural adjustment. Guyana signed an IMF agreement in 1990 and was slated to receive US$7 million in food aid and US$1 million in structural adjustment support funds in the US fiscal year 1991.

Until the late 1970s, US policymakers regarded the small islands of the Eastern Caribbean as a political backwater, guarded by the ageing but still dependable British colonial system. The United States gave little economic assistance to the sub-region before 1979. The Reagan administration took a new look at the islands of the area, perceiving them as the gateway to the Caribbean Basin: Central America, northern South America and the insular Caribbean. AID spending in the sub-region climbed, reaching a peak in 1984, when AID spent more than US$114 million in the Eastern Caribbean, including US$48.4 million for its post-invasion Grenada program. Spending on AID's Eastern Caribbean Region program in 1990 totalled US$29 million.

AID explained the rationale for maintaining some expenditures there in the face of pressure to shift US funds to Eastern Europe:

> Threats to democracy and US security in the region have not been as great [in the Caribbean] as in Central America. Events in Grenada not long ago, however, remind us that we must always be alert to the possibility that hostile forces could take advantage of opportunities to threaten large volumes of US trade — particularly in petroleum — that pass through Caribbean sea lanes.[6]

US overt direct military aid to the Eastern Caribbean jumped from zero in fiscal year 1981 to US$7.6 million in 1986. This figure only partially reflects the increase in US military presence in the sub-region. Much of the costs of the US-sponsored war games now held annually there, as well as part of the costs of training Eastern Caribbean paramilitary police units and expanding US bases and other installations, are covered by other budget items and do not appear as foreign military aid.

The Uses of AID

Privatization has been the overarching theme of AID's projects in the Caribbean and worldwide since 1981. As interpreted by AID, privatization entails the shift of resources — tax revenues, public land, government-owned enterprises, public utilities, the time and attention of civil servants, and foreign grants and loans — to private hands and to uses intended to stimulate private investment. An array of AID projects provide direct and indirect subsidies to commercial businesses, mainly investors from outside the Caribbean and especially US-based corporations. For example, factory space is rented to manufacturers at rates below the actual cost of constructing and maintaining the facilities. Potential entrepreneurs are matched with loan sources and Caribbean investment opportunities by bureaucrats paid with AID funds. Related AID projects promote changes in Caribbean government policies, such as revisions of tax laws, designed to make private enterprise more profitable. Other AID projects aim to create new, pro-business institutions or to reshape existing institutions so that they will carry out the privatization strategy after AID projects are discontinued. The impact of such policies on Grenada, Dominica and Jamaica is detailed in chapters 7, 8 and 9.

Another category of AID funding in the Caribbean (and globally) provides grants directly to governments closely allied with the US. Some of these grants are for specific projects, such as electric power systems. Others are lump sums of money to help pro-US governments cover their budget deficits and pay their debts. Either way, these grants increase the chances for re-election of governing parties supportive of the United States and its policies. They are part of the international patronage system that rewards US political allies.

A sub-theme in AID's Caribbean programs, and AID programs worldwide, is 'basic human needs'. Projects in the dwindling AID basic needs portfolio include small grants to repair schools, provide water to rural communities, operate health clinics and provide temporary public works jobs. In part, this emphasis is a carry-over from an earlier trend in AID strategy; in part, it is an effort to contain the social and political crises that are intensifying as a result of the lack of significant economic growth and of the shared benefits of growth.

An ideal project, from AID's point of view, addresses all of these goals. A network of newly resurfaced roads, for example, helps private companies to get export crops to the dock, makes transportation easier for the rural population and lends prestige to the co-sponsoring government. Most AID grants for infrastructure are designed to stimulate investment in export agriculture and manufacturing by private entrepreneurs. In addition, roads, power plants, port construction and similar large projects are 'highly visible activities' (AID's term) which serve as advertisements for the United States.

Caribbean aid for US investors

AID grants recycle funds back to US-owned businesses, such as the consulting firms and construction companies which get the bulk of the contracts for planning, carrying out and evaluating AID projects. For example, the USAID grant agreement to the government of Dominica for a US$12.1 million road repair project stipulated that US$10 million of the AID funds had to be used for the purchase of materials, equipment and consultant services from US firms. Similar conditions tied to an AID grant for privatization of agriculture in Grenada required the use of US-made vehicles and equipment that were not compatible with the tools and equipment being used in Grenada. The Jamaica Agricultural Development Foundation, set up with US$7.5 million in AID funds in cooperation with the US dairy firm Land O' Lakes, netted numerous benefits to Land O' Lakes, reportedly including a US$400,000 contract to provide cheese to Jamaica — a country capable of producing its own cheese — at three times the market price.

AID's newsletter describes the benefits of agency programs to US entrepreneurs and investors:

> AID Missions often apply resources directly to assist U.S. businesses. Under the Commodity Import Program, the Agency makes money available to developing countries to import U.S. products such as tractors and the equipment used in irrigation systems. The agency's development programs also call for the use and export of U.S.-made products, including agricultural equipment. In 1985, bilateral U.S. economic assistance to developing countries directly generated about $6 billion in U.S. exports of goods and services.[8]

In addition, the quasi-public AID-affiliated agency is chaired by AID's administrator and has a board composed of eight US business representatives and seven US government officials. The Overseas Private Investment Corporation provides corporations with risk insurance to protect US investors against expropriations or political turmoil and ensures that profits and capital can be converted into US dollars. OPIC also has a credit program under which US firms can obtain loans and loan guarantees as high as US$50 million for a single project.

AID's newsletter and other publications spotlight AID's Caribbean program, in conjunction with CBI trade legislation, as a leading example of the successful promotion of US business opportunities.

> The CBI has focused attention on trade opportunities in the region and has bolstered the prospects of U.S. firms. The bottom line: U.S. exports to

AID-assisted Caribbean countries have also grown, from $3.9 billion in 1984 to $4.9 billion in 1987.

The newsletter notes that 'non-traditional' exports from AID-assisted Caribbean countries increased between 1983 and 1987. It fails to mention that, *overall*, exports from the same countries to the United States over the same period declined, reducing the region's earnings and adding to the Caribbean's dependence on imported food and foreign financing.

There is a fundamental discrepancy between the major AID goal of promoting US business interests in the Caribbean and the goal of increasing employment, economic development and stability in the countries which receive US aid. AID recipient countries are required to purchase US exports, but US products are costly; buying them undermines Caribbean countries' ability to keep their economies afloat. Imports of US goods tend to weaken Caribbean economies because they displace local products, often forcing producers out of business. US investments in the region provide too few jobs, and at wages that are too low, to make up for the economic losses resulting from AID grant restrictions.

The acting USAID Caribbean and Latin American head, Marilyn Zak, alluded to this dilemma in 1988 when she said of AID's Caribbean programs:

> It's not so much local government policies on foreign investment that are posing a problem for us, since the foreign exchange generated [by US-owned industry] goes right back to the United States. What's important to us here is job creation, which is a problem because wage rates [in the Caribbean] are too high.

One AID-supported program that, in theory, increases local employment by promoting small businesses was the establishment of National Development Foundations (NDFs) in the Windward Islands, Antigua, Barbados, Montserrat and Belize. Dominica's NDF was headed by Anita Bully. According to Bully:

> AID is supposed to provide support for the private sector here, including medium, small and micro-enterprises. Yet what you see is financial support for a series of US-based agencies. You can't say 'AID is giving us $10 million' when most of that cake goes back to the US. . . . There's a need for a limited amount of foreign investment, especially joint ventures, but if you want to create an independent and strong private sector — if that's what they really want to do — then it has to be a *Dominican* private sector.[9]

Aid for consultants

AID's operating procedures have been a source of frustration to Caribbean businessmen, government officials, representatives of non-government organizations, heads of Caribbean projects funded by AID and even many AID staff. They fault the Agency for, in particular, its heavy reliance on US consulting firms, its imposition of criteria and plans developed in Washington and its failure to consult intended project beneficiaries or to draw upon Caribbean expertise.

Veteran AID Eastern Caribbean official Peter Medford acknowledged that, 'There is validity to the criticism of AID for setting up new institutions that pull human resources out of existing institutions by offering better salaries and benefits.' Vincentian trade unionist Burns Bonadie told a US Congressional delegation that, through the CBI and USAID, Caribbean organizations and governments 'are saddled with prescriptions from outside'. Marcus DeFreitas, ex-Trade and Industry minister of St Vincent and the Grenadines, believes that while 'AID's intentions are good', its effectiveness is undermined by 'so many AID conditions that are forced upon us' by the Agency's own priorities and by non-Caribbean AID consultants with ill-informed preconceptions. Says Vincentian Ministry of Agriculture planner Hugh Phillips, 'AID comes in with their minds made up. Then they try to finesse you into asking for what they already have to offer. There's no real dialog.'[10]

According to Castine Quashie, Director of St Vincent's NDF, part of the reason for AID's failure to stimulate more small business development lies in the Agency's 'vague, confused, and contradictory' funding criteria. It is simply not logical, he said, to set ambitious goals for employment-generating investments and then constrain potential enterprises by requirements such as the use of US vessels for shipping. He called such policies indicative of AID's 'lack of any long-term view' for Caribbean development. Another problem, Quashie says, is the agency's own administrative inefficiency: 'AID tells you what you need, what time you need it. But then, because of the agency's crazy bookkeeping, the grants come through after the program is already over.'

The ineffectiveness of AID private enterprise promotion in the Eastern Caribbean has been documented by the Agency's own evaluations. A 1988 study reported that the Agency paid a multinational consulting firm to implement the Project Development Assistance Project (PDAP), an effort to seek employment-creating investment for the region, at a total cost of US$16 million. The evaluators estimated that PDAP had influenced the creation of a total of 2,782 jobs, meaning that each job for which the consultant might claim some credit cost AID US$5,751, considerably more than the Caribbeans employed are likely to have earned. The net export earnings possibly stimulated by the project totalled US$12.5 million, less than the cost of the project.[11] The main beneficiary seems to have been the consulting firm, which had its contract renewed despite the dismal results reported in interim evaluations.

In any case, AID's method of calculating job creation is highly misleading. Castine Quashie said that AID procedures required him to list any employment related to an NDF-funded business as one 'job created', even in cases when the job, such as painting a store-front or clearing a plot of land, lasted only a few days. His observations were confirmed by the directors of the Grenada and Dominica NDFs.

AID's Eastern Caribbean Testing Ground

Social and economic crisis is as acute today in much of the English-speaking Caribbean as in the rest of the region, despite the particular history of these former British colonies. Their political independence came about relatively recently and was achieved peacefully, although after a long political struggle.[12] By the time they obtained sovereignty, the English-speaking Caribbean islands had elected legislatures and other Westminster-style political institutions, educational structures modeled after the British system, a relatively low level of political violence and repression, a common language and other cultural ties with the hemisphere's dominant power, the United States, and they were not burdened with powerful and costly military establishments. These supposed advantages have not spared the English-speaking Caribbean from worsening poverty, social disintegration and political instability.

Following the official departure of the British, the United States moved to extend its influence in the region. It spent an average of US$52 million yearly from 1980 through 1989 on its Eastern Caribbean program, which covers Antigua/Barbuda, Dominica, Grenada, St Kitts/Nevis, St Lucia and St Vincent and the Grenadines, in contrast to an annual average of only US$11.3 million during the period 1962–82.[13] The decade also saw rapid expansion of the US military role in the Leeward and Windward Islands. These small Eastern Caribbean nations, along with Barbados, are the furthest outposts along what Pentagon and White House strategists have called the 'third border' of the United States. In their view, these island outposts had to be fortified and drawn into the US military network. Increased militarization has added an ominous new factor to the political equation in a region where, until recently, peacekeeping was carried out mainly by police forces armed only with batons.

Along with Jamaica, the Eastern Caribbean has been a testing ground in the English-speaking Caribbean for the US policy of privatization, an unregulated free market and the aggressive promotion of US business interests. But these policies, vigorously promoted by the Eastern Caribbean office of USAID, have increased the pressures on the poor and heightened the islands' vulnerability to external economic forces. The experiences of Grenada and Dominica, described in chapters 7 and 8, provide revealing lessons about the perilous consequences for poor nations of AID's development doctrines.

In the context of these policy failures, USAID is working with other industrial countries and international lending agencies to require Caribbean governments to adopt economic austerity policies as a means of coping with growing deficits and unpayable foreign debts. Among Eastern Caribbean countries, Dominica, Grenada, Guyana, and Trinidad and Tobago have become the staging ground for externally designed and coordinated programs of structural adjustment (see chapter 6).

AID's analysis of the problems and prospects of the Eastern Caribbean is much like that of the colonial administrations which shaped Caribbean economies through the mid-20th century. AID equates the region's potential for development with its ability to produce and supply resources — crops, minerals, labor and tourist attractions — for other parts of the world: 'Economic growth will depend to a great extent on increasing export earnings, particularly to markets outside the region.'[14]

AID concedes that major constraints prevent the Caribbean, especially the small states of the Eastern Caribbean, from producing exports cheaply enough to compete with those from other countries. To cope with these 'comparative disadvantages', AID's 1985 Strategy Statement for the sub-region called for government actions to aid private business, including: fewer restrictions on corporations and their rights to take profits out of the host countries, reduced taxation of corporations and higher-income individuals, and elimination of reduction of import duties on parts and materials imported by private companies for assembly and re-export. These policy changes, AID predicted, would entice entrepreneurs to produce more and cheaper exports.

These AID recommendations do not address the built-in limits, cited by AID itself, to the international competitiveness of Eastern Caribbean exports. These include high production costs, declining world demand for the region's traditional exports and the absence of linkages between export businesses and the rest of the islands' economies. Nevertheless, driven more by ideology than reason, AID has pressed Eastern Caribbean governments to strive to make private industrial enterprises more profitable. AID recommends the transfer or sale of publicly owned land, utility companies and other government-run enterprises to private owners, and increased government spending on infrastructure, such as factory buildings and port facilities, to support private export enterprises.

To finance such programs, and compensate for reduced corporate taxes and duties, AID's strategy statement calls for increased, more regressive taxation of the majority of the countries' populations. (Regressive taxes are those which require low- and middle-income people to pay a higher percentage of their incomes than do the wealthy.) AID also insists upon reducing government spending for social services and lowering public-employee wages, with two purposes: to shift government revenues toward support for private business and to put a downward pressure on wage rates throughout the economy. In essence, AID advocates greater subsidization of businesses, especially foreign firms, by Caribbean taxpayers and workers, supplemented by AID funds derived from US taxpayers.

AID versus Caribbean institutions

Geographic, economic and political fragmentation is one of the greatest obstacles to greater Caribbean self-reliance. This is especially true in the small, scattered states of the Eastern Caribbean, where regional coordination is essential to development. The thrust of AID's program, however, is in the opposite direction. The US government has used AID grants not only to reward some governments and isolate others, but also to manipulate Caribbean regional institutions into adopting US political criteria. The politically discriminatory nature of such grants presses regional bodies to choose between

US dollars and their integrity as institutions representing the region as a whole.

In 1981, USAID proposed a Basic Human Needs Project grant for the Eastern Caribbean, to be administered through the Caribbean Development Bank (CDB). The funds were offered on the condition that Grenada, which had a pro-socialist government at the time, be excluded from the grant benefits. Unwilling to accept this form of interference, the CDB declined the funds. According to William G. Demas, who was president of the CDB at the time:

> We rejected that money because we cannot discriminate against any one political system. Even in the last years of the Carter administration, US policy shifted toward more bilateral funding and less support for Caribbean regional institutions. Reagan's entire aid thrust has been a deliberate attempt to discourage regional integration.[15]

Typically, USAID bypasses Caribbean regional institutions to set up alternate bodies more reflective of US political philosophy and amenable to US influence. Soon after the CDB rejected the AID grant that required the exclusion of Grenada, the US supplied funds to establish the Caribbean Financial Services Corporation (CFSC) as a more compliant conduit for US funds to the region. AID provided US$17.3 million in loans and a US$400,000 grant to establish the CFSC as an offshore bank to provide financing to businesses in the English-speaking Caribbean, some of which already had ties to branches or firms in the United States. Some AID staff objected to the project because it 'appeared to be solely in support of well-established businesses and having little developmental impact', according to an AID-commissioned evaluation. Audit reports by the office of AID's Regional Inspector General found that the CFSC project fell far short of its goals, and cited evidence of 'self-dealing' and other conflicts of interest among the clique of businessmen involved.

Similarly, AID chose to establish its own institution, the High Impact Agriculture and Marketing Project (HIAMP) Trust Fund, to subsidize private investment in Eastern Caribbean agricultural exports. AID could have chosen to work with the already-established, Caribbean-led Caribbean Food Corporation (CFC), and its subsidiary, CATCO, a joint public/private sector enterprise which provides technical assistance to Caribbean farmers and markets Caribbean agricultural products to Europe and within the Caribbean. Instead, HIAMP was set up to embody AID's principles of support for profit-making enterprise and to promote exports primarily to the United States. Most often, AID simply ignores Caribbean regional structures and efforts at economic planning and cooperation, or treats them with disdain.

In its dealings with Caribbean organizations, even those supported by AID itself, the Agency shows little respect for local initiative or democratic process. For example, AID provided funds to seven Eastern Caribbean countries for re-lending to small local enterprises. At AID's direction, coordinating committees were to be established to oversee the loans in each country. In Dominica, an AID representative met with more than 40 private sector organizations and several NGOs: 'We told them to come up with a structure, so they did,' the representative later reported. The Coordinating Committee held an election to choose its officers, but after the election AID disappeared from the scene. More than a year later, the elected committee officers learned from another source that a new committee had been selected. Asked why, the AID representative stated bluntly, 'Miss Charles [the conservative prime minister] didn't like it [the election result], so we canned it.'[16] Asked the same question, an AID official who helped design the loan project replied with sarcasm about the Dominica election: 'It was a real zoo. That's what happens when you let democracy take its course. They had elections without any guidance from us about which groups could have a real impact. They went right ahead and voted.'[17]

AID and Agriculture in the Eastern Caribbean: A Garden in the US Backyard?

The Eastern Caribbean countries depended at least as heavily on earnings from a few unprocessed agricultural crops at the end of the 1980s as when they gained independence 10 to 15 years earlier. Only in St Lucia and Antigua had the proportion of earnings from non-agricultural activities, mainly tourism and manufacturing, risen significantly. In 1988, the region was importing about US$370 million more worth of food from other countries than it was producing locally, according to USAID estimates. AID noted that this 'negative food balance' cost the equivalent of half of the region's annual current account deficit (the amount of red ink accumulated yearly).[18]

In the Windward Islands of the Eastern Caribbean, events during the first decade of independence drove home the lesson of the danger of excessive reliance on export crops. Severe hurricanes in 1979 and 1980 devastated coconuts, bananas, citrus and other tree crops. Periodic droughts and epidemics of pests and diseases caused serious export losses. Prices for the region's agricultural exports were unstable and beyond the control of local farmers and governments. Yet AID encouraged the same policies that had rendered the Eastern Caribbean colonies so vulnerable.

Some unusual circumstances allowed post-independence governments in the Windwards to postpone reckoning with the dangers of depending on a few export crops. Banana prices paid to farmers rose to record high levels beginning in 1986, mainly because the value of the US dollar fell in relation to the British pound. Grenada enjoyed windfall gains from nutmeg sales in 1986 and 1987, largely the result of a cartel agreement with Indonesia, then the world's only other large-scale producer. The banana boom and the nutmeg bonanza enabled the governments of Dominica and Grenada to ignore the overall continuing decline of agricultural productivity and the stagnation of manufacturing in both countries. This statistical magic, along with the tangible impact of increased cash in the hands of banana and nutmeg growers, helped to disguise the underlying weakness of the islands' economies. But for those able to see past the smoke and mirrors, these quirks of fortune only accentuated the vulnerability of Eastern Caribbean economies, based on the export of unprocessed crops, to factors beyond the islands' control.

Nearly all concerned Caribbean citizens, particularly non-government organizations working with the rural poor and the farmers themselves, agree that a more varied agriculture, with greater local control over prices and markets, is needed urgently. Earlene Horne, a banana farmer and General Secretary of the National Farmers' Union of St Vincent and the Grenadines, observes:

> We have a history of slavery, and now that slavery's abolished we're still depending on external masters, expecting them to buy our one or two export crops. Instead, I'd like to see us produce a variety of crops, process them locally to meet our own needs, and then sell the surplus abroad.[19]

John Elwin, an agriculture specialist at the CDB, said:

> When we look at our food import bill, we can see the very real danger of our dependency on traditional exports, especially bananas. We have to make a transition toward more self-reliance and self-respect . . . Instead of looking primarily toward selling more goods to industrialized countries, we need to generate demand in our own economies. We need a practical import substitution strategy.[20]

USAID, however, spurns any reorientation of Caribbean agriculture toward meeting local and regional needs first. Analysis of AID agriculture projects in the region, and of the US trade regulations on which their success depends, shows that the United States is promoting continued dependence on the export of traditional crops; alternative agricultural exports get little attention, and the production of food for local and regional needs gets even less.

- Increased national or regional food self-sufficiency is totally lacking as a priority in AID's program.
- Many AID agriculture projects are specifically geared to increasing the production and export of traditional crops such as bananas and cocoa.
- AID projects and policies with regard to land tenure and distribution, such as the Grenada and St Lucia Model Farms projects, have encouraged continued production of traditional exports.
- Those AID projects which purport to promote agricultural diversification, such as HIAMP, do little to enhance the ability of small-scale farmers to produce new crops and almost nothing to help develop reliable markets in the medium or long term for non-traditional exports.
- To the extent that AID does address the problems of marketing, its policies tend to reproduce exploitative relations between most farmers, on the one hand, and agribusiness firms and shipping companies, on the other.
- AID's policy of aiding the 'most efficient' farmers favors larger, wealthier

growers at the expense of the landless and land-poor. Among Caribbean farmers, the wealthier growers generally have the least to gain from contributing to the food security of the majority by growing crops for local and regional markets.

- AID projects often create new institutions which bypass and weaken existing regional structures, such as CARICOM, the purpose of which is to promote intraregional trade and cooperation for development and greater self-reliance.
- AID in the late 1980s had become a vehicle for promoting structural adjustment policies geared to increasing exports, including traditional agricultural products at lower prices (see chapter 5).
- AID's main selling point with Congress and the US public is its promotion of opportunities for US businesses, especially those exporting food, feed grain and other goods to countries of the South. By promoting exports of the relatively low-priced products of the heavily government-subsidized US agricultural system, this policy undermines the ability of small farmers to sell their own crops in the Caribbean region.

Diversification doubletalk

Nearly all AID planning and evaluation documents related to Eastern Caribbean agriculture stress the need for countries in the region to diversify their agricultural exports.[21] The Agency reported that the value of Eastern Caribbean exports supported by AID increased by an estimated 28 per cent from 1985 to 1988, to US$165 million. However, the value of non-traditional exports, including mangos, papayas, vegetables, aloe vera, avocados, pepper sauce and flowers produced with AID assistance, declined by 23 per cent during the same period, from US$6 million to only US$4.7 million.

According to AID projections, the Agency expected to be supporting production of US$171 million worth of traditional exports from the Eastern Caribbean by 1990, a further increase of 29 per cent. In the same period, the value of AID-supported non-traditional exports was projected to increase by 127 per cent, to US$10.6 million. Such an increase is doubtful in light of the past failures and clouded future of AID's largest agriculture diversification project in the region, HIAMP. But even if such an increase were to occur, earnings from AID-supported agricultural diversification would amount to only 6 per cent of the Eastern Caribbean's modest earnings from traditional crop exports.

Neither of AID's current top-billed agriculture projects for the Eastern Caribbean, HIAMP nor TROPRO, encourages local processing of tropical fruits or vegetables. The agro-processing industry can provide employment and preserve seasonal crops for local storage and regional distribution by canning, bottling, drying, chilling and the manufacture of juice concentrates. This reduces the need for expensive food imports and can add to the value of surplus crops to be exported.

Agro-industry and regional food marketing, however, are not AID priorities, for reasons that are fundamentally political and ideological. More important to AID than promoting regional self-reliance are short-term export earnings that help pay debt bills and provide profit opportunities for US businesses. Neither agro-processing nor the regional distribution of fresh produce generally yields the kind of quick results and high profit margins expected by most US investors and demanded by lenders.

In addition, successful food production for local and regional consumption in the Caribbean requires time, planning and coordination among small-country governments. In many cases, such projects may be best implemented by regional organizations, governments, joint public–private ventures or cooperatives. The persistence, despite the lack of government encouragement, of food-processing co-ops such as Grenada's Grenfruit venture attests to the interest among rural Caribbean women in cooperative income-generating activities. But the support of government-assisted or cooperative enterprises runs directly counter to AID's philosophy of private sector-led growth as the path to development. Also, AID is more interested in fostering bilateral ties and business ventures between US and Caribbean entrepreneurs than in strengthening regional institutions and facilitating cooperation among them.

Meanwhile, AID officials are determined that the fate of agriculture in the Eastern Caribbean must remain subject to the Agency's control and consonant with Washington's privatization and free-market development ideology. They responded angrily, for example, when the Secretariat of the OECS expressed its intention to take responsibility for agricultural diversification efforts in the region. In a memorandum prepared for the June 1988 meeting of the Caribbean Group for Cooperation in Economic Development (CGCED), AID strongly urged the OECS governments 'to reexamine this decidedly statist position'. At the same time, the Agency acknowledged that 'the private sector has been unable or unwilling to take the lead in agricultural diversification'.

The failure of AID's strategy in the Eastern Caribbean

Many of AID's recommendations have in fact been adopted by AID-assisted Caribbean governments, although not always in full. Moreover, the CBI, which promised to open US markets to Caribbean exports, has been in effect since 1984. These programs and policy changes to promote export-led growth have failed. Significant expansion of industry and diversification of agriculture, upon which AID says the region's future depends, has not occurred in most Caribbean countries, and certainly not in the Eastern Caribbean.

AID has been forced to acknowledge that its optimistic predictions of economic growth in the region have not come to pass. The agency's Congressional Presentation on the Eastern Caribbean for fiscal year 1989 begins with the admission that,

> The English-speaking islands of the Eastern Caribbean have so far been unable to take advantage of the trade and tax provisions of the Caribbean Basin Initiative and other opportunities for achieving rapid and sustained long-term growth. . . . The small size and isolation of these islands impede the effort to attract the significant foreign capital required for expanded investment.

This admission, however, has not led AID to alter its insistence that the answer to the region's problems lies in increased exports to the US and other countries of the North. The possibility of developing Caribbean agriculture and industry to meet local needs and to strengthen local and regional markets does not seem even to occur to AID officials. As a farmer in Dominica observed, 'For years the United States has seen our country as part of your backyard. Now it seems you want to make that yard into your garden.'

The goal of export-led growth has proved elusive, but in its official statements AID continues to present a rosy picture of development prospects if its privatization policies are implemented fully. More candid comments by AID officials reveal a very different attitude. An AID official who headed the Agency's agriculture program in Grenada in the mid-1980s remarked, 'Once you accept the need [for Caribbean countries] to earn foreign exchange, you're stuck with tourism and export agriculture.[22] An official whose job has been to oversee a US$12 million program to support businesses in the Eastern Caribbean was equally cynical: 'None of these islands is viable. . . . Only tourism and drug traffic keep these islands from going down the tubes.[23]

Notes

1. The political–strategic basis of US foreign aid is even more clearly shown in per capita terms. In 1989 African countries south of the Sahara received about US$1.90 per person in US economic and military aid, on the average. In contrast, the four Central American countries most closely allied with the United States received more than US$40 per person from AID, and Israel received US$632 for every resident of that country. (USAID *Congressional Presentation* for fiscal year 1991.)

2. USAID *Highlights*, Vol. 5, No. 3, 1988.

3. Thomas Barry and Deb Preusch, *The Soft War*, Grove Press, New York, 1988.

4. USAID, *Congressional Presentation* for fiscal year 1991; figures for supplemental appropriations provided by the AID Caribbean office in the US Department of State; USAID, *Overseas Loans and Grants*, Washington, 1986.

5. USAID, *Overseas Loans and Grants*, Washington, 1986.

6. USAID, *Congressional Presentation* for fiscal year 1991, 1990.

7. Timothy Ashby, *Missed Opportunities: The Rise and Fall of Jamaica's Edward Seaga*, Hudson Institute, 1989.

8. USAID, *USAID Highlights*, Washington, September 1988.

9. Author interview, December 1987.

10. Author interviews, 1987–88.

11. AID Evaluation Summary PDKAL940.

12. The independence dates of the nations of the English-speaking Eastern Caribbean today are: the Windward Islands — Dominica 1988, Grenada 1974, St Lucia 1979, and St Vincent and the Grenadines 1979; the Leeward Islands — Antigua/Barbuda 1981, St Kitts/Nevis 1983; Barbados, to the east of the Windwards, 1966; Trinidad and Tobago, off the coast of Venezuela, 1962; and Guyana on the South American mainland, 1966. The Leeward Islands of Montserrat and Anguilla remain under British rule. The English-speaking Caribbean as a whole, including Guyana on the northern coast of South America

and Belize in Central America, as well as the English-speaking islands, has a population of 5.3 million.

13. Calculated from USAID, *Overseas Grants and Loans*, 1986, and from the estimated 1989 expenditures reported in USAID's *Congressional Presentation* for fiscal year 1990, Washington, 1989. The estimates do not include Barbados, Guyana or Trinidad and Tobago, which received negligible amounts of US aid during the 1980s.

14. USAID, *Congressional Presentation* for fiscal year 1988.

15. Author interview, December 1987.

16. Author interview, February 1988.

17. Author interview, November 1987.

18. USAID, 'Eastern Caribbean 1989/90 Annual Action Plan', Washington, 1988.

19. Author interview, November 1987.

20. Author interview, December 1987.

21. USAID Eastern Caribbean Regional Statements for 1985 and Annual Action Plans, 1985–90.

22. Author interview, November 1987.

23. Author interview, February 1988.

Part III
Adjusting The Caribbean

5. The IMF/World Bank Prescription

The devastation wreaked upon the Caribbean peoples, through economic policies whose true purpose is hidden from us, is crushing our hopes for a better future. It is increasing poverty, especially among women, breaking up families, and deepening the cries and pain of our children, even those yet to be born. The dependency syndrome purposefully designed to favor US interests has tied our economies in debt that each one of us is forced to pay until we reach our death bed. It is really a recolonization by the North of the South.

Josephine Dublin, Caribbean Association for Feminist
Research and Action

USAID's Caribbean policy, with its emphasis on privatization and market-led growth, has failed to stimulate the increases in employment and investment promised by US policymakers. With the CBI discredited, the elusive goal of free-market development appears dim on the horizon, while the region's trade deficits and swelling debts loom large. In this context, AID has increased its emphasis on structural adjustment as a way, in the words of one AID official, 'to postpone the big crunch', of a drastic fiscal crisis for US allies in the Caribbean.

Structural adjustment is the economic strategy currently being promoted, not only in the Caribbean, but also in the majority of indebted nations in the South, by the US government, the World Bank, and the IMF. Its purpose is to improve the fiscal balance sheets of governments and stimulate economic growth, mainly by increasing exports. The idea is that impoverished countries will thus be able to dig their way out of debt and become paying customers in the global marketplace. Structural adjustment redirects resources away from consumption by the citizens of indebted countries in the South and toward debt payments to foreign lenders. It shifts capital, minerals, land and labor away from production for local needs and towards increased production for export.

Its proponents call it strong economic medicine which the ailing countries of the South must swallow for their own good. The economy doctors of the World Bank and the IMF, backing their pronouncements with computer projections, warn of dire consequences for the patients who do not swallow their medicine. The sponsors of structural adjustment also contend that it is urgent and essential to the preservation of the current global economic system. 'As the 1980s draw to a close, economic turbulence and uncertainty persist,' noted the World Bank in its 1988 *World Development Report*. The adoption of Bank-recommended policies by the North and the South for 'global adjustment', the report states, 'provide the best chance to avoid a worldwide economic downturn'.[1]

The Caribbean has been a structural adjustment testing ground. Jamaica was among the first countries to accept economic re-programming by the sponsors of adjustment; as of 1988, it had received more funds per capita in World Bank structural adjustment lending than any other country in the world. Other Caribbean countries getting the adjustment treatment include the Dominican Republic, Haiti, Dominica, Grenada, Guyana, and Trinidad and Tobago. The World Bank and IMF are eager to administer the same remedy to Caribbean nations that, until recently, seemed to be prospering, particularly Antigua and Barbados.

An Attack on the Majority

Structural adjustment programs typically require Caribbean governments to adopt policies intended to increase their exports (for example, allocating more land and resources to export crops) and measures to lower the costs of producing them, such as ceilings on wages. Some structural adjustment programs also require the devaluation of Caribbean currencies. This makes the devaluing countries' exports cheaper on world markets and discourages imports from other countries by making them more expensive. Adjustment programs usually require Caribbean countries to aid foreign investors by reducing taxes and increasing government spending on factory buildings and port facilities.

These policies, however, worsen the vulnerability of Caribbean economies to external economic forces which they cannot control, such as falling commodity prices, footloose investors and fickle tourist preferences. They intensify the pressure on struggling small farmers by raising the costs of imported tools, fertilizers and pesticides, putting many of them out of business. The result is an increase in the adjusting countries' dependence on foreign sources of food. Structural adjustment austerity measures also hurt workers and their families by reducing their poverty-level incomes even further.

Among the most directly damaging effects of structural adjustment programs are required reductions in government spending on public and social services. This means cuts in education, health care, and nutrition monitoring. It entails reducing or eliminating subsidies that have helped to keep food prices low. These policies, along with currency devaluations which increase the cost of living, shift the burden of adjustment onto those least able to bear it.

Because structural adjustment programs cause tremendous hardships for the poor, they have been met with resistance, ranging from peaceful protests to bread riots, in the Caribbean and in dozens of countries in Asia, Africa and Latin America. UN agencies, major church leaders, trade unions and international development organizations have also drawn attention to the terrible human toll taken by the programs.[2] Jamaica and the Dominican Republic are the two Caribbean countries whose people have experienced the most drastic decreases in incomes and living standards in conjunction with IMF stabilization and World Bank structural adjustment policies. In both countries, the imposition of new austerity measures on people who were already desperately poor triggered street demonstrations to protest IMF austerity measures. A general strike in the Dominican Republic in August 1990 left at least 14 dead. Structural adjustment austerity has precipitated major labor strikes and a coup attempt in Trinidad and protests in Guyana.

Caribbean grassroots organizations, especially movements representing low-income and working women, have become vocal and articulate critics of structural adjustment and its devastating impact on the poor. Joan French, representing the Jamaica women's organization, Sistren, told a US Congressional symposium, in Barbados in January 1989:

> Structural adjustment is an attack on the majority of the population in every country where it is being imposed. There is a basic contradiction between structural adjustment and growth, and an even greater contradiction between structural adjustment and development.[3]

The evidence is strong that structural adjustment has not succeeded, and cannot succeed, in promoting economic development in the Caribbean or in the majority of poor countries. A closer look at the theory, history and practice of structural adjustment and the related strategy of export-led development reveals why.

The Origins of Structural Adjustment: New Debts for Old

The structural adjustment strategy evolved in the late 1970s and early 1980s as a response to the global debt crisis. During the preceding decade, governments in Asia, Africa and Latin America had incurred large debts to commercial banks in the United States, Europe and Japan, which they took on with the active encouragement of the banks themselves and at the urging of the governments of the North. The private banks held excess dollars, accumulated as a result of the expansion of world trade, itself financed by debt and government subsidies, and the rise of oil prices. The banks were eager to profit by lending their stores of petrodollars, particularly to countries in the South that were rich in mineral resources. The bankers believed their loans were as sound as the mineral wealth that lay beneath the soil of the borrowing countries, which in effect was their collateral. The rich-country governments themselves proffered loans as well as grants, primarily for the purpose of protecting and enhancing their own commercial and industrial interests in the former colonized nations.

Multilateral lending agencies also offered large loans to governments in the South. The World Bank, as well as the IDB and other regional lenders, made huge sums available. Many of these loans were earmarked for the construction of roads, ports, dams and power plants, and for the expansion of government services. Such projects, the lenders and borrowing governments believed, would enable the former colonized nations to take off on their own toward industrialization and economic growth. The proceeds of this growth, they expected, would provide the countries of the South with funds to repay the loans.

Meanwhile, the IMF was advancing billions to many of the world's poor nations to help them cope with their balance of payments deficits. These deficits reflected the gap, which had developed during the years following the independence of most former colonies, between the borrowing countries' earnings from their exports of raw materials and their costs of importing the manufactured goods which they could not yet produce themselves. The IMF predicted that this gap would be closed gradually and that its loans could then be repaid with the proceeds of industrialization and increased exports. The fact that prices for many commodities exported by the South were rising during the period of most active lending in the 1970s, after a long period of decline, made this scenario seem plausible to some. These raw material exports were then, and are still, the main source of income for most indebted countries.

By the end of the 1970s, however, it was apparent that the debt-paved path to prosperity was much steeper than anticipated. The prices of the mineral and agricultural commodities exported by the South resumed their decline. At the same time, the prices of manufactured imports, including those needed to build the planned roads, dams and factories continued to increase. Consequently, many of these large infrastructure projects proved too expensive to complete, while those that were completed typically failed to generate enough money to cover the cost of constructing them.

In addition, the rapid rise of interest rates saddled borrowing nations with annual debt bills that had doubled or tripled over the course of a few years. The World Bank estimated that developing countries' real interest rates rose 30 per cent in just two years (1980 to 1982).[4] Soon many debtor nations were forced to borrow immense sums merely to cover the interest payments they owed on previous loans. As the combined total of Third World debt edged towards US$1 trillion in the mid-1980s, it became obvious to borrowers and lenders alike that this tremendous debt bill could not be paid. Bankers, finance ministers and heads of state worldwide became alarmed. At stake was not only the wealth of the commercial banks and the health and prestige of the multilateral lending agencies but also the stability of the global economy and faith in the free enterprise system as the basis for economic development in the South.

Adjustment in the 1980s: A New Level of Control

At the end of the 1970s, the economic experts of the World Bank seized upon structural adjustment as the solution to this looming crisis. Their reasoning was that underdeveloped countries that could not pay their debt and import bills were living beyond their means. The immediate causes of the borrowing countries' insolvency, falling commodity prices and rising interest rates, were outside the debtors' control. Moreover, the loans now overdue had been urged upon Southern governments by the banks and lending agencies themselves. Despite this, the World Bank and other lenders determined that impoverished debtor nations would now have to pull their belts tighter. They had to be compelled to consume less and to increase their export earnings at the same time. Structural adjustment was the tool for making sure that they did so. If indebted country governments could come up with enough revenue to make payments on some of their debts, the big lenders would then agree to roll over the remainder until some future date.

Most of the parties involved realized that the debts, especially the commercial bank loan bills now bloated by soaring interest charges, would never be repaid at their full face value; but, by refinancing their loans and by enforcing structural adjustment, the World Bank and IMF could postpone the day of reckoning. In the meantime, the commercial banks could recover as much as possible of their paper losses and the illusion of a stable international financial system could be maintained.

Structural adjustment lending had already been initiated by the IMF. During the 1970s, the IMF had devised a set of more or less standard stabilization policies which the Fund required as a condition for refinancing past loans and extending new ones. At the core of these infamous IMF conditionalities were sweeping austerity measures intended to force borrowing countries in the Third World to spend less and earn more. (The largest debtor nation of the North, the United States, has never been subjected to similar pressure, despite the financial instability and the widely recognized danger to the global economic system created by the huge US government debt.)

By the early 1980s, these austerity programs had already provoked massive protests in some countries and contributed to the demise of a number of governments. Nevertheless, IMF austerity policies were the foundation upon which World Bank-sponsored adjustment programs were built, and the two agencies continue to work hand-in-hand in designing and implementing those programs. The two mega-agencies deny that they enforce cross-conditionality — the practice of requiring World Bank loan recipients to meet IMF conditionalities before Bank loan funds are released, or vice versa. However, the Bank and the Fund not only hold joint annual meetings and coordinate their general policies but also cooperate intimately in monitoring debtor country finances and in planning and supervising structural adjustment programs. In the Caribbean and elsewhere, the World Bank negotiates structural adjustment loans in conjunction with IMF Structural Adjustment Facilities (SAFs), a loan category devised by the Fund in 1985. Cross-conditionality has in fact become standard practice.

From 1979 through 1987, the World Bank advanced 121 adjustment loans, totalling US$15.3 billion. These include 51 structural adjustment loans and 70 sectoral adjustment loans, which are used to restructure particular sectors of the borrowing countries' economies, such as trade or agriculture. The adjustment loans ranged in size from US$500 million to Mexico to US$3 million to Dominica. The total amount of World Bank adjustment lending alone in 1987 was double the amount spent by the United States for development assistance worldwide in the same year. In 1988, World Bank adjustment lending increased further to 25 per cent of all new World Bank loans that year. The Bank is pleased with the policy clout it has achieved through its adjustment lending:

Adjustment lending has become a major part of the Bank's development program . . . It has involved the Bank, for the first time on a significant scale, in addressing short- and medium-term economic policy issues through its lending operations.[5]

The World Bank-sponsored structural adjustment programs of the 1980s far surpassed the scope of IMF austerity policies. In addition to regulating the finances of indebted countries, the major task of the IMF, the Bank stepped in to regulate the internal economic policies, the distribution of resources and even political and social priorities within the countries undergoing adjustment. The degree of control assumed by the Bank has in many cases approached that of the former colonial powers over their subject nations.

During the 1980s, USAID became increasingly active in planning and enforcing Caribbean structural adjustment policies, both in conjunction with the World Bank and IMF, and also independently. A 1988 AID memorandum asks:

Is there any possibility that not only governments contemplating structural adjustment, but also the opposition parties and other interests in the societies, can be brought into the process? The important thing is not the analysis, but that the analysis convince all concerned of the costs and benefits of structural adjustment.[6]

In its Caribbean program budget request for 1988, AID noted that, 'Although some structural adjustment measures have already been adopted, major additional adjustments are needed.' This emphasis was reiterated in AID's 1989–91 programs.[7] AID now makes certain of its Caribbean project grants contingent on the recipient countries' compliance with IMF and World Bank conditionalities. The Agency also attaches structural adjustment requirements of its own to the budgetary support grants it gives to Caribbean governments, and even as a condition of US food aid. As shown in chapters 7 and 8, AID has taken a leading role in designing and implementing structural adjustment programs in Dominica and Grenada.

Components of Caribbean Structural Adjustment Programs

Structural adjustment programs typically require the governments of indebted countries to adopt policy changes to achieve the following:

Reduced local consumption. This goal can be accomplished by various means, including currency devaluations which make imported goods more expensive. Such measures can be especially harmful to the populations of countries which depend on imported food. Another means of forcing needy people to consume less is by the reduction or removal of subsidies or price ceilings that many governments use to limit the prices of staple foods and other basic goods.

Whether the means employed are currency devaluation or the removal of subsidies or price controls, the result is the same: prices rise and most people cannot afford to buy as much. The adjustment experts describe the policy goal of reduced consumption in terms such as 'tightening of domestic demand' or 'reduced local absorption'. This abstract economese obscures the fact that the direct intent of these measures is to force already-impoverished populations to get along on even less.

Higher personal taxes and other means of increasing government revenue by collecting more from the poor and middle classes. Many structural adjustment programs include new forms of indirect taxation, such as sales or value-added taxes (VAT) that fall disproportionately on the poor. Adjustment programs generally discourage taxation of businesses and high-income individuals. This is to encourage increased domestic savings by allowing the better-off sectors of society to retain more of their incomes. According to adjustment theory, the wealthy will then invest these savings locally in economically productive activities. In reality, however, business people and large-scale landowners frequently invest their higher incomes and profits abroad, or spend them on luxury consumption and speculation. Deregulation of the uses of foreign exchange and the *laissez-faire* thrust of structural adjustment programs leave affected countries with few means of preventing these practices.

Government subsidies to the private sector. To qualify for most adjustment loans, governments must agree to spend a larger proportion of both local revenues and the foreign assistance they receive on projects to aid private investors, particularly foreign corporations. Such projects typically include construction of port facilities and roads to expedite the shipment of exports and the provision of water, electricity, government services and factory buildings, often at rates below their actual cost, to businesses engaged in export manufacturing. Such measures are designed to entice foreign investors to channel local land, labor and capital into export production. These policies, however, also reduce the ability of local enterprises, which often cannot compete with large foreign corporations, to provide jobs and to supply local products to meet local needs.

In structural adjustment terminology, such spending priorities make up an adjusting country's Public Sector Investment Program (PSIP). This term refers to spending by the public sector, not primarily for public needs, but rather for the private sector. While some components of PSIP programs, such as better roads, are undoubtedly needed by the adjusting countries, priorities within the PSIP, such as where new roads are to be built, are determined more by their potential enhancement of export profits rather than by the needs of the local population for greater economic self-reliance and food security.

Lower taxes on businesses and tax holiday periods of 5–20 years, during which time new investors are not required to pay taxes to host country governments. These and other financial incentives are designed to attract investors, especially foreign investors, by making the production of exports more convenient and profitable. The tax revenue losses to host countries, however, especially when added to the expenses incurred under PSIP programs, often end up costing countries much more than they gain from new foreign investment. And foreign corporations frequently pocket the proceeds of government subsidized low-wage manufacturing, then move their operations elsewhere when tax holiday periods expire.

Removal or reduction of tariffs and levies on exports. Such taxes have been used by governments to tap some of the wealth generated by the exporters of agricultural and mineral commodities. Since they may, however, counteract the structural adjustment goal of maximizing exports at all costs, they are discouraged or forbidden under the terms of most structural adjustment programs.

Decreased public spending on services to local citizens, including health, education, sanitation and housing, and on other activities that do not directly enhance export earnings. In addition to, or in lieu of, structural adjustment loans, the World Bank sometimes arranges sectoral adjustment loans to be used by governments to 'rationalize' health, agricultural extension, education and other programs.

Sectoral adjustment programs in public service sectors attempt to reduce government spending by means such as raising school fees and the prices of books, reducing the numbers of teachers and scholarships, and charging new fees for services, such as health clinic visits and vaccinations, which were previously provided free of charge. The sponsors of adjustment tend to view these services as unaffordable luxuries, even though they address the needs of the world's poorest people and even though the governments of the South already spend a much smaller portion of their revenues on social services than do the industrialized nations.[8]

The dismantling, scaling down, or sale of government-owned enterprises, except those which directly or indirectly support the private sector, and the sale of publicly owned lands, utilities and industries at low cost to private investors. In view of the adjustment experts, agricultural cooperatives, as well as government-owned farms, factories, power companies and marketing corporation are, by definition, inefficient. However, no standard yardstick of efficiency is used to evaluate and compare the operations of private corporations, or of aid projects or public agencies that support and subsidize private enterprise.

Reduction of the number of government employees. Like the selling of government enterprises, public sector retrenchments (lay-offs) are intended to increase efficiency, reduce public spending and balance government budgets. But since, at the same time, governments are required to provide increased services to businesses, it is those services that benefit the poor majority of citizens which typically suffer most as a consequence of reduced government payrolls.

Lower wages, especially for workers in export agriculture and manufacturing. By keeping a lid on public employees' salaries, freezing wages or failing to enforce minimum wage laws, and by doing whatever is necessary to reduce the influence of trade unions, governments are expected to improve the business climate for foreign investors.

Adjustment experts frequently blame the failure of poor country economies to grow on the high cost of doing business there and, in particular, on non-competitive wages. World Bank emissaries exhort the governments of adjusting countries to freeze real wages or to enact currency devaluations, which have the same effect of lowering workers' incomes, in order to compete in attracting investors with other poor countries which are lowering their own workers' wages in response to identical advice from the Bank.

Opening of domestic markets to foreign-based exporters of manufactured goods and food. One way of doing this is by eliminating import quotas and tariffs that are sometimes used by governments to raise the prices of imported products and thus to protect their countries' industries from foreign competition. Such protectionist policies violate structural adjustment doctrine. The World Bank contends that, 'An outward-oriented strategy is superior to one in which trade and industrial incentives are biased in favor of production for the domestic market over the export market'.[9] This is an updated version of the time-worn economic development theory of comparative advantage. According to this theory, Third World countries will do best by producing bananas or baseballs for export, while importing things like wheat and radios, leaving the production of these and most other goods for local consumption in the hands of the developed countries.

Foreign corporations, World Bank economists still insist, can better supply most consumer goods, machinery and even food to poor nations than can local producers. Low-income nations, they say, should confine their economic efforts to the export of what they are currently best at producing, mainly unprocessed agricultural and mineral commodities and the products of low-wage assembly industries. The outcome of such advice in case after case has been the reinforcement of dependency and of poverty-creating patterns of trade.

Expanded Tourism. The Caribbean version of structural adjustment also calls for the expansion of tourism, with few restrictions or guidelines other than the goal of bringing in foreign currency. The region's tourist industry has already despoiled the environment, contributed to increased drug abuse and prostitution, replaced farms on prime agricultural land with hotels, and placed many beaches and scenic areas off-limits to local people. But tourism does bring in dollars that can help pay debts, and that is the adjustors' main concern.

The Caribbean Precedent: Region-wide Orchestrated Adjustment

Oscar Allen, leader of the Rural Transformation Collective in St Vincent and the Grenadines, observed at a meeting of development organizations in the Eastern Caribbean in March 1988:

> The stranglehold on us by foreign institutions today is more total than under the colonial situation, because it is cultural and social as well as economic, and because it includes cooperation and coordination among Caribbean governments under terms dictated by the IMF and the World Bank.

The Caribbean is the only area of the world, thus far, where the structural adjustment programs of an entire group of nations are being orchestrated by a region-wide organization dominated by outside forces. This body, the Caribbean Group for Co-operation in Economic Development (CGCED), is led by the IMF and the World Bank, and includes more than 30 government and multinational agencies and 22 Caribbean states. Through the CGCED, the United States, other governments and the multilateral lending institutions coordinate decisions about how much and what kind of aid the indebted Caribbean countries will receive, whether countries will be allowed to postpone some debt payments and what kinds of policy changes will be required as a condition of the aid given or the debt rescheduling permitted.

AID is an active member of the CGCED and, while not bound by CGCED decisions, generally pursues policies parallel to those of the CGCED. The CGCED's resources, especially those of the World Bank and IMF, far outweigh those of AID, and the consortium has been more effective in promoting AID's privatization and structural adjustment priorities than AID itself. This has been particularly true since 1988, when AID budget cuts reduced the Agency's influence over the details of adjustment programs for the region. Until 1988, AID had been using ESF grants to help plug the budget gaps of the United States' Caribbean allies in return for those countries' promises to implement structural adjustment measures. The bulk of Caribbean ESF funds were, however, eliminated from the 1988 US foreign assistance budget. Zak explained that the Caribbean ESF cuts were made because, 'They're small countries, they're in our backyard, and the US has no overwhelming security interest there at present, since Grenada is no longer a problem.'

The lack of ESF funds reduced AID's bargaining power in the CGCED. 'Nobody believes them [AID] any more,' remarked an official of the World Bank's Caribbean program. AID complained to Congress that, 'In effect, the elimination of ESF in FY [financial year] 1988 to the Caribbean takes AID out of the macroeconomic policy dialogue, AID's highest priority in the Caribbean region.' The ESF cuts prompted AID to attach more stringent structural adjustment requirements to other types of aid, including PL 480 food donations and development assistance. According to David Cohen, then AID's

Caribbean Program Director, however, 'The economic issues are the same, whether the agency dealing with them is AID, the IMF, or the [World] Bank.'

The CGCED: Caribbean adjustors' club
The CGCED usually meets for one week every 18 months in Washington. The IMF and the World Bank set the group's agenda and chair its meetings. Attending the ninth CGCED meeting in Washington in June 1988 were representatives from 17 Caribbean recipient countries, 10 donor nations (Canada, France, Germany, Italy, Japan, the Netherlands, Spain, Britain, Brazil and the United States), and 9 international aid or lending institutions. More than 350 delegates and observers, the majority from the North, attended. Non-government organizations from the Caribbean member countries were not permitted to attend. Between meetings, the World Bank and IMF send monitoring missions to examine the finances and economic policies of the Caribbean member states. Recommendations resulting from these missions become the basis for discussions and decisions made at CGCED sessions and sub-committee meetings on the various member countries.

The donor governments and agencies, of course, have their own agendas. They hold bilateral negotiations outside of the CGCED context, and do not always comply with CGCED recommendations. One World Bank official complained after the 1988 CGCED meeting that some member governments are giving too much aid to certain Caribbean states:

> The availability of financing by other donors inhibits countries such as Antigua and Barbados from accepting the need for structural adjustment. It allows them to postpone the inevitable. . . . if a country is not ready to put structural adjustment in place, the Bank abstains from lending, or we go in with minor involvement until they accept the need to adjust, and the social costs of investment. It's not just a question of cutting public expenditures, but also of providing adequate incentives and a framework for foreign investment.[10]

In general, however, the IMF and World Bank have used the CGCED successfully as a means of getting donors to line up in support of structural adjustment in the region. According to CGCED chairman and World Bank Vice-President S. Sahid Husain, 'the Group has increasingly provided a useful forum for policy dialogue and for coordinating external finances for adjustment'.

Many Caribbean leaders see it differently. 'What is referred to as "policy dialogue" is a method of manipulation,' says William G. Demas, a respected Caribbean economist and former head of the CDB:

> To the extent that AID and the multilaterals veer away from project lending and into policy dialogue — in which they impose their own policies, with their lack of knowledge of the region — it doesn't work. Their simplistic structural adjustment policies, stressing growth above all else, have led to a

depressing of demand and the suffering of the poor. When you make the poor suffer, you erode the human capital on which development depends.[11]

Through the CGCED, the multilateral agencies have succeeded in imposing their own policy priorities on many Caribbean governments. Ricky Singh, a Guyanese journalist and astute observer of Caribbean politics, comments that, 'The multilaterals are refining their technique, trying to get governments to institute IMF-type policies as if the governments themselves were requesting them.'[12]

According to a World Bank position paper prepared for the June 1988 CGCED meeting, 'Most of the CGCED countries are small. . . . Smallness means that economic growth must inevitably be export-led, at least in the long run.' This view seems to have been accepted by nearly all the current leaders of Caribbean governments, who, in their presentations to the CGCED, stress their eagerness to comply with related adjustment criteria. World Bank economist Roger Robinson, at the time assigned to Jamaica, noted in 1988 that the 'policy dialogue' between the Bank and Caribbean governments on the issue of export-led development has been 'intense' but effective. Immediately after the June 1988 CGCED meeting, Robinson remarked with an air of satisfaction that, 'Most of the governments in the CGCED now see that the main potential for growth is external.' In this context, even countries which do not have official World Bank or IMF-sponsored structural adjustment programs, such as St Vincent and the Grenadines, come to the CGCED donor consortium to request funds and to report on their policies.

The policies of the seven member nations of the OECS are subject to the tight scrutiny of a CGCED sub-committee called the Tighter Consultative Group (TCG).[13] 'The TCG has Caribbean staff, including economists, but they must play by the USAID rulebook,' observed University of the West Indies political economist Dr Neville Duncan.[14] The failure of Grenada to satisfy the criteria of the TCG is the reason given by both World Bank and US officials for the lack of support for Grenada by the IMF and the Bank, and for the slashing of Grenada's USAID program.

As part of their effort to overcome the smallness which, in the World Bank's view, sentences them to eternal export dependency, the OECS countries asked the CGCED in 1985 to deal with them as a group, coordinating funding and related adjustment measures through the OECS secretariat. The World Bank would not agree. According to the USAID official responsible for structural adjustment in the Eastern Caribbean, Robin Phillips, 'No multilateral, and probably not AID, would put money into something controlled by someone else.'

CGCED decisions are made behind closed doors. The conditions and terms on which they are based are rarely made public, even though they often have a direct impact on Caribbean taxes, wages, prices, social services and living conditions. When the World Bank commissions studies and projects in connection with structural adjustment programs, the relevant documents are made available to consultants and bidders for the contracts, but not to the

Caribbean citizens whose futures are at stake.

The arm-twisting that takes place at CGCED sessions is hidden behind a public facade of jovial diplomacy and consensus among equals. This secrecy helps Caribbean governments to preserve the illusion that it is they, and not their creditors, who set policies for their nations. The CGCED reflects the degree to which the sovereignty of the region has become (or, more accurately, has remained) subordinate to the powers and priorities of governments and institutions outside the Caribbean. The coordinator of a non-government development agency in St Vincent and the Grenadines, Cecil Ryan, commented at a 1988 meeting on development goals:

> What we are facing is a new form of an old problem. The mechanisms to withdraw resources from our countries have become more sophisticated. Now international capital is being used to extract value from the Caribbean through regional institutions, and our own governments are cooperating more in going along with it.

In the eyes of many Caribbean observers, the extent of control by the World Bank and the IMF over the economic options of Caribbean states represents a new stage in a process of recolonization. As such, the CGCED may be an ominous precedent for other impoverished countries, particularly those in sub-Saharan Africa whose weakened economies, high levels of non-commercial foreign debt and lack of political bargaining power may make them subject to similar mechanisms of outside control.

Adjusting to the Power of International Capital

The immediate goal of adjustment is to give indebted governments quick cash to stave off bankruptcy, make payments on their debts and avert a collapse of the banking system in the North. To a limited extent, this goal has been achieved. By the World Bank's accounting, the less developed countries (LDCs) of the South paid to the banks and governments of the North US$43 billion more in 1988 than they received in aid and new loans.[15] The net flow of financial resources from South to North, out of poor countries and into wealthy nations, corporations and institutions, has accelerated yearly since 1985. This has helped ease the mood of near-panic among bankers and finance ministers in the North but it has not resolved the debt crisis.

The long-term goal of adjustment lending is to restructure poor-country economies to give maximum advantage and a free hand to private investors. With the private sector at the helm, propelled by the winds of free trade, poor countries will, the adjustors contend, be able to steer a course towards rapid economic growth. Corporations and business owners, they say, are better able to take the steps, especially the wage reductions, necessary to make poor countries' exports cheaper and thus more competitive in world markets.

This international competitiveness, in the opinion of the sponsors of structural adjustment, is the key to economic growth. Economic growth, in their view, is the essence of development. Whether most of the low-income indebted countries can achieve growth, much less development, by increasing their exports is doubtful, but it is particularly unlikely in the case of the small, fragmented economies of the Caribbean. 'We're told we must have free trade,' Arnhim Eustace of the CDB told the author, 'but there's no way we can compete internationally on those terms.'

Whether viewed as stranglehold or stewardship, the imposition of structural adjustment has failed to produce sustainable development in the Caribbean. Some countries have experienced short-term inprovements in balances of payments, reduced government budget deficits, and modest GDP growth, but at a terrible cost to social infrastructure, environment and prospects for longer-term or broader-based development. The pattern is not unlike that elsewhere in Latin America and in Africa. In September 1989, the UN Commission on Trade and Development (UNCTAD) added its voice to that of the UN Economic Commission on Africa (UNECA) and the growing number of international development agencies and analysts who challenge World Bank claims of structural adjustment success.[16]

The Bank itself has not yet conceded failure but it has begun to shift its emphasis from structural adjustment programs *per se*. In March 1990, World Bank Vice-President and then chief economist Stanley Fisher announced that the Bank was planning to reduce the proportion of quick-disbursing structural adjustment loans in its portfolio while increasing the total amount of its lending for specific projects. (Part of the Bank's motive in steering away from structural adjustment loans is the realization that such reforms are failing, that highly indebted countries may be unable to pay these and other World Bank loans, and that this could threaten the Bank's own high credit rating.)[17] As the case of Jamaica illustrates, however, increasingly the Bank ties such project loans to the same conditionalities that are contained in structural adjustment agreements.

Adjustment-related measures, especially the rescheduling of poor-country debts, may indeed have helped to postpone a global financial catastrophe. But almost everywhere it has been attempted, structural adjustment has been accompanied by increased poverty and unemployment, declining export incomes, higher debts and political unrest. This is clearly true in the Caribbean, where the results of adjustment experiments suggest that for impoverished nations, structural adjustment medicine is likely to worsen the conditions it is intended to cure.

Notes

1. World Bank, *World Development Report*, Washington, 1988.

2. Giovanni Andrea Cornea, Richard Jolly and Francis Stewart, *Adjustment with a Human Face*, UNICEF, Clarendon Press, 1987; Susan George, *A Fate Worse than Debt*, Food First/Grove Press, 1988; 'The Berlin Statement' by NGOs to the joint

annual meeting of the World Bank and the IMF in Berlin in 1988.

3. Congressional Consultation sponsored by the House of Representatives Subcommittee on Western Hemispheric Affairs and the Washington-based development advocacy agency, The Development GAP.

4. World Bank, *World Development Report*, Washington DC, 1988.

5. 'Lending for Adjustment', *World Bank News*, Special Report, Washington, April 1988.

6. USAID 'New Initiatives', unpublished memorandum.

7. USAID *Congressional Presentations*, 1988–91. According to Marilyn Zak, Acting Director of AID's Caribbean and Latin America program: 'There's been some improvement in government policies in the region because of structural adjustment programs worked out with the IMF and the World Bank. We see progress toward our goals in privatization, divestment, and tax policy reform.' (Interview with the author, June 1988, Washington DC.)

8. World Bank, *World Development Report*, 1988.

9. World Bank, *World Development Report*, 1987.

10. Author interview, June 1988.

11. Author interview, December 1987.

12. Author interview, November 1987.

13. The OECS includes the independent nations of Antigua and Barbuda, St Kitts/Nevis, Dominica, St Lucia, St Vincent and the Grenadines, and Grenada, and the British crown colony, Montserrat.

14. Author interview, November 1987.

15. World Bank, *World Debt Tables*, Washington, 1989.

16. UNECA, August 1989; UNCTAD Report, 1989.

17. *Washington Post*, 15 March, 1990.

6. Free Trade Zones: States within States

Industries with value added rates lower than 30 per cent and paying wages lower than what any US student earns working at McDonald's can hardly set a solid base for the expansion of domestic markets and the accumulation of capital needed to attain a self-sustained capitalist development. The benefits of this type of industrialization are far greater for US industries than for the countries of the Caribbean Basin.

Emilio Pantojas-Garcia

'Today I didn't make my quota because I was feeling sick, so I'll have to work all day instead of half of Saturday to make it up. I'm supposed to do seven big bundles of bras an hour. My job is to sew on one strap.' Women who work in Jamaica's FTZ export assembly factories were meeting in a small house where four families of mothers and children share a common kitchen.

'It takes a lot of pressure,' another said. 'Last week all of a sudden the needle went right through my fingernail. But you can't use a thimble, it would hold you back.'

'The minimum wage [then equivalent to US$14.29 weekly] just covers the basics, like flour, cornmeal, rice and a little sugar and milk for the children. You have to work a lot extra to pay your bus fare and the rent, or if you expect to eat chicken once in a while, especially now that our dollar's devalued again.'

'You can't be too old, or too tired, and especially you can't get pregnant. If they find out they fire you, but they wait until 3 pm on the last day of the pay period, so you lose your last two weeks wages.'

'What scares me is so many of us packed in there with the fire door blocked.'

Asked whether such practices were legal, one of the workers replied, 'The government has said we can't bring Free Zone problems to them because what goes on in there is the owners' business. The Free Zone is a state unto itself.' Said another, 'This government is bending over backwards for the Free Zone factory owners just like the last one did, even though they know our local factories are going out of business. It's because of the IMF and all that pressure to expand the zone.'

The workers have the story right. Jamaica's export processing zones are a model of the type of unregulated trade, investment and employment policies endorsed by the sponsors of structural adjustment. In the IMF and World Banks' free trade dream world, criteria of profitability would determine the allocation of global resources. The multilateral lenders frown upon 'anti-export biases', such as export duties, import restrictions to protect local industries, trade unions, and government involvement in setting minimum wages or health and safety standards. Elimination of these annoying obstacles, they contend, would enable the free market to determine the utilization of land, labor, technology and capital in a way that would maximize efficiency. Conditions in today's free trade zones and other export processing zones

(EPZs) prefigure the tremendous human and environmental costs that such an unrestricted global free trade system would entail.

The Entrepreneurial Spirit

Jamaica and the Caribbean as a whole have been falling behind in the worldwide export race. Total exports from CGCED member countries to Canada, Europe and the United States fell in value from US$8.4 billion in 1980 to US$4.9 billion in 1986, a 41 per cent decrease. But within this trend of declining exports is an exception: from 1980 to 1986, manufactured exports from the Caribbean to Western Europe and North America grew by 10.2 per cent in volume and 11.1 per cent in value. The manufactured exports from Jamaica, the Caribbean country which experienced the most rapid increase, rose by 16.6 per cent in volume and 17.6 per cent in value during this same period. Jamaica's clothing and textile exports to the United States grew at an average annual rate of 38.8 per cent. Light manufactured exports from the Dominican Republic, Haiti and some Eastern Caribbean countries have also increased, especially exports from these countries' expanding EPZs. Exports from Jamaica's EPZs grew twice as fast as its other manufactured exports.

At first glance, export assembly industry appears to be a way to make up lost ground in the global race for export markets. 'Why are textiles working so well?' asks World Bank Program Officer for the Caribbean, Christian Del Voie. His answer:

> The investors already have the marketing channels, to Bloomingdale's and other stores. All the investor then has to do is to look at the cost of labor. Local labor skills are not important, and local inputs are not an issue, because all they are doing is cut-and-sew.[1]

The most important condition is low pay. The Bank cites the correlation between low wages and increased manufactured exports as a sign that Jamaica and the other Caribbean countries which have managed to reduce real wages are on the right development track. Wages in Jamaica, Haiti and the Dominican Republic are about equal to or below those of Mexico, Brazil and Central America, notes a World Bank 1988 report on Caribbean exports. Before-tax wages in Jamaica cited with favor by the Bank in 1988 were US$.63 per hour, only one 24th of the wages of US workers in the same category. Caribbean wages are substantially higher, however, than export industry wages in Thailand, Sri Lanka, the Philippines and China.[2]

For export assembly industries to succeed in the South, the adjustors say, industrialized countries must open their markets to exports from the Caribbean and other low-wage countries. The United States has done this to a limited extent. Before the CBI, other US trade provisions were adopted to help US-based companies take advantage of low factory wages in the South. These provisions, mainly sections 806.30 and 807 of the US Tariff Schedule, reduced US import duties on goods, mainly textile and metal products, assembled abroad using US-made components. Additional non-CBI tariff provisions enacted in the 1980s have extended further duty exemptions to certain goods assembled in the Caribbean with US-made inputs. According to a 1990 study by Policy Alternatives for the Caribbean and Central America (PACCA), on US–Caribbean relations, this was done to counteract the decline in the competitiveness of US industry:

> As a model of industrial organization, this outward-looking development strategy favors US interests by encouraging the location of US multinational corporations' processing facilities in low-wage areas to maintain the US competitive edge. This was achieved without the US having to administer any foreign aid, as in the Alliance for Progress, or public transfer of funds, as in Operation Bootstrap [in Puerto Rico]. . . . What has spurred the relocation of labor-intensive manufacturing operations to the [Caribbean] region has been the lure of cheap labor and incentive schemes granted to US corporations by Caribbean governments.[3]

World Bank economists stress that in order for US tariff provisions such as 807 and the more recent 'super 807' to be effective, countries such as the Dominican Republic and Jamaica must maintain political stability, 'flexible exchange rates' (willingness to devalue their currencies further) and a 'positive investment climate'. According to the Bank, the most effective of these export-promoting policies undertaken by Caribbean governments have been the currency devaluations, required as a condition of IMF and World Bank structural adjustment loans, that so depressed wages and living standards in Jamaica and in the Dominican Republic in the mid-1980s.

A Model for Global Free Trade

Exports of products assembled in the EPZs have grown approximately twice as fast as other manufactured exports from the same countries. Says the Bank:

> Both Jamaica and the Dominican Republic are in the midst of a manufacturing export boom centred in their rapidly-expanding EPZ factories. Somehow these zones — with their special legal and unusual physical framework — allow efficiency criteria to predominate.[4]

What are these special legal and physical characteristics that, in the Bank's view, make EPZs more efficient? Essentially, they are conditions which facilitate the exploitation of low-paid women workers. They are made possible by the fact that in FTZs, manufacturers are not subject to the same taxes, tariffs and regulations that apply to factories outside the zones. In the words of St Vincent Industrial Development Corporation head Claude Leach, 'Export processing zones are states within states.' In most cases, EPZ investors are exempt from paying import duties and taxes on stock dividends, and are free to remove their profits from the host countries. In addition, they typically receive generous incentives, including tax holidays of up to 20 years and the provision of factory shells and utilities at rates below their actual costs. Thus, EPZs are a model of the type of unregulated trade, investment and employment practices that the Bank believes ought to be in effect worldwide.

A new form of slavery
Rawwida Baksh-Soodeen of CAFRA described the conditions typical in export factories:

> Women put together these garments . . . in a sweat shop where women are cramped, each woman spending an entire eight- or nine-hour day stitching a dart, tacking a seam, or doing any of the micro-tasks into which the assembly of any single garment has been fragmented to maximize production, and hence the profit margin and the competitive edge of the company, which is usually a subsidiary or a sub-contracting firm of a multinational corporation.
>
> Women are paid by piece work. They often have no access to basic facilities like lunchrooms. When they need the toilet, they are 'frisked' or checked and on top of that, they are monitored and allowed to go only once a day . . . . The conditions under which these women work are reminiscent of earlier forms of colonialism like slavery and indentureship.[5]

The health hazards and exploitative conditions faced by women workers in export processing factories in St Vincent and Dominica have been documented by Cecilia Green, a sociologist from Dominica:

> The foreign factory owners rely on our local governments to keep the workers' unions from being effective. As a result the conditions in some of the factories are horrible. There are hazardous chemicals and little ventilation, and safety regulations aren't enforced. [Far from strengthening local economies] the primary effect of export processing is to give US investors a place in our Caribbean sun, subsidized by our own taxes and savings.[6]

More than 80,000 women work in the rapidly growing free trade zones in the Dominican Republic, for only about US$20–30 a week. Women employees in unionized industries in the Dominican Republic earn an average of 23 per cent more than their counterparts in the non-unionized EPZs.[7] Workers in at least 40 per cent of the Zona Franca (FTZ) factories in the Dominican Republic have tried to unionize, according to Magaly Pineda of the Centro de Investigacion Para la Accion Feminina (CIPAF). She says that factory owners usually succeed in firing the workers who start organizing the recruitment drives because the workers have no legal backing. 'Factory owners often tell free zone workers that unions in export processing zones are illegal.' Because the factory owners are foreigners, mainly North Americans, they can threaten everyone with moving their factories elsewhere if workers demand better pay and better working conditions.[8]

A 1988 survey of workers in the Kingston, Jamaica, FTZ found that 80 per cent of the workers, who are almost all female, earn less than US$15 a week. In contrast to the myth that women take jobs outside the home in order to supplement their husbands' wages, the survey found that four out of five of the female EPZ workers have full responsibility for supporting their children. Almost 70 per cent of the EPZ workers surveyed said their basic pay is so low that they have no choice but to work overtime.[9]

Other special features of EPZs that make them so profitable include poor or no health benefits, lack of facilities for lunch breaks, sanitation or rest, and the prerogative of the employers to require long working days and forced overtime. The physical separation of the zones from communities and other workplaces makes effective trade union representation more difficult. According to the World Bank, this is another positive aspect of the EPZs: 'The excessive labor militancy and strong unions with rigid work rules in some countries, and the work stoppages in others during recent political turmoils, are examples of labor situations that have seriously undercut competitiveness.'[10]

USAID has also begun to champion the cause of EPZs. The success, despite the social costs, of the zones in stimulating exports, in contrast to the failure of the CBI to do the same, has spurred AID to follow the lead of the World Bank in pressing for their expansion. A 1988 AID memorandum on Caribbean development states that, 'The countries that have benefited the most from the CBI are those that have established Free Trade Zones. Investors like them. We believe other countries in the region should consider having FTZs.'

Export industrialization has been one theme stressed by AID in what it euphemistically terms 'policy dialogue' with Caribbean governments. The Agency makes the release of its funds contingent on the adoption of AID-recommended policy changes to aid foreign investors. It underwrites the advertising in the United States of Caribbean 'investment opportunities' and the wining and dining of potential investors. AID provides grants and loans to Caribbean governments to finance industrial parks, contingent upon the recipient countries' agreement to policy changes favoring US businesses. Other AID-sponsored programs teach young women the minimal skills required for export assembly and cover their daily stipends, which, at US$1.85 a day can hardly be called wages, during 'training periods' that last as long as nine

USAID, which takes the official position that the CBI has been a success, blames Caribbean countries for not making it more of a success. The 1988 memorandum states:

> Caribbean countries could do more for themselves to attract investment to their shores. They could, for instance, eliminate restrictions on foreign ownership, withdraw curbs on remittances, remove exchange and trade controls, loosen moratoria on new construction, roll back excessive taxes on business, and revise depreciation rates on facilities. . . . Investment would be much easier to attract if wages were not so high.

The Costs of FTZs

Meanwhile, there is no clear evidence that the net contribution of FTZs to Caribbean economies is positive. The low proportion of value added to the export products by Caribbean workers means that the zones contribute little foreign exchange to the host country economies. According to Peter King of Jamaica's government investment promotion agency, 'For every US$100 exported [by Caribbean export assembly industries] only US$20 remains in the Caribbean and US$80 goes to the United States industry.'[11] The lack of linkages to other economic sectors means that the zones have little or no effect in creating additional jobs outside the export factories. Most of the jobs created are temporary, lasting only as long as incentives and low labor costs add up to a more profitable deal than that offered by competing would-be exporters. The skills learned by export assembly workers are typically not transferable to other productive activities.

The number of jobs created in export manufacturing does not begin to make up for the number of jobs lost as a consequence of structural adjustment. As employment grows in the EPZs, jobs disappear as public sector employment is reduced and as businesses close because of competition from foreign producers and the scarcity of foreign exchange needed to buy machinery and inputs. And, as low as wages for women in Caribbean factories are, they are two to three times higher than those of export factory workers in the low-wage Asian countries of Thailand, Sri Lanka and the Philippines (see chapter 10). This helps to explain why, while the total amount (as measured by value) of manufactured exports from the Caribbean grew by an average of 8 per cent yearly from 1980 through 1986, the amount of factory-assembled goods exported by other countries of the South grew faster, at an average annual rate of 10.8 per cent.[12] This fact alone casts doubt upon the notion that the export assembly industry is the key to Caribbean development.

Jamaica and the Dominican Republic have seen dramatic decreases in living standards as a consequence of the very structural adjustment policies, especially currency devaluations, which have made them attractive to export assembly industries. It is no coincidence that the Caribbean countries, which have shown the greatest success in export manufacturing are also the countries which have experienced the most political turmoil. Haiti's living standards and wages were already the region's lowest. All three countries have also been the scene of organized protests and spontaneous uprisings in response to structural adjustment austerity measures.

Women Fight Back

Women's organizations, including CIPAF in the Dominican Republic, Sistren in Jamaica, and Women Against Free Trade Zones in Trinidad and Tobago, have exposed and fought for the improvement of the conditions of export processing industry workers. Beyond this, they have been among the few organized groups that have questioned the contributions of this type of export-oriented industry to national development. (In Trinidad and Tobago, the Oil Field Workers Union has also advanced a profound critique and ground-breaking proposals for development alternatives to structural adjustment and export-oriented industrialization.) Says Asha Kambon of Women Against Free Trade Zones:

> We do have to export, but the questions are: what do we export? Why, where, to whom, on what terms? We do need hard work, and we need to make sacrifices, but who is sacrificing, and what do we gain? In Trinidad and Tobago, we have challenged the policy of export processing zones not only because of their exploitation of women, but also [because of] their questionable role in national development. It's raised a hornet's nest of controversy. Now we take up every issue that comes to national attention in terms of whether or not and how it contributes to or detracts from development.[13]

Before these questions were raised, writes Marilyn Jones in *CAFRA News*:

> few people understood that Free Trade Zones or Export Processing Zones form part of structural adjustment programmes recommended by the IMF, the World Bank, and other US-controlled agencies, which result in enhanced profits for a few and further underdevelopment for the majority. Few understood the system to be a creation of transnational companies requiring cheap labor and an escape from the health and occupational safety laws of their own countries. People were unaware that workers in developing countries are being made to become the 'hands' in a system where the 'brains' are concentrated in the developed world; that under that system, 'Third World' countries remain woefully ignorant of the new technologies that are never shared with them.[14]

Jamaican women have shown themselves willing to work, and to work long and hard, in their struggle to sustain themselves and their families. But many have been unwilling to accept without complaint the sub-poverty wages and dangerous working conditions of many of the free zone factories. Nor have they been willing to submit meekly to indignities, such as abusive language by factory managers and body searches, carried out, factory operators say, to detect stolen cloth or thread. For three days in March 1988, more than 2,000 women from the Kingston FTZ participated in demonstrations protesting conditions in the garment factories. Prime Minister Seaga responded by naming a joint union–management council to investigate their complaints, but then backed down in response to pressure from factory owners.

The struggle of Jamaican women against exploitation in the FTZs continues. As word of their movement has spread, they have linked their efforts with women in other Caribbean countries who face similar conditions, including the

Dominican Republic, Antigua, Montserrat, and the nations of the Windward Islands. The plan of the government of Trinidad and Tobago, pressed by USAID and the multilateral lenders to establish EPZs in Trinidad, has met with strong protests by Trinidadian women. Because of their ties to the Caribbean regional women's movement, women in Trinidad are already familiar with the consequences of such a strategy.

The Jamaican women have not confined their protest to the issue of FTZ factory conditions. Organizations in the anti-free zone movement point out that the exploitation of women in the FTZs is a central part of the structural adjustment solution. 'The economic arrangements demanded by the IMF and other US-controlled lending agencies and the economic objectives of the CBI are part of the same economic policy aimed at redesigning the Caribbean to suit US interests,' says Sistren member Joan French.

The promotion of EPZs employing low-paid women workers is self-defeating as a means to foster development, many Caribbean women contend. They point out that women are the heads of 50 per cent or more of Caribbean households. Sisters, grandmothers, aunts and daughters, whether or not they are the household's main breadwinner, do many essential tasks in the home. Many women also work in the informal economy, as vendors, seamstresses, artisans, and at other occupations. All this work by women, although not recognized in official production statistics, is essential to the sustenance of the family, including family members who are part of the officially employed population.

When women are forced to work long hours in export factories, they are less able to carry out these other productive activities. As a result, the health and well-being of the entire population, and therefore the productivity of the economy as a whole, are undermined. Says Rawwida Baksh-Soodeen:

> In the Caribbean, we have always had the support network of extended families; but that institution itself is cracking under the onslaught of urbanization and industrialization. In addition to exploiting cheap female labor, governments — as part of their structural adjustment programmes — are shrinking all other support services women depend on to make ends meet.

The Bank Knows Best

The experts at the World Bank dismiss the protests and warnings of these Caribbean women with undisguised contempt. Says the Bank's former Caribbean Program Director Christian Delvoie, 'The World Bank knows the needs of the Jamaican economy better than some local women's association. We can't direct the development of the Jamaican economy on the basis of the needs of these women in Kingston.'

The World Bank experts resent the intrusion of Caribbean women and other workers onto the Bank's plush-carpeted turf. Export assembly workers have no role in the Bank's version of 'policy dialogue' and development planning, even though it is upon the labor of these workers that the Bank is basing its scenario for the economic future of Jamaica and the rest of the Caribbean. 'Our policy dialogue with the government of Jamaica has been very intense,' cautions World Bank Jamaica economist Roger Robinson:

> Now local non-government organizations want to get into it, including many with very little financial resources to devote. The local NGOs are saying they want to be part of the policy dialogue [between the World Bank and the government], but they're too tied to small constituencies, such as farmers and women.

Clearly, to Robinson, it is financial clout, and not numbers or contribution to economic production, that determines whether a sector of the population is 'small'.

Delvoie, too, is critical of the efforts of NGOs to influence economic policy, particularly in view of the fact that non-government development agencies, trade unions and grassroots organizations, in his view, 'have very few resources to contribute' in comparison to the World Bank's billions: 'Everybody wants to get into the policy game now, and that's dangerous. But let's remember who has the comparative advantage here: the Bank does.'

Notes

1. Author interview, 13 June 1988.
2. World Bank, *Caribbean Exports*.
3. Policy Alternatives for the Caribbean and Central America (PACCA), *In the Shadows of the Sun*, Westview Press, 1990.
4. World Bank, *Caribbean Exports*.
5. *CAFRA News*, Vol. 2, No. 3, Port-of-Spain, Trinidad and Tobago, September 1988.
6. Interview with the author, February 1987. Green's study, *The New Enclave Industries and Women Workers in the Eastern Caribbean*, was jointly sponsored by the Caribbean People's Development Agency (CARIPEDA) and the Canadian agencies Canadian University Service Organization (CUSO) and Centre for Caribbean Dialogue.
7. Helen Safa, 'Women and Industrialization in the Caribbean', University of Florida, Gainesville.
8. Magaly Pineda, 'La Fuerza Obrera Feminina en la Republica Dominicana', CIPAF, Santo Domingo.
9. This survey, cited in *Sistren* magazine, Vol. 8, No. 1, was conducted by the pastoral team of St Peter Claver church and compiled by Dr Patricia Anderson of the University of the West Indies (UWI).
10. World Bank, *Caribbean Exports*.
11. Quoted in *South* magazine, March 1990.

12. World Bank, *Caribbean Exports*.
13. Consultation on Structural Adjustment sponsored by CARIPEDA and Oxfam America, St Georges, Grenada, March 1988.
14. *CAFRA News*, Vol. 2, No. 3, September 1988.

Part IV:
Aid and Adjustment in Action

7.   Grenada: Development by Conquest

> The US created expectations for better incomes and jobs, but the US assistance consisted mainly of rebuilding some of what they bombed, finishing the airport and roads we were already constructing, and pouring budgetary support into the new government. This is window dressing, not development.
>
> Grenadian businessman Lyden Ramdhanny

On 25 October 1983, 6,000 US troops invaded Grenada, a country only twice the size of the District of Columbia with a population of fewer than 110,000. The US government termed the invasion the 'joint intervention' in reference to the token participation of police and military from six Caribbean countries. US President Ronald Reagan vaunted the military conquest of this tiny nation as a major victory for the United States. He characterized the US intervention, which ended Grenada's three-and-a-half-year experiment with a pro-socialist government and a mixed economy, as a 'rescue' of the country and the Caribbean from a new communist threat.

The White House and State Department assured the American public and the people of Grenada that the return of the island to US favor would now unleash the power of private enterprise to foster development. Foreign investment, thousands of jobs, and progress on the path toward North American-style prosperity would soon result, the US government said. While the interest of American public and press in the island's fate faded as fast as the invasion-week banner headlines, the myth of the successful rescue of a grateful Grenada lingered.

In 1986, Reagan and his entourage of more than 500 paid a highly publicized visit to the island. A major purpose of Reagan's four hour and twenty minute visit, a presidential aide told the *Wall Street Journal,* was to 'show people how important defense spending is and also why we need to take a strong position in Central America'.[1]

By the fall of 1988, after five years of US stewardship, almost none of the development goals set by the US had been met. Grenada was deeper in debt than at any time in the nation's past. AID-sponsored efforts to balance the government's budget had failed. The country's tax system, after being thoroughly re-designed by US consultants, had largely collapsed. AID was withholding promised grants to Grenada's government in an effort to force it to comply with structural adjustment conditionalities. Unemployment, estimated by AID at 30 per cent of Grenada's work force, was at an all-time high.[2] Agricultural productivity continued its long-term decline, and Grenada's manufacturing sector remained small and stagnant. 'It's like the whole country's in a coma,' observed one young man, who recounted the three-year search which finally won him a steady job. Hard-drug use, household burglary and violent street crime, all of them rare in Grenada before the mid-1980s, were becoming widespread.

Six years after having helped put Herbert Blaize in power, the US appeared to be dumping the ailing prime minister in much the same way it had abandoned Jamaica's Edward Seaga the year before. The new US favorite was the majority opposition party, the National Democratic Council (NDC) led by George Brizan and Nicholas Braithwaite, to which many business interests had switched their support. Blaize died on 19 December 1989. In the elections held in March 1990, the NDC won enough seats to patch together a government. Like Michael Manley in Jamaica, Blaize's successors inherited, along with conditional US support, a decaying economy, unpayable debt and strong pressure for tighter economic austerity.

Force-fed Growth

Grenada's US-sponsored economic plan had been buttressed by more than US$102 million in development assistance by USAID over a period of less than five years, millions more from other foreign donors and lenders, and help from the Commerce and State Departments, the White House, and committees of powerful US business executives. US personnel, including army construction brigades, Peace Corps volunteers, and retired IRS officials, were visible in nearly every town and government office during the aftermath of the invasion; many were still there in 1988.

During the two years after the invasion, AID spent at least US$37 million on 'emergency' construction and re-construction. The largest expenditure was US$22.1 million for completing the Point Salines airport. The airport, built to aid Grenada's tourism and commerce, was already 85 per cent finished, thanks largely to loans, training and construction assistance from Cuba. Condemned by President Reagan as a major military base, the airport had been one of the main justifications cited by the United States for its military intervention. Nevertheless, the airport was opened under the stars and stripes, complete with a plaque thanking the US (but not Cuba) for its construction, on the first anniversary of the invasion. This and other US-financed construction gave a temporary boost to Grenada's economy.

AID and the US military did make some efforts to win Grenadian hearts and minds by means of what the Agency terms 'highly visible activities'. But total AID allocations for social services and basic human needs, repair of buildings, agricultural research and extension, and community self-help added up to less than 7 per cent of AID spending in Grenada. A rural development worker said:

> We hear over the radio all the time that the US is giving us so many thousands of dollars for this project or that. But by the time the experts and bureaucrats take their share, we don't see any results from it. That's why, when people hear these announcements, they say, 'Here comes more of that radio money', because that's all it is — money you hear about on the radio.[3]

During 1984–87, the period of maximum USAID involvement in Grenada, one sign at least appeared positive: Grenada's GDP registered annual increases in its growth rate in the years 1985–87. This resulted primarily, however, from two special factors: US aid funds, which one economist described as the 'force-feeding' of the economy, and a jump in the prices of two major exports, nutmeg and bananas. In any case, the benefits of this windfall accrued mainly to US contractors, foreign-owned shipping and manufacturing companies, and a small stratum of Grenada's élite.

For sale: one island
George Shultz, US secretary of state in the Reagan cabinet, arrived in Grenada soon after the invasion. One of his first remarks after sighting the town of St George's, with its backdrop of mountains and picturesque harbor, was 'It's a lovely piece of real estate.' In the opinion of US officials, too much of Grenada's real estate was government-owned. In fact, nearly all the country's industry and commerce and 80 per cent of its farmland remained in private hands under the People's Revolutionary Government (PRG).[4] Nevertheless, the guiding principle of AID's Grenada program was 'privatization'.

A top AID priority in Grenada was to dismantle or sell all government-owned enterprises. Among the public facilities slated by AID for disposal were the government carpentry shop, machine shop and central garage, the government printing office, the national electricity and telephone companies, a quarry, a housing construction materials plant, and small factories for grinding spices and coffee and processing fruits and vegetables. One of the first enterprises to go was the Spice Isle canning plant, where local produce had been processed into jams, juices and sauces for local consumption and for export. The canning plant had been important to many Grenadians because it employed local people, provided a market for small farmers and made use of local crops that would otherwise have gone to waste. The local processing and preserving of fruit and vegetables had both increased the country's food supply and added value to the crops it exported by preserving and packaging them in Grenada.

The Spice Isle plant embodied the type of economic activity that the PRG had hoped would increase the country's earnings and reduce its dependence on expensive food imports. The canning plant linked agriculture, the main source of wealth and livelihood in Grenada for centuries, to industry, one of the keys to the country's development. Thus, to many Grenadians, the plant symbolized a development strategy that would build a bridge from Grenada's impoverished past to a more prosperous future, without sacrificing the present generation.

According to Lyden Ramdhanny, one of a considerable number of local landowners and entrepreneurs who supported the Bishop government, the closing of the agro-processing operation was a foolish loss:

> The US called the plant a failure because it was not yet making a profit. But in less than three years, its sales were growing fast. Many private factories

get tax concessions and are still operating at a loss after five years, but the same people don't consider them failures.

When it came time to sell many of the other publicly owned facilities, such as small factories and hotels, few buyers were interested: 'AID tried to put most of the country up for sale, but there were no takers,' businessman Robert Evans observed.[5]

Invitation to exploit

According to AID's version of free market economics, it is wrong for governments to participate directly in production or commerce, but it is proper and necessary for governments to prepare the ground for profitable economic activities by private corporations. While pressing the government of Grenada to do more to help private businesses, the Agency itself spent approximately US$44 million in three and a half years on projects intended primarily to attract and benefit foreign investors. In one such project, AID paid US contractors nearly US$1.8 million to create the Frequente Industrial Park, by converting warehouses into factory buildings to be rented by private manufacturing companies. At the end of 1988, many of the new factory shells remained empty. AID's plans for another industrial park farther from the capital were more likely to succeed, Grenada AID chief Peter Orr predicted. 'Country people are more willing to sit all day by a sewing machine or do other tedious work,' he explained.[6]

AID spent another US$1.5 million to install a new system to remove sewage from luxury hotels and restaurants along Grenada's main tourism strip, Grand Anse beach. There, AID expected, private entrepreneurs would step in to expand and revitalize the industry. 'We've saved one of the world's great natural attractions from pollution!' Orr declared proudly. He did not mention that some homes in the nearby Grand Anse valley still had no plumbing facilities at all, that few Grenadians could afford to patronize posh beachfront facilities, that the beach was still polluted or that tourism had barely increased.

If AID was unable to script a foreign investment success story in Grenada, it was not for want of trying. AID advertised the opportunities for profit-making in Grenada to US companies, and rolled out the red, white and blue carpet for prospective investors. The agency received help in these efforts from the US business consortium Caribbean/Central America Action, from the US Commerce Department, from the White House Office of Private Sector Initiatives, and from two US government-sponsored business finance and insurance companies, OPIC and Eximbank. But even when, in addition to being 'allowed to operate freely', potential investors were offered sizeable subsidies, they were not inclined to come in and develop Grenada. US Chargé d'Affaires John Leary reported that 'Some investors came in just to support the [Reagan] administration, and others came down to have a look, but not too many have stayed.'[7]

By 1989, several investors had come and gone after the collapse of their get-rich-quick schemes, which took advantage of the pro-business climate and government credit. At least three left owing debts to the Grenada or US government. Asked in 1988 to list US companies currently operating in the country, USAID and embassy officials could name only four, which together provided only about 200 jobs. The few new jobs created were far outweighed by the jobs lost as a result of public-sector layoffs and discontinued social programs and public enterprises.

Meanwhile, leaders of Grenada's own private sector reported that they faced more obstacles from AID and from US trade and structural adjustment policies than they had faced under the Bishop-led government. Most private investment since the invasion had been by local businesspeople, they said, without US help. According to Chamber of Commerce president De Bourg, 'AID doesn't work with the private sector here because they already have their minds made up.' De Bourg said:

> We're told that the leftist regime was intending to stifle the private sector and that the present one is trying to support it. This has not been our experience . . . The Bishop government had its act in gear; they were much more motivated. Since then, AID has not created a very palatable situation for Grenada's private sector.[8]

According to Manufacturers Association spokesman Adrian Redhead, 'When we were in the process of the revolution, it was clear. Those guys told us, "profiteering is out, but as long as you share your profits with your workers, you're OK". At least we could plan in that situation.' In contrast, said Redhead, 'AID encourages outside individuals who come in looking for cheaper labor. They want to pay 10 or 15 per cent of what they pay in the US. That leads to labor unrest and kills productivity.'[9]

Meanwhile, small business promotion, described by AID as a top priority, got short shrift. AID allocated US$12 million for one project to help small and medium-sized enterprises in the Eastern Caribbean. But the director of Grenada's AID-funded small-enterprise program, the NDF, soon felt thoroughly frustrated by AID. In his opinion:

> AID puts so many conditions on a project that they stifle it. It's as if the people who work for AID don't feel we should get anything, and that their job is to block aid. There is a lot of money paid to Americans for consultant fees, but little for local loans.[10]

AID's Reluctant Land Reform

AID spent more than US$1.7 million to 'revitalize' farming in Grenada, where the total arable land is only 35,000 acres, less than the size of many private ranches and corporate farms in the United States. AID's primary concern was to make sure that the country's agriculture was privatized. Its main target was the Grenada Farms Corporation, a publicly-owned company that included 32 farms and plantations and provided employment for 990 workers. Most of these estates had become government property not under the PRG but under the previous government of Sir Eric Gairy. Under the PRG, the employees benefited from increased wages, paid sick days, holidays, maternity leave, pension and death benefits, and farm visits by nurses sponsored by the State Farms Health Program.[11]

AID first tried to return the Farms Corporation estates, along with cash grants and free fertilizer, to their previous owners. According to AID Mission head Peter Orr, 'We expected people to want their farms back, but there wasn't exactly an outpouring of interest in agriculture from the private sector.'[12] At the urging of its consultants and with the encouragement of the then minister of agriculture in the Blaize government, George Brizan, AID agreed that the estates would be transferred to selected small-scale farmers, about a fourth of the number employed by the Grenada Farms Corporation before the US intervention. AID was reluctant to take this course because, in the words of a former senior official in the Grenada AID Mission, 'AID doesn't want to support anything right now that could be construed as land reform.'[13] No provision was made in the new plan for the majority of the Farms Corporation employees who would not receive land. Said one Grenadian woman farmer:

> Right now we have so much wasting. Tomatoes, cabbages, dasheen are rotting because we can't get transport or sales for them. I'd put in more tree crops, but I don't know if I might lose the land. It seems like the government wants to give the estates to rich Americans, or they'll sell plots for people living overseas to build houses, but there's no way for farmers like us to get land.

As of March 1988, plots had been assigned to the selected farmers on only three of the Farms Corporation estates slated for privatization. Individual farm plans for some of these plots had been drawn up by technical consultants, but the plans had not yet been shown to the farmers. The farmers, an AID/World Bank study noted, nevertheless 'had carried out an immense amount of hard labor in land preparation'.[14]

Mrs Agnes Hope (not her real name) and her husband were among the fortunate few who been designated a Farms Corporation plot in December 1987. The plot is larger than many and is close to a passable road. Mrs Hope is also fortunate in having a husband and sons who were able and willing to work the land with her. As of March 1988, she had no deed, however, nor was she told what she would have to pay for the land if and when she were permitted to buy it. After waiting weeks to borrow a chain saw shared by several dozen farmers, the family had managed to clear space for planting. They were eager to plant tree crops, but worried that if they did, the assessed value of the land would be raised to an amount they could not afford.

Within a few months, Mrs Hope and her family had planted about 480 vegetable plants, using their savings for seed and fertilizer. Now her concern was with selling the produce. 'The government doesn't really help us to market short crops [as opposed to export crops such as bananas and cocoa]. I just hope some of the things I put in will pay.' Another problem for the family was lack of access to safe water. The Blaize government had promised to install a standpipe, but after several years there were no results:

> We have to go to a stream a long way off, or catch water from the drain along side the road. Sprays like furadan [a plant fungicide] and gramoxone [paraquat] get into that water, and that's the water we have to drink [Mrs Derry said] We don't mind if we have to pay for the land, but to get started we need help with fertilizer and transport. Then we can advance. Right now the government doesn't have the back-up people they should have. It was working alright when Bishop was in office, but since then it's just been going down. If you want your children to grow up strong and well, you stick with them. This government doesn't stick with us the way they should.

Farms Corporation Manager Terrance Beddeau reported that, as of November 1987, all AID funds available to the Corporation had been used and that AID officials had told him no more money would be forthcoming. 'AID brought us just so far, but they're not seeing us through. I would like to see an AID that's genuinely interested in dialogue, and willing to stay around long enough to get some understanding,' Beddeau said.[15]

In its zeal to reverse what it thought were the anti-private property policies of the PRG, AID paid almost no attention to what was, and continues to be, the foundation of Grenada's economy: Grenada's 8,000 independent, mostly small-scale farmers. These producers, many of whom lack title to the plots they farm and receive little or no government assistance, nevertheless are the source of most of the country's earnings and much of its food.[16] One farmer remarked that, 'When the government gets money from abroad for agriculture, it doesn't reach the farmers. Maybe a little of it gets to the extension officers, but we *never* see them.' 'If we small farmers could get just a little fraction of the help big landowners get from the government and from other countries, you'd see some real changes around here,' added another.[17] Nor was AID concerned with the majority of rural Grenadians who are landless or very land-poor. Many work on small farms or on agricultural estates where technology and social structures have changed little since the era of slavery.

These hard-pressed agricultural workers and small-scale farmers have produced most of Grenada's wealth for centuries and continue to produce it today. Their labor, until recent decades, fed most of the island's population. Their work has been the original source of the generally modest riches accumulated by Grenadian estate owners and merchants, the core of the island's elite, and of the greater gains of the absentee estate owners, financiers, and international merchants and shipping companies which have garnered the greater part of the profits of Grenada's export agriculture.

AID's Grenada Agriculture Sector Revitalization Project produced more than a dozen thick volumes of feasibility studies and consultants' reports. Throughout these reports, there is barely any mention of the living conditions, needs or opinions and aspirations of the country's poor rural majority. One sub-sector of Grenada's low-income rural population ('entrepreneurial' smallscale farmers) is singled out in the AID reports as worthy of support, although little actual support has been forthcoming.

By 1988, most of the US$1.7 million allotted for the project had been absorbed by consultants' fees, equipment imported from the United States, feasibility studies for the Farms Corporation project, land surveys (re-done several times), and 'training and technical assistance' to government personnel. AID's reluctant land reform was stalled in the mud.

The Dependency Syndrome

Most AID-financed projects were carried out with little consultation of the people affected. Members of a committee of parents, grandparents and teachers in a village told of the dubious help they received in building a pre-school. A new school was needed for the 40 pupils who, in the teacher's words, had been 'jammed like herring' in a tiny, tin-roofed shack. The committee had begun raising funds for a building by holding benefit parties when, one day, a construction team arrived unannounced and began building the foundation for a new pre-school in a broad gully by the steep village road. Said one building committee member:

> Anybody who lives here could tell you that the place where they set those pillars turns into a river in the rainy months. Children playing there would have been swept away. But nobody consulted us, except to approach our treasurer for the $600 we had got together.

The committee finally completed a new pre-school in a safe location, but the pillars built by the construction team remained standing like tombstones in the eroded gully, monuments to the folly of development by outside experts.

While scrimping on funds for social needs, AID failed to tap the most valuable resource of all — the skills and ideas of Grenadian people. Under the government led by Maurice Bishop, literacy, teacher training and other programs had linked schools and communities, mobilized local skills and served as focal points for political activism and debate. The popular health and social welfare projects, developed by the PRG with help from Cuba and from citizens of other Caribbean countries, from Europe, and from a few North American non-government agencies, inspired many Granadians to contribute time and skills, working unpaid overtime or as volunteers.

After the US intervention, nearly all of these programs were discontinued. Mass-based organizations, such as the National Youth Association and the National Women's Association, were disbanded. Cooperatives engaged in farming, food processing, fishing and handicrafts were discouraged and denied access to credit, which was directed, ineffectively, to private businesses. Many of the country's most dynamic young leaders, particularly those who were associated with the previous government or who spoke critically of the new one, were laid off, denied licenses to practice their professions, or even forced into exile. Demoralized by the loss of leadership and by the dissolution of the popular organizations, many Grenadians withdrew skills and energies they had contributed under the PRG. A former government employee said, 'It used to be that we'd work up to three in the morning sometimes, and we didn't complain because we wanted to get the work done. Now a lot of people are going home grumbling at three in the afternoon.'

Neither AID nor the New National Party (NNP) government put forward a plan for developing the country's economy using Grenadian skills and local materials. There was no effort to build structures to allow grassroots participation in decision-making, nor were poor Grenadians encouraged to identify their own needs and to take action on their own behalf. AID tended to assume it knew what Grenada needed better than Grenadians did, while the Blaize administration perceived grassroots organizations as a political threat. Lyden Ramdhanny notes:

> People need to learn and think about the problems involved in things like, for instance, how water is treated and supplied, instead of taking that sort of thinking for granted or looking to foreign so-called experts. One legacy of the revolution is that now people understand things like that much better.

Whether or not the Bishop-led government could have brought prosperity to Grenada, it did recognize an essential element of any such effort: the value of local resources, both human and material, and the need to mobilize Grenadians to take responsibility for their own future. Neither US advisors, with their smug assumptions of superiority, nor Blaize's NNP, subservient to a foreign patron, were able to motivate and inspire the population as the previous, proudly Caribbean nationalist government had done.

Retooling the Economy

During the five years following the invasion, USAID transferred US$22.2 million in hard currency directly to the government of Grenada in an effort to jump-start the country's stalled economy. (Grenada's annual GDP is only about US$20 million.) AID negotiated five separate grant agreements with the Government of Grenada, all with the general purpose of promoting private sector-led growth and providing 'a more secure basis for undertaking structural adjustment'.[18] To this end, the grants were made conditional upon economic policy changes designed to turn the country's rusty, recycled government into a lean development machine, fueled by generous investment incentives. These policies, AID hoped, would put the private sector in the driver's seat and enable business to steer Grenada into the free enterprise fast lane.

Grenada's creaking economy failed to pick up speed. To AID's dismay, the only sector of the economy that was growing in 1985 was the public sector; increasing government payrolls were funded by borrowing from private banks in addition to the AID cash grants. AID tried to get tough. AID structural adjustment conditions became increasingly specific and severe with each subsequent cash transfer. The third in the series was an Economic Stabilization Grant (ESG III) of US$7 million. As with other AID budgetary support grants, this one required the Grenada government to purchase US goods or services from a list approved by AID, worth at least the total of the grant within one year of receiving it.

Other conditions of the grant were: (1) decreased government involvement in 'decisions on the directions of investment, particularly foreign investment' and delegation of authority from the cabinet to an AID-designed Industrial Development Corporation; (2) faster privatization of publicly-owned assets, including the state-owned farms; (3) less government regulation of import/export trade and local commerce, including elimination of ceilings on interest rates and price controls on many staple foods; (4) increased 'policy dialogue' with AID, including monthly meetings and regular written cash flow reports; (5) a major new program of 'fiscal reform', to be developed under AID supervision; (6) design of a 'comprehensive development strategy', the purpose of which, AID said, was not to 'plan the economy, but to assist government in formulating a policy environment consistent with its market-oriented development aims'.[19] AID estimated that these directives would reduce government spending by US$10 million. AID's grant of US$7 million would make up the rest of the government's projected US$17 million budget deficit. The IMF later reported the actual fiscal deficit for 1986 as US$24 million.

Fiscal fiasco
AID's Grenada Fiscal Reform Project, started in 1986, brought in American business executives, former IRS employees, and business consulting firms to show Grenadians how to transform their country into a free-enterprise paragon. A major part of their plan was to take more from poor and middle-income Grenadians to offer as investment incentives to the prosperous. The AID fiscal reform project reduced corporate taxes, eliminated the country's moderate but progressive income tax and a variety of other indirect taxes, and replaced them with a property tax and a complex and cumbersome 20 per cent value-added tax (VAT). While trying to get the government to decrease its deficit by raising more revenues, AID was pressing the government not to spend less but rather to shift spending priorities from public needs to private-sector benefits.

The new, made-in-the-USA tax system was so poorly understood by the Grenadian officials who spoke in public to explain it that US consultants nearly always stepped forward to answer questions. At the same time, the US consultants understood Grenada so poorly that the tax system they designed proved impossible to implement and had to be discontinued after two years. The 20 per cent VAT led to price hikes for consumers. Some goods cost 300 per cent more at the retail store than their price at the port of entry, after the VAT was added each time the product changed hands. Elimination of the modest tax formerly applied to exporters of cash crops meant an annual revenue loss of an estimated US$7.5 million, while reduced corporate taxes cost the government millions more.

Soaking the poor

AID fiscal reformers advised the government to make up for the fall in tax revenues from corporations and the rich by charging more for services used mainly by the poor. Grenadians, US officials said, had the misguided notion that just because certain services were paid for by their taxes, they ought to be offered free of charge. US Chargé d'Affaires John Leary observed that, 'Water here is traditionally free; they ought to meter it. You can walk into a clinic here, get your eyes checked, and not be charged!' His tone made it clear that the situation offended his sense of economic propriety. In addition, Leary said, 'They [Grenadians] ask for things they can't afford. The fellow in charge of the hospital said they want an ultrasound machine, but it's not really needed.' (Ultrasound machines are part of the basic equipment of hospitals and many private obstetrical practices in the United States.)

To help fill leaky government coffers, AID's fiscal reform team prepared a lengthy list of user fees and other charges. Among them were many imaginative means of making public services and citizens' rights into commodities to be sold, including licenses for market vendors, fees for veterinary services to farmers, charges for birth certificates, for the right to reside in Grenada, to become a citizen or to renounce citizenship, and higher charges for cemetery plots, especially for those on hills. An AID memo noted that fees for delivering babies, at an average of 1000 births per year, would yield US$26,000 annually, while upgrading of hospital staff and facilities could justify higher charges. Other recommended revenue sources were higher fees for lab tests, dental care and X-rays.

The health care system illustrates the effects of AID-recommended cutbacks in social services. Emphasis was shifted away from decentralized primary and preventive care serving rural areas. PRG health care and insurance plans, such as those provided to cooperative farm workers and their communities, were eliminated or reduced drastically. Training for health workers comparable to the long-term scholarships provided by Cuba was not offered. Thanks to dental drills installed by Cubans in parish clinics, many Grenadians had had tooth cavities filled for the first time. Five years after the invasion, most of the drills were no longer in service because no funds were available to buy replacement compressors, and dental workers again had to extract teeth that could have been repaired. Grenada's hospitals had to get along with a few second-hand X-ray machines (and none in the outlying islands), shortages of syringes, solutions, medications and gloves. One Grenadian citizen took up the opportunity this created in the true spirit of free enterprise. For just 25 Eastern Caribbean dollars, paid well in advance, he offered a 'health insurance policy' that promised a seat on the next outgoing plane to any Grenadian facing a medical emergency.

In spite of the AID Fiscal Reform Project and social service reductions, Grenada's government budget deficit remained stubbornly high. According to AID Grenada Mission Director Orr, the reason was obvious: 'Grenada has been living at a standard above its means. There's fat in all areas — education, health, public works, agriculture, everywhere — but there's no willingness to tighten belts.'

Unable to pressure the Government of Grenada to implement the full US austerity program, AID turned to the World Bank and the IMF to help carry out the job. AID's 1986 Grenada Structural Adjustment Program (SAP) Support grant of US$4 million, intended to help make up for government's tax revenue shortfall, carried the explicit requirement that Grenada cooperate with the World Bank in planning its structural adjustment program. AID's grant conditions also directed Grenada to participate in the TCG, the subcommittee of the CGCED established by the World Bank and other Northern agencies to monitor Eastern Caribbean economies. However, an AID memorandum prepared for the June 1988 CGCED meeting stated: 'The government has been reluctant to implement fully its planned civil service retrenchment plan and it has yet to join in the Tighter Consultative Group arrangement. Hence, Fiscal Year 87 funds conditioned on these actions remain undisbursed.' As of early 1991, no structural adjustment agreement had been signed, but politics prevailed when AID released most of the held-back SAP funds in the period prior to the 1990 elections.

USAID was unable to impose its entire structural adjustment agenda on Grenada, in part because of the ineptitude and corruption of the Blaize administration, combined with the political protection it enjoyed from Washington in the post-invasion years. During the Reagan years, the short-term political goal of keeping the 'rescued' nation afloat outweighed the economic goal of enforcing structural adjustment. The Blaize government also had to contend with the expectations of Grenada's people, heightened by the revolutionary experiment. The political price of meeting AID's retrenchment quota was more than the Blaize administration was ready to pay.

Pulling the Plug

After four years of US involvment, many Grenadian civil servants and business people — the local representatives of the private sector that US officials said was the key to the country's future — had lost patience with Grenada's patron from the North. Said Grenada Chamber of Commerce president George de Bourg:

> Under the PRG, the government was much more aggressive in support of economic programs, but we were squeezed out of access to foreign capital. . . . AID has a lot of programs in theory, but in practice the money is tied up in consultancies. The designers aren't sure what they're doing or why, so they produce all manner of reports that don't reach the intended beneficiaries, and not much in actual assistance.[20]

Many Grenadian working people were disillusioned, too. Said a part-time construction worker, 'The same ones who've been exploiting we [poor people] are back in power now. They get you in the lumber yard, they get you in the supermarket, at the bank, in the insurance, and now they get you in your taxes, too.'

By 1988, the US government was in the process of abandoning its protégé nation. AID funding in Grenada had been slashed to about a fifth of the amount spent in the year following the invasion; further cuts were planned. AID officials were stalling the release of promised budgetary support funds because of the country's failure to comply with AID's own structural adjustment program for Grenada, and because of Grenada's alleged unwillingness to cooperate with the World Bank-led economic coordinating committee for the Eastern Caribbean, the TCG.[21]

AID officials in Washington spoke with thinly veiled contempt of the Government of Grenada and its 70-year-old prime minister, Herbert Blaize. A harried AID official, charged with overseeing AID's structural adjustment funding in the Eastern Caribbean, received a telephone call at the State Department AID office from Blaize, enquiring whether and when Grenada would receive an expected check for several million dollars from AID. When the official asked what to say to the prime minister, he was told by his superior, 'If he [Blaize] doesn't get the message that we don't take him seriously, tell him to turn up his hearing aid.'[22]

USAID officials in Grenada, busy packing their files and computers in preparation for closing the special Grenada AID Mission, also blamed the Grenada government for the country's sad condition. The last official in charge of the Grenada AID Mission remarked, 'This government has no political backbone. They've been raising people's expectations when they should have been telling them to prepare for hard times ahead.' But hard times were the opposite of what the United States had promised Grenada only a few years before. The same Grenadian government that so appalled AID officials had been virtually hand-picked under US supervision in the year following the invasion. Its budget and economic strategy had been shaped under AID tutelage to follow the principles of privatization, free trade and market-driven development.

'What Can You Expect from the Americans?'
In retrospect, the failure of the US development model in Grenada appears unavoidable. Most Grenadians, whether they had been supportive, critical or, as were many, critically supportive of Bishop and of the PRG, at least had thought of the PRG as *Grenada's* government. The United States sought to establish a government that was compliant and willing to act as a US surrogate; thus, the new regime was inevitably weak, incapable of inspiring Grenadians to make the economic sacrifices required to carry out structural adjustment. The gap between the hype and hoop-la that accompanied the US takeover and the harsh cuts in living standards required by the free market model only made the failure of that model more obvious.

The privatization principles which guided US development directives could not catapult Grenada out of poverty. Investors realized, even if AID did not, that chances of making a profit were slim in a small country where the costs of importing and exporting were high and where most people remained too poor to be good customers for products sold locally. The interest of US companies in Grenada's investment opportunities stretched only as far as funds available through AID for construction and consultation contracts. These projects and policies, which used public funds to underwrite the costs of private enterprise, represent the type of endeavors that AID, the World Bank and the IMF want the government of Grenada to continue as AID pulls out. To the extent that AID is leaving Grenada with any development strategy at all, that strategy boils down to this: depend on outsiders to develop your economy and give them all you can to make it worth their while to do so.

American values and the material rewards for which Grenadians were expected to work, symbolized in the mind of the US embassy chief by consumer electronics, are glorified daily in Grenada by one of the most visible results of the US intervention: 18 daily hours of commercial television beamed from the United States. The influence of the US media is a cause of great concern to many Grenadians. A member of the Grenada Popular Theatre Organization observed:

> We're being bombarded by TV with a message that says that to have anything worthwhile, we have to go to the US, and that nothing we have here in Grenada is worth having. That message is causing a lot of people to turn to alcohol, and young people to turn to drugs.

Said Lyden Ramdhanny:

> US promises have created hopes for jobs, and the US media feed expectations for a US style of living. TV ads create desires for the latest stereos and styles. The commercials get us hooked on the products of their economy so we will consume *their* products.

Even if a taste for US goods could be construed as a step toward development, few Grenadians could afford them.

Five years after the invasion, some AID Grenada veterans had become sceptical. 'We still try to slip in a few traditional basic needs projects when we can,' one AID staff member confided. But top AID officials and US policymakers remained too beholden to the ideology of private sector-led development to recognize their failure or alter their dogma. Instead, they blamed the government they had helped to create, and the Grenadian people themselves. US Chargé d'Affaires O'Leary told a group of US visitors in 1988 that as a consequence of slavery, Grenadians lack initiative. 'They need to learn that if they want a stereo, they'll have to work for it.'

Vyra McQueen, general secretary of the Grenada Union of Teachers, is from the countryside and has taught in Grenada's schools for 23 years:

People in Grenada are not lazy. They're very willing to take action. We have a tradition of rural co-operatives and grassroots credit unions. Things like this are the real local base of development.

With all the speed and hustling you see today, you don't see as much of this kind of cooperation as during the PRG. Then, there was a willingness of parents and community members to assist, because people had a clear idea of where money was coming from and where it was going. Today it's more like it was under Gairy, when people knew there was money but didn't know where it was coming from or where it was going. The PRG didn't have much time or much money, but we had our own government. Everyone had a sense of belonging, so there was more willingness to come out, on Sundays if necessary, to get things done.[23]

Notes

1. *Wall Street Journal*, 20 February 1986.
2. USAID, 'Project Assistance Approval Document', 543K603, July 1985.
3. Author interview with Judy Williams, director of the Grenada Community Development Agency (GRENCODA), March 1989.
4. The PRG was the official name of the government headed by Maurice Bishop. It was formed and led by the New Jewel Movement, which took power from the eccentric autocrat Sir Eric Gairy in a nearly bloodless coup on 13 March 1979.
5. Author interview, March 1988.
6. Author interview, November 1987.
7. Meeting with US visitors, March 1988.
8. Author interview, November 1987.
9. Ibid.
10. Author interview, November 1987.
11. Background information was provided by Grenadian researcher and former manager of one of the model farms, Ambrose Phillip.
12. Author interview, November 1987.
13. Author interview, November 1987.
14. Leon Hesser, Evaluation of the Grenada Agricultural Sector Revitalization Project, Agency for International Development, 30 June 1987.
15. Author interview, March 1988.
16. Agricultural exports, mainly of cocoa, nutmeg, bananas, and mace account for more than 90 per cent of the cash-strapped country's export income. Full-time and part-time farmers, many of them women, also produce a substantial portion of Grenada's food.
17. Women farmers' workshop, 8 March 1987, Gouyave, Grenada.
18. AID agreements for cash transfers to the Government of Grenada included
19. USAID Program Assistance Approval Document for Grenada Economic Support Grant III, July 1985.
20. Author interview, November 1987.
21. Interviews with USAID officials in Bridgetown, Barbados, St George's, Grenada, and Washington DC, February and June 1988.
22. 13 June 1988.
23. Author interview, April 1988.

8. Dominica: The Plunder of Nature Isle

> Dominica will never be able to provide optimal services. Our health service is satisfactory now. . . . Some people are asking for another pediatrician, but we don't require two pediatricians in the country. We can't afford to send every child to a pediatrician. People expect this, but they'll have to learn otherwise.
>
> Prime Minister Eugenia Charles

In September 1989, Hurricane Hugo ripped across Dominica, destroying 80 per cent of the island's banana crop and demonstrating the danger of the country's dependence on bananas for the bulk of its export earnings. The lesson was not a new one: just 10 years before, Hurricane David had stripped much of the small Eastern Caribbean island nearly bare of vegetation. But it was a lesson that went unheeded by USAID.

In 1980, Dominica's banana industry had nearly collapsed in the wake of a leaf-spot epidemic and another severe hurricane that year. Here was an opportunity for the United States to support a transition from precarious dependence on bananas to a more diversified and self-reliant economy. But also in 1980, conservative Eugenia Charles was elected prime minister of this English- and French Creole-speaking nation. With the Grenada and Nicaragua revolutions a fresh memory, and other political storms brewing through the region, the United States was far more eager to shore up a Caribbean political ally than to address the underlying causes of Dominica's poverty and dependency.

Rather than funding crop diversification and staple food production, AID chose to spend US$1.7 million to prop up and privatize Dominica's banana industry. In so doing, the agency poured cash and US fertilizer into the economy, enabling the Charles government to postpone a crisis and ignore the calls by farmers and others for a sounder development strategy. AID thus helped lock Dominica more tightly into the vicious cycle of debt and dependency on cash crop export earnings to pay for imported food and basic consumer goods.

Prime Minister Eugenia Charles has pointed to superficial signs of prosperity — increased car sales on credit and construction fueled by the banana boom and foreign aid — as evidence of debt-defying leaps of economic progress. But her Thatcheresque, stiff-upper-lip optimism cannot disguise the growing anxiety at the top of the society, nor can it hide the worsening plight of the country's poor majority. Citizens of Dominica have responded to economic pressures with great resourcefulness. They have tripled their production of marketable, unblemished bananas in less than a decade, extending cultivation into treacherous terrain and exceeding challenges that might have daunted the most determined North American farm pioneers.

Many dedicated teachers and nurses have stuck bravely to their posts, under terrible working conditions, in crumbling buildings, for abysmal pay. But ever-longer lines of Dominicans seek visas to work abroad; others have joined a new outflux of Caribbean boat people.

Natural Riches, Needless Poverty

USAID officials say the country is 'not viable'. World Bank economists dismiss it as a 'micro-state'. But there is nothing natural nor inevitable about Dominica's poverty. Because of its rugged terrain and the frequency of heavy rains and hurricanes, Dominica is not well-suited for large-scale export agriculture. The soil is bountiful and could, if handled carefully, feed more than the country's 81,000 people. Instead, Dominica now depends largely on imported food and on subsistence farming, much of it done by women using tools and techniques unchanged for centuries. The best farmlands, flat areas near the coast, along roads or in sheltered valleys, have been owned for generations by foreign companies or landlords living in town or abroad, who have frequently left their land idle. Meanwhile, Dominica's poor, and the nation as a whole, remain heavily dependent on the earnings of emigrants to nearby Caribbean or Latin American countries, to Britain, Canada and, increasingly, the United States.

The country's agricultural estates have specialized in a succession of export crops: cocoa, coffee, sugar, essential oils, limes and other citrus fruit, coconuts and, now, bananas. Small-scale farmers, too, have usually grown some export crops to obtain cash for goods they have not been able to produce themselves. As one export crop has taken the place of another, Dominica's plantation owners and small-scale producers have had no control over the prices and markets for their exports. They have shifted crops repeatedly in an effort to meet fickle international demand and to out-compete other exporters. Neither estate owners nor small farmers have had control over the costs of the tools, machinery, fertilizers, and other inputs they have needed to import from abroad.

Over the years, the country as a whole has continued to sell cheap and buy dear, essentially operating at a loss. For more than 200 years, Britain was willing to cover some of that loss in exchange for the country's militarily strategic location and the riches it produced for a small number of British investors. But by far the greater part of the loss was, and still is, absorbed by the peasants and farm workers, the fruits of whose labor have been sold for a fraction of their value. Meanwhile, the local elite skimmed enough of the profits of the plantation economy and the import–export trade to live in relative luxury. It still does.

Today, both bananas and coconut, the country's second most important earner of foreign exchange, can be grown at lower cost in larger Asian and Latin American countries. This leaves Dominica extremely vulnerable to external forces it cannot control: weather, unstable international commodity prices and politically determined aid and trade preferences. A preferential banana marketing agreement with Britain temporarily guarantees above-market prices for West Indian bananas. This, plus heavy foreign and local borrowing and USAID grants, has kept its economy from collapse since Dominica became independent in 1978. Meanwhile, 'The government doesn't even recognize, much less develop, our agricultural potential,' maintains Dominican agronomist Neville Graham. Graham notes that many agricultural estates slated to be privatized and sold for industry, housing and tourism 'were once productive and diversified entities'. They could be the centerpiece of a national plan for a more self-sufficient economy, with certain land set aside for livestock, other land for beans, potatoes and other crops. Instead, says Graham, 'piecemeal planning has allowed Dominica's agriculture to be undermined and buffeted about in response to shifting market incentives and private sector priorities'.

Dominica remains poor, but its poverty has been created and recreated over the years since colonial conquest by economic and social structures that have robbed the island of its wealth and skills, prevented farmers and workers from earning enough to sustain their families, stunted the growth of local institutions and isolated the country from its Caribbean neighbors. These same structures of power and patterns of trade, reinforced by AID, British government, IMF and World Bank policies, perpetuate Dominica's poverty today.

The road not taken
The pre-independence years of the 1970s had brought Dominica to a crossroads; would its best land, labor and skills continue to produce wealth mainly for outsiders, or might those resources be redirected to meet the needs of Dominicans? Could the country begin to work itself free from extreme dependence and, by linking with its Caribbean and Latin American neighbors, overcome the obstacles of its small size and colonized economy? This option has not yet been given a chance.

Those Dominicans who have the greatest decision-making power have least incentive to change the country's or the region's subordination to Northern countries and foreign corporations. The governing élite is largely still tied to colonial interests and constrained by a neo-colonial outlook. Many are managers for, or junior partners of, the foreign corporations that have reaped the greatest profits from Dominica's soil. Others have made their fortunes from import trade, export agriculture and land speculation. Only a far-reaching restructuring of the economy could enable Dominica to reduce, and perhaps ultimately to overcome, its poverty and vulnerability.

Eugenia Charles did not aspire to lead her country along any major change of course. As a lawyer and a daughter of the landed and commercial élite, she was part of a class that benefited from the status quo. Charles herself had been outspokenly opposed even to political independence. In addition to promises of continued, albeit reduced, support from Great Britain, Charles had a new patron: the United States. When the administration of US President Ronald

Reagan took office in January 1981, it already had close ties with Charles and her party.

The IMF, too, saw an opportunity in Dominica to pursue its global free trade policies. In Dominica as elsewhere, it was willing to plug the balance of payments deficit with IMF debt, to postpone, although not to solve, the problem. In 1981, the IMF proffered a loan of US$11 million, on the condition that the country adopt an IMF-supervised program of 'economic stabilization'. It required Dominica to reduce government budget deficits by cutting payrolls, social services and public enterprises, and adopting more regressive taxes. The government was also required to open the country to more imports from abroad and to work with the World Bank on a plan to aid foreign investors. Prime Minister Charles says her government had no problem with these IMF conditionalities: 'The things the IMF wanted us to do were the same things we wanted ourselves. . . . We believed in privatization before the IMF and World Bank were here.'[1]

The IMF was relatively lenient in its dealings with Dominica, as it often is with conservative US allies. It permitted Charles to strengthen her political base by using part of the US$11 million loan to cover wage arrears of government employees. It negotiated a second deal with Dominica in 1984, a stand-by agreement, even though the country had not met the targets for economic growth under the previous agreement. Dominica's growth rate did increase in the mid-1980s, but at the cost of a doubling of the country's debt, to nearly 60 per cent of GDP by 1989. 'We have to get deeper into debt in order to get out of debt,' said Charles.

The US Buys Support

USAID funds flowed freely through most of the 1980s to the Reagan administration's closest friend in the Eastern Caribbean. Prominent among AID grants during the Charles administration have been US$24.5 million for road rebuilding, $1.7 million for the restructuring of the banana industry and US$4.7 million for expansion of Dominica's electricity system. A special AID fund has supported what the agency calls 'highly visible activities', such as small road and water projects and school repairs in rural towns. That the main motive behind this AID support has been to strengthen a US political ally is obvious to many Dominicans. The head of Dominica's Economic Planning Division remarked:

When people in the Caribbean talk about the 'miracle' of economic growth in Taiwan, they shouldn't forget that Taiwan got huge amounts of US aid in reaction to the revolution in China. Here, the revolution in Grenada got us one big road. I'd hate to have to wait for communism to take over Haiti to get more.[2]

It was not long before the Reagan administration received a big payoff for its modest investment in Dominica. It came in October 1983, when the US needed official backing in the Caribbean for its invasion of Grenada. Administration officials were delighted when Prime Minister Charles stood staunchly beside President Reagan in Washington. She told the world that the US invasion was being carried out with her full endorsement and at the request of the OECS, over which Charles was presiding at the time.[3]

AID also had its own agenda for the Dominican economy. 'We need to keep favorable governments in power long enough to maintain privatization,' explained Robin Phillips, the AID official in charge of AID's structural adjustment support programs in the Eastern Caribbean.[4] To this end, AID gave the Government of Dominica a series of direct cash transfers beginning in 1983. The AID mission indicated that continued budgetary support would be 'contingent on Dominica's success in negotiating an accord' for privatization and deregulation with the IMF, and that 'These [IMF-required] reforms are a model for the rest of the Eastern Caribbean less developed countries.'[5] To get US cash grants, Dominica also had to purchase US goods and services worth the amount of each grant, offer a better deal to US businesses in Dominica, publicize the US government as its benefactor and use local revenue to cover the costs of all the administration and paperwork involved.

Enter the World Bank

The USAID program in Dominica did not begin to address the country's underlying economic plight. In 1985, Dominica's earnings from its exports still covered only 51 per cent of its import bills. In the same year, the World Bank spearheaded plans for a new, more far-reaching structural adjustment program within the CGCED framework. The carrot offered in conjunction with the familiar austerity stick was US$8 million in below-market interest rate loans from the Bank, the IMF and the CDB. USAID made a 'verbal commitment' to add at least US$4 million in SAP grants to the package. AID did provide most of the promised funds, several years behind schedule.

The World Bank plan called for 'policies that will create the right environment for productive investment by the private sector and for export growth'.[6] The Bank recognized the obstacles caused by 'the very small island economy, difficult terrain, paucity of financial and human resources', over-dependence on fragile bananas and vulnerability to hurricanes. Yet somehow, this tiny, storm-battered country had to be launched upon the rough seas of international free market competition; the Bank could conceive of no alternative to an export-led development strategy.

Low wages are central to that strategy. According to the Bank, Dominica's 'lack of international competitiveness', makes it essential that the government 'place primary reliance on controlling the growth of real wages. This policy will maintain the attractiveness of Dominica's low-skilled labor for labor-intensive light manufacturing and help contain the costs of its tourism product.' In line with this goal, the Freedom Party-dominated parliament enacted labor legislation that allows employers to make separate contracts with individual workers, avoiding trade union bargaining units.

In other 'adjusting' countries, including Jamaica and the Dominican Republic, the World Bank and IMF have dealt with the problem of 'too high' wages by requiring currency devaluations, which have the double effect of reducing workers' real incomes and of making the adjusted country's exports cheaper. Because Dominica's currency is pegged to the US dollar and tied to that of other OECS countries, devaluation is politically difficult, a fact repeatedly bemoaned by Bank officials.

Other adjustment program measures required the government to freeze Dominica's minimum wage, toughen its stance toward the civil servants' union and reduce the number of public employees. The World Bank specifically urged elimination of 30 per cent of the jobs in the country's Central Water Authority, despite the fact that broken sewers and lack of piped water plague many urban and rural communities. The government reorganized the authority with fewer and lower-paid employees. Another public body, the DOMLEC power corporation, was partly privatized. The national Housing Development Corporation was dismantled. Said a senior government official, 'We're raising water and electricity rates, but we can't raise them fast enough to please the World Bank.'

A particular contribution of USAID to Dominica's adjustment program has been a tax structure revamped under supervision by USAID consultants, with some input from Canadian experts. Although taxes on the majority of Dominicans were already relatively high, AID official Robin Phillips explained, a revenue source was needed 'to make sure that the new tax reforms [i.e. cuts in corporate and high income-bracket tax rates] wouldn't reduce the total tax take and thereby create disincentives for investors. . . . The IMF wanted a VAT; AID recommended a sales tax, and Miss Charles bought into this.' As Charles has made clear, the essence of the tax law changes has been 'downstreaming', a euphemism for the shift of the overall tax burden from higher-income Dominicans and foreign investors to lower-income Dominicans.

Many Dominicans are disturbed by the impact of adjustment on their beleaguered economy. As head of the Dominica Hucksters Association, Cecil Joseph deals daily with struggling small-scale traders, many of them women, who sell produce to Guadeloupe and other nearby islands. Says Joseph:

> The higher customs duties and taxes have increased the cost of living at the same time that government employee cuts have reduced overall economic activity. The result is more unemployment, more emigration, and acceleration of the brain drain. . . . The government has been saying that if it weren't for the IMF, we couldn't pay for this project or that one. But who do the projects really benefit? We get a glossy picture, but never the true picture of how much we owe, who is gaining, and the sacrifices we're making.[7]

Passengers on a rural bus expressed their anger in no uncertain terms: 'It shameful what the government is doing to we poor people!' One elderly woman exclaimed, 'Now they're taxing even our food! It pains you especially when you know that there's aid money coming into the country, but none of it reaches down to where it's really needed. It's the ones at the top who are collecting.'

Trauma to the system
Worsening health care services are one price the poor are paying for structural adjustment. The number of beds in the country's main hospital was reduced by 21 per cent from 1978 to 1987.[8] The country's promising rural health clinics, established in the early 1980s, are now seriously understaffed and undersupplied. Doctors at the Princess Margaret Hospital report constant shortages of essential supplies, forced by strict new budget controls. Cloth dressings must be used and recycled, and surgical and other wards have been combined. As a result, said one physician, 'a child who comes in for a circumcision is very likely to leave with measles or another infectious disease, and come back sicker than before'. Although the hospital's main lobby has been redecorated, operations must sometimes be done with assistants holding the lights by hand and forceps falling off blood vessels during surgery. Some patients have had to sleep on the hospital floor; many others have been sent home, their surgery postponed repeatedly, because of the shortage of beds or the lack of oxygen. (Many better-off Dominicans facing medical emergencies fly to Martinique or Miami.)

Badly overworked nurses in Dominica's clinics and hospitals have left in droves, many in response to campaigns to lure them to US hospitals, where even as nurses' aides they can earn more. Instead of improving nurses' pay and working conditions, the government responded by eliminating government financial aid to nursing trainees, on the theory that it is a waste of money to train nurses who may leave the country.

Education is also a casualty. The number of pupils enrolled in primary schools declined by 23 per cent from 1978 to 1987, although the population grew by 9.9 per cent. For many who complete primary school and do well in the placement exams, there are no secondary school places. Said a teacher, 'It's really sad to see what happens to the ones who can't go to high school, even though you know they could do the work. Sometimes they get depressed and disappear for days. It's as if their fate is sealed.' According to Prime Minister Charles:

> People need education in order to be fit to earn a living, not in order to get into secondary schools and come out with a white collar but no job. That kind of education is pointless. We need to stream people into the kind of employment that's available.

Dominicans who want to acquire scientific and technical skills generally must seek training outside the country. Those who manage to do so often cannot find jobs at home. As a consequence, Dominican teachers, nurses, doctors, architects and engineers serve foreign institutions, while Dominica either does without their badly needed skills or depends on foreign agencies and expensive experts from abroad.

Health care and other service cuts may help achieve short-term budget savings and meet structural adjustment targets but they damage the prospects for genuine development. They greatly increase the burden on women, who must make up for the loss of public services by increasing their own labor in nurturing the sick and educating the young, at the same time that they and their sisters must seek wage labor or increase their export crop production to keep up with the rising costs of food, transport and taxes.

The effects of adjustment policies on export-oriented industry 'have not been promising' in the words of the World Bank. According to a senior official in Dominica's Ministry of Trade, most of the AID funds spent on investment promotion by consultants paid by AID have amounted to 'money gone down the drain'. Consultants from a multinational firm hired by AID, he said:

> were here to attract US investors, but the kind of investments they promoted were the cut-and-sew type, that have a limited and very short-term benefit to the economy. What we need are industries where there is more value added in Dominica. But the only criterion they had to report to AID was the number of jobs.[9]

At the airport, a large billboard asks would-be investors, 'Need Skilled Workers? Call the Youth Development Division.' Just down the road stands a vacant cinderblock building where 200 women worked during the late 1980s. Faced with rising living costs, many of the young women eagerly accepted jobs in the new Silver Star garment assembly factory, although their wages barely covered the costs of getting to work. Some of the trainee workers received daily stipends of about US$1.88, paid by USAID to save expense to the employer. Trained machine operators earned a daily wage of US$5 or more. The Silver Star factory followed several of its predecessors, closing its doors in 1990 and throwing its AID-trained workforce off the job.

After five years of AID-funded efforts to persuade foreign investors to set up export operations in Dominica, only 472 new jobs had reportedly been created in the new AID-backed industrial estate, according to an AID evaluation report. Given the costs of incentives and foregone taxes, the net economic gain to the country from the factories is probably negative and there is nothing to stop export companies from moving to other countries that offer even lower wages or more lucrative deals.

Agricultural Reaganomics

Another damaging consequence of structural adjustment is the further erosion of Dominica's food security. The full impact of the country's increased dependence on unreliable export markets will be felt in the 1990s, when Britain's entry into the European common market is likely to bring the phasing-out of the preferential UK market for West Indian bananas and the end of Dominica's banana boom. Under a system of genuine free trade, Dominican bananas would easily be priced out of the world market. Thoughtful Dominicans have been pointing this out for years; AID finally acknowledged it in an internal 1988 memorandum that states, 'Dominica will be devastated by adverse changes in the banana market and has only a few years to prepare for them.'

The World Bank has been urging agricultural diversification, although it has done little to promote it. The government of Dominica and other governments in the region have finally acknowledged the problem. Dominica's Deputy Chief Agriculture Minister, Errol Harris, said, 'We're desperately trying to find something other than bananas that the free market will accept.'[10] AID has belatedly joined the chorus, after helping prop up the banana industry in the 1980s.

There are many traditional as well as new crops that, from a technical viewpoint, could be grown for export in Dominica. According to Edward Lambert, manager of a fruit-processing factory jointly owned by the government and several private firms:

Dominica's climate is ideal for citrus and many other tree crops, and there is a great potential market in the region for our fresh fruit, juice concentrate, and chilled fruit sections. We could easily sell six to eight times what we're selling now. Instead, countries in the region, including Trinidad, St Vincent, and Barbados, are importing grapefruit and concentrate from Miami.[11]

But there has been relatively little support for citrus production and processing. AID officials confirm that the agency will not assist Dominica's citrus industry because Dominican fruit or juice exports might compete with the products of US citrus growers.

Like others, Lambert asks, 'Why should we be exporting unprocessed cocoa when we could be manufacturing chocolate? This kind of industry can be planned so that different countries in the region can process different crops, so we don't compete against each other.' According to Errol Harris, Dominica already produces most of the components for small animal feed and could produce more. But, Harris says, 'We can't get money from AID to develop a feed factory. . . . It's hard to get assistance to support our own livestock production because industrial countries produce too much meat and want to sell it to us.'[12]

A senior Dominican civil servant places the blame equally on the policies of Dominica's government:

It pains me to see our country importing EC$50 million yearly (about US$19 million) worth of meat and chicken. . . . Resources are not put into this kind of development because there's a lack of will at the highest political levels, where entrenched commercial interests benefit from the import and distribution of frozen chicken.[13]

Little has been done by the government, and nothing by AID, to expand regional markets for other Dominican products, such as root vegetables and citrus fruits. Foreign markets, too, are weak because of quotas, tariffs and competition from other countries selling fresh produce at lower prices. In addition, the lack of secure land tenure and the inflation in land prices, problems exacerbated by privatization policies, discourage many farmers from planting other tree crops, which take years to bear fruit. 'I'd like to plant permanent crops instead of bananas,' said one farmer who does not have a deed to the land she has cultivated for years, 'but I can't take the risk because I might lose the land.'[14]

As banana fever has swept Dominica, forested slopes, pastures and vegetable fields have been dug up and replanted with banana trees. Imported foods have replaced many traditional food crops. Production of tannias, plantains, breadfruit, cassava and other local staples has declined. One mountain village was once known for the high quality of its dasheen, the tubers, leaves and stems of which are edible and nutritious. But there are few markets near the village for the sale of dasheen and other local foods, and no system for regularly transporting them to the capital town or to nearby islands where such crops are in short supply. Loans, fertilizer and technical assistance for growing these foods are not available on a scale anywhere near that of the services and infrastructure provided for banana production. As pasture land shrinks, less local livestock can be raised, and imported beef, chicken and animal feed add to the country's balance of payments deficit.

The unhappy result is that Dominican farmers who would like to grow other crops lack both the means to do so and adequate channels for selling them, while other Caribbeans who would like to eat Dominican and other regionally grown produce either cannot find it or cannot afford it. According to Neville Graham:

This government has blindly followed Reaganomics, instead of building on what we already have, feeding ourselves first, and developing our own agro-industry. For instance, we know that there are many other uses, such as rope and packaging materials, that can be made from banana by-products and other local resources. The extra earnings from the banana industry ought to be used to develop these kinds of industries, which would provide jobs, reduce import costs, and benefit us much more in the long run. But as far as this government is concerned, if an idea doesn't come from the US or Western Europe, it's no good.

Banana Blindness

AID's Dominica Banana Company Project (1982–87) is a prime example of the agency's promotion of traditional exports at the expense of crop diversification and food self-reliance. AID evaluators describe the project as a development success. If short-term economic growth constitutes development, they are right. Banana production in Dominica more than doubled between 1983 and 1987, when bananas accounted for 71 per cent of Dominica's export earnings and thousands of tons of unsold fruit were dumped into the sea. Dominica's GDP grew by more than 4 per cent annually from 1986–88, primarily as a result of increased banana sales. Banana industry expansion reflected British assistance, currency fluctuations and Dominicans' hard labor as well as AID's intervention. AID's role was chiefly important in strengthening the position of those who benefit from the industry's top-heavy, exploitative structure.

Cultivation of bananas, directly or indirectly, employs half the active workforce of the English-speaking Windward Islands. When the scheduled arrival of the banana boat is announced, activities throughout the countryside shift to banana harvesting. Many children stay home from school to help. Small-scale farmers spend the night in line at inland buying depots to be sure their crop will be purchased and transported to the dock. Heavily laden trucks of boxed bananas careen along narrow roads and form long lines at the ports.

Geest Industries, a British-based corporation, has monopolized the region's banana trade since 1952. Geest's monopoly has been guaranteed by agreements which restrict the amount of bananas imported into the UK from other sources and by contracts with banana growers which ensure that Geest carries little risk of losing money. Between World War II and the mid-1980s, Geest grew from a small company shipping fruit in two rented boats to become Britian's ninth largest private company, even though the world real market price of bananas as well as prices paid to growers fell during most of this period.[15]

The Geest Corporation prospered by reaping the fruits of the increased labor of banana farmers. But bananas are grown more cheaply today on a far larger scale on flatter lands in Ecuador, Columbia and Central America. These crops, already imported into Europe via Germany, and French banana imports from Guadeloupe and Martinique, are likely to price Windward Islands bananas out of much of the European market as most intra-European tariff barriers are eliminated. Geest itself, now widely diversified, is said to be eager to get out of the Caribbean banana business. In the meantime, it is pressing for policies that would eliminate the majority of small-scale farmers, whom the corporation calls 'less efficient'.

Most Windward Islands bananas are grown by paid laborers or self-employed small-scale farmers. Ownership of farm land in the Windwards is sharply skewed. In Dominica, St Lucia, and St Vincent, the majority of banana growers has access to less than one acre, while a few large-scale growers have many acres planted in bananas. In Dominica, 2 per cent of all farms occupy more than 50 per cent of the island's farmland, while more than 4000 farmers work plots of five acres or less.[16] Much of the banana crop is raised on such plots, often on steep, erosion-prone mountainsides.

Producing a steady supply of high-quality fruit in such a terrain is extremely difficult. Farmers must prepare the soil and dig holes for the young plants, remove weeds from around the plants by hand or with chemical herbicides, pluck the blossoms from each developing fruit, spray the leaves with fungicides and encase the maturing banana stems in chemically treated blue plastic to protect them from insects and disease. Much of this tedious work, especially on small family farms, is done by women. At harvest time, smaller bunches must be cut one by one from the main stem. The cut stem of each bunch must be sealed with a putty-like substance to prevent rot. The fruit must be washed and carefully packed in boxes weighing up to 32 pounds. The boxed fruit must then be carried to the roadside and transported, often at high cost to the farmer, to the seaside loading dock.

At the dock, fruit that is blemished or not uniform in size and degree of ripeness is rejected by Geest representatives. Since each banana tree produces only one bunch of bananas and then dies, farmers must clear and prepare the soil and plant new trees after each harvest from a particular plot. They must do this without knowing for sure how much of the crop they will be able to sell nine months to a year later, when the next crop from that plot is ready. 'In banana farming you can't afford to take a day off or you might lose your whole crop, and even then there's no guarantee,' said one farmer at the dock in Dominica.

Banana production not only absorbs land and resources that might otherwise be applied to food for local needs; it is also causing environmental damage, including loss of soil fertility, erosion of slopes and contamination of watersheds and streams. A farmer in the south of Dominica noted that in the years before the banana boom:

> The soil was much richer. Vegetables would grow almost anywhere. But now, as you can see, there are no vegetables, except maybe on a Sunday morning you might get some, and then they are so expensive people can hardly buy them. The amount of fertilizer being thrown onto the crops is a terrible thing; it makes the soil so dry and poor.

Others have remarked on the disappearance of once-common species of lizards, toads and fresh-water fish, and voice concern about the effects on their children. Structural adjustment-related cuts in the budget of the government's Department of Environmental Health have made it impossible to carry out adequate monitoring of environmental hazards.

A quick fix by AID

AID-sponsored restructuring increased the control of the banana industry by Dominica's élite. AID's strategy, of course, was privatization. Instead of focusing on the structure of the industry as a whole, AID zeroed in on the one sector of the industry that appeared to violate AID's guiding principle of free market economics. This, of course, was not Geest Industries, a paradigm of private enterprise success. Nor was it the farmers; although many banana growers were losing money or barely breaking even, they were doing so as individuals selling goods on the free market. Instead, AID's target was the Dominica Banana Growers' Association (DBGA).

The DBGA, like parallel bodies in the other Windwards, purchased fruit from individual farmers for resale to Geest, sold fertilizers and other inputs, and collected fees from farmers to cover services, such as insurance for limited crop loss. The DBGA, like other producers' associations in the region, was operating at a loss, mainly because banana prices were falling while Geest's profits and the cost of inputs were not. In AID's view, the root of the problem was that the DBGA was not 'commercially oriented'.

Without consulting the farmers, AID called for the establishment of a more 'business-like' body, the Dominica Banana Marketing Corporation, to take over the key functions of the DBGA. Although dominated by the larger growers, the DBGA had given small farmers access to information and a chance for some involvement, through their elected representatives, in negotiations over the terms of banana sales. The new corporation, dominated by large-scale landowners, merchants, bankers and government appointees, now buys and resells Dominica's bananas to Geest Industries. As a consequence, the small-scale growers, who comprise the majority of banana farmers, have even less say over how prices are set, how fruit is graded, how much is purchased and how profits are used and distributed. In spite of AID subsidies and donations of US fertilizer, the new marketing corporation has also lost money. But by papering over the cracks in the banana economy, AID helped ensure a steady supply of fruit and profits for Geest.

AID also insisted on the privatization of banana boxing plants, putting hundreds of women out of work with meagre or no compensation. The plants, formerly owned by the DBGA, were closed or turned into buying depots for boxed fruit. In AID's word's, 'the boxing plant function is being divested back to the individual grower'.[17] This greatly increased the workload of banana farmers, who must pack the fruit in the field. Farmers carry more of the costs and risks of production, while Geest operates virtually risk-free. Related changes fostered or applauded by AID, such as the increased use of imported chemicals and packaging materials, raised the cost of producing bananas, speeded environmental decline and steered profits from AID-subsidized fertilizer purchases to the US oil and chemical company Texaco.

The illusion of economic progress based on higher export crop earnings is both deceptive and dangerous, warns Atherton Martin, who has served in the past as minister of agriculture in Dominica:

This blind rush into producing more bananas is making us more dependent on Geest and on foreign loans. When you take into account the debts we took on to 'revitalize' the industry, the fees paid to foreign consultants, and the costs of purchasing chemicals from abroad, we suspect the cost to us of growing these bananas has been much higher than what we've earned. At the same time we've become more dependent on expensive, processed food imported from the US and Britain. What these countries give to us in loans and aid is more than taken back through the money we pay to buy their products. We've become a much more fragile and vulnerable economy than before the so-called banana revitalization, as the next strong gust of wind will demonstrate.

Martin's prediction, made in 1987, was borne out when Hurricane Hugo struck the island in September 1989.

Ultimately, bananas continue to dominate the economy of Dominica and the rest of the Windward Islands because interests outside of the Caribbean continue to dictate the policies of governments in the region. The flow of financing in the form of loans, grants and investment subsidies has been made contingent on the government's ability to reduce its short-term deficits and make payments on its debts. This stance prolongs and worsens banana dependency because, largely as a result of past AID, World Bank and Dominican government policies, banana exports remain the surest means of earning the required income.

Jerome Durand, of Castle Bruce on Dominica's windward coast, has been farming long enough to remember the days before banana was king: 'The other day I was telling a young boy that after 1992, we can't expect to depend upon selling bananas. That boy said to me "That can't be! There have always been bananas in Dominica." I told him, "If you keep believing that, I'm sorry for you."'[18] The designers of AID's Banana Company Project arrived in Dominica at about the time Durand's young neighbor was born. Like the boy, they had a limited understanding of the country's history and a short-term perspective on its future. Perhaps if they had listened less to the Geest Corporation and more to farmers such as Durand, Dominica's economic prospects would not be as precarious as they are today.

Notes

1. Author interview, December 1987.
2. Author interview, December 1987.
3. Robert Woodward, *Veil*, New York, 1989. Woodward also reports allegations that Eugenia Charles herself received a payoff of US$100,000, arranged through the US State Department.
4. Author interview, December 1987.
5. USAID Project Paper, 'Program Assistance to Dominica', September 1983.
6. World Bank, 'Dominica Structural Adjustment Program Paper', Washington, 1985.
7. Author interview, December 1988.
8. Government of Dominica, 'Statistical Digest: Ten Years of Growth: 1978–1988', Roseau, Commonwealth of Dominica, 1988.
9. Author interview, December 1987.
10. Author interview, February 1988.
11. Author interview, February 1988.
12. Ibid.
13. Ibid.
14. Author interview, March 1988.
15. Between 1950 and 1982, the real world market price (adjusted to take account of inflation) dropped by 46 per cent. Dr Allan N. Williams, *The Banana Industry: National Development or Rural Impoverishment*, draft of a paper for the Association

for Caribbean Transformation Ltd; Robert Thompson, *Green Gold*, Latin America Bureau, London, 1987.

16. UN Food and Agricultural Organization, *The World Banana Economy*, Rome, 1986, cited by Thompson, *Green Gold*.

17. AID Evaluation Summary, 'Dominica Banana Company Project', January 1985.

18. Author interview, April 1988. The author is also grateful to Josephine Dublin, Bertilia Henderson, and Martha Joseph for their outstanding case studies of women in Dominica's agriculture.

9. Jamaica: The Showpiece that Didn't Stand Up

> The policies of the 1980s have reinforced old structures, especially dependence on imported food. We have seen none of the promised upsurge in production. The high-tech agro-export projects have failed. What little growth we have seen is based on a tremendous increase in debt, while the vulnerability of the economy to external forces is greater than ever.
>
> Richard Bernal,
> President of the Jamaica Workers' Bank

A newly appointed US ambassador to Jamaica, William Holden, announced his mission at his swearing-in ceremony in November 1989. It was, once and for all, 'to silence the trumpets of socialism' in Jamaica and the Caribbean. In the 1970s, such a declaration by the chief emissary of the US or any foreign country would have been met with strong protest, if not expulsion. Jamaica's government in the 1970s was run by the social democratic PNP and its charismatic leader, Michael Manley. But the government of the 'new Michael Manley,' elected in February of 1989 after eight years out of power, had little reason to object. The trumpets had long been laid aside.

Manley and the PNP returned to power over a state with its independence greatly curtailed by foreign control and a society choking in the stranglehold of debt. To regain sovereignty over Jamaica's economic and political affairs, the government would have had to confront the world's most powerful economic institutions, the IMF and the World Bank. It would have had to risk a showdown with the economic power, and very possibly the military might, of the United States.

As the decade opened, no trumpets blew louder than those of the White House and State Department prophets of privatization. No drum was banged with more clamour than that of 'free market democracy'. But the very policies which the US government dictates in the name of freedom are a grave threat to genuine democracy. Even as it slashed its own aid to Jamaica, the US was tying its limited support more tightly to the austerity requirements of the multilaterals. By pushing impoverished people over the brink into hunger, these policies are bound to result in social chaos and political upheaval, which can ultimately be contained only by authoritarianism and repression.

During a decade of structural adjustment, the people of Jamaica were forced to make great sacrifices to keep their nation in the debt-refinancing game, watching resources and capital flow out of their country into the coffers of Northern creditors. Unless the rules of the game are changed, or until Jamaica, along with other governments, refuses to play, their suffering will be in vain. But in the face of enormous odds, the PNP appeared to lack not only the means but also the political will to attempt to break out of debt bondage.

Jamaica: 'Open for Business'

Toward the end of his first tenure as prime minister, Manley had first tried to apply, and then had resisted, an IMF stabilization program. Manley's PNP lost the violently contested 1980 election to the Jamaica Labor Party, led by Edward Seaga. Seaga, a Boston-born, Harvard-trained businessman with close ties to US presidential candidate Ronald Reagan, came into office with the full support of Washington. During the election campaign, Seaga boasted of promises of substantial new loans and aid from the IMF and the US government.

The Reagan administration pulled out all the stops to assist Seaga and keep its new Caribbean free enterprise showboat afloat. US economic aid jumped from US$38 million in 1978–79 to US$208 million in 1981–82, making Jamaica the third largest per capita recipient of US aid in the world.[1] USAID warned in 1983 that:

> The failure of the [AID] program in Jamaica would confirm the view of those in the Caribbean and elsewhere in the third world that cooperation with the IMF and stimulation of the private sector is a hopeless endeavor.[2]

By 1985, AID was spending US$48, for Jamaica projects, for every person in Jamaica. This was 27 times more per capita than AID provided to sub-Saharan Africa that same year, the peak year of AID funding for Africa.[3] USAID spent more on its Jamaica program — an average of almost US$120 million yearly from 1981 to 1989 — than on any other Caribbean country.

The spigots of international lending also opened. Seaga borrowed more during his first two years in office than Jamaica had borrowed in the entire preceding decade. A new IMF deal, which originally promised US$698 million over three years, was accompanied by more than US$400 million in new funds from other members of the CGCED.[4] World Bank aid to Jamaica in 1981–82 constituted more than 67 per cent of the Bank's total lending in the Caribbean. In contrast to their policies toward the Manley government, the multilaterals at first were lenient with Seaga. Despite Jamaica's failure to meet IMF economic targets, the Fund agreed to a series of additional loans. The World Bank advanced five more adjustment loans between 1983 and 1987. A major factor in these decisions was the United States, which controls the largest share of voting power in both the IMF and the World Bank.

US banker David Rockefeller assembled a high-profile Business Committee on Jamaica to attract investors to the country. The US government dropped its warning against tourism to Jamaica. Reagan urged the world to 'watch Jamaica', declaring that 'Free enterprise Jamaica, and not Marxist Cuba, should be the model for Central America in the struggle to overcome poverty and move toward democracy.' Buoyed by this flood of support, Seaga proclaimed Jamaica 'open for business'.

Free enterprise débâcle

The linchpin of Seaga's economic strategy was to seek new foreign investment in order to increase Jamaica's exports. To make that investment more convenient and profitable, he reduced government protection of Jamaican producers and opened the country to more imports from abroad. He promoted expansion of the country's FTZ, state-of-the-art sweatshops where Jamaican women, with no union representation, earn as little as 50 cents an hour for assembling garments for export. Seaga played down the loss of jobs resulting from the closure of Jamaican-owned factories unable to compete with the foreign manufacturers for credit and foreign exchange. To reduce demand for legal foreign exchange, channel dollars to favored interests and supporters, and resist pressure for further devaluation of the Jamaican dollar, Seaga allegedly condoned import and resale of dollars from the profits of the ganja (marijuana) trade, estimated to be the country's second highest source of foreign exchange earnings.

Unfettered free enterprise, however, did not stanch the haemorrhage of wealth from Jamaica. Instead, the outflow increased. Between late 1980 and the end of 1982, Jamaica's trade deficit tripled. New IMF loans to plug the gap were made contingent on stronger austerity measures. The Jamaican dollar was devalued by 43 per cent, greatly reducing the buying power of the poor. Nevertheless, after a brief period of increase in Jamaica's GDP in 1983, economic growth again ground to a halt. The rate of inflation accelerated to 30.1 per cent in 1984/85.[5] Unemployment climbed to 30 per cent overall, and to 78.6 per cent and 58.6 per cent among females aged 14–19 and 20–24.[6] In 1985, in the context of low world market prices for bauxite and alumina, Kaiser/Reynolds and Alcoa shut down their operations in Jamaica. (Jamaica again experienced limited GDP growth in the second half of Seaga's term, mainly from increased tourism, laundered ganja dollars, lower fuel import costs and the partial recovery of world market prices of bauxite and alumina.)

By 1988 the country's external debt had reached US$1,875 for every Jamaican, one of the highest per capita levels in the world. The IMF loans and the accompanying conditions failed in their primary objective. Rather than increasing, Jamaican earnings from exports to the United States, Canada and Europe fell by 2.6 per cent from 1980 to 1986. Moreover, the conditions attached to the stabilization and structural adjustment loans were so harsh that even Seaga himself protested: 'Jamaica,' he said in 1985, 'is not a country that has the large-scale capital resources that can indulge in a totally free economy.'

The social side effects of structural adjustment medicine were severe. From 1981 to 1985, total government per capita spending on health fell by 33 per cent. As a consequence, according to a study by the ACE:

> Health capital stock and equipment have deteriorated badly; hospital services have been closed; real incomes of doctors, nurses and other health personnel have fallen; charges have been introduced in public hospitals; patient care has deteriorated; and patients are often asked to take their own linen and food to the hospitals.[7]

The study notes that:

> Over the period January 1981 to June 1985, the consumer price index for housing increased by 95 per cent in the capital city and by 115 per cent in the rural areas. The minimum wage, if earned by the two adult members of the household, covered less than 40 per cent of the cost of the basket [of minimum essential foods] over this period. . . . A fifth of the public workforce was let go in just one year, from October 1984 to October 1985.[8]

All this was more than many poor Jamaicans were willing to withstand. For three days in January 1984, after the Seaga government announced yet another austerity measure, a gasoline price increase, the capital city of Kingston and much of the rest of the country were paralysed by road blockages and demonstrations which left at least 10 people dead or wounded.

The US tightens the screws

After 1986, the Reagan administration and its corporate supporters became disenchanted with their Jamaican free enterprise paradise. The administration blamed 'statist attitudes' of the Jamaican government and Seaga himself for failing to bring about private sector-led growth. Assistant Secretary for Interamerican Affairs, Elliot Abrams, reportedly warned Seaga to 'get off the dime' and complete the privatization of state shares in Jamaica's industries, banking, land and tourism enterprises.[9] Seaga's subsequent efforts did not satisfy Washington. Moreover, by 1988, the Caribbean was no longer a US foreign policy priority.

In the 1980s, AID had tried to make privatization a condition of its assistance, particularly the ESFs given to help finance Seaga's government budget. ESF cash grants averaged US$62.6 million yearly from Seaga's first year in office through 1986. According to AID's 'Overview of US Assistance to Jamaica':

> One of the major goals of USAID's ongoing policy dialogue with the government of Jamaica is to bring about structural adjustments which will permit private market functions to lead Jamaica's drive for economic expansion and growth. ESF is one of AID's major instruments of influence in this policy dialogue.

ESF funds were used by Jamaica to purchase imports from the United States. Thus, the ESF program served the double purpose of promoting privatization and subsidizing US exporters of goods and services to Jamaica. But in the late 1980s, ESF funds were cut almost entirely, except for limited doses released after Hurricane Gilbert in 1988 and following a visit by US Vice-President Dan Quayle in 1989. In a 1988 memorandum, AID vowed to continue to press for privatization and austerity by tightening the conditions attached to US PL480 Title I food aid. In this way, the memo explains, 'Food assistance is used to obtain leverage in our negotiations and, therefore, constitutes a key tool in our ongoing policy dialogue with the Government of Jamaica.'

At the end of Seaga's term, Jamaica's GDP was no larger than it had been in 1980. From 1986 through 1988, Jamaica had paid out a net total of US$881 million to its foreign creditors, including US$349 million to the IMF alone. Yet its external debt stood at US$4.4 billion, one of the highest, per capita, in the world. More than half had been accrued by Seaga's government. The World Bank's senior economist for Jamaica, Roger Robinson, acknowledged in 1988 that Jamaica's 'social and economic infrastructure is worse than it was in the 1970s'. Nevertheless, he maintained, 'The government is still spending more than they can afford.' Robinson recommended 'rationalization, by recovering more of the costs from the users' of hospitals, schools and other services. As a result of Seaga's fiscal sleights-of-hand, the government had become the nation's biggest bad debtor; it failed to pay bills for maintenance of hospitals, the university and other public institutions, and allowed the Jamaica Commodity Trading Corporation to accrue huge deficits.

By AID's own accounting, as of March 1988, Jamaica had 'a crippling debt burden', with an economic output 'far below the production level of 1972'. It was a country where 'distribution of wealth and income is highly unequal . . . shortages of key medical and technical personnel plague the health system . . . [with] severe deficits in infrastructure and housing . . . [and where] physical decay and social violence deter investment'. This grim assessment was made six months before Hurricane Gilbert dealt Jamaica its devastating blow.[10]

Manley's Return: 'You Can't Go Back Easily'

By early 1988, Seaga was so unpopular that World Bank officials apparently concluded that it was preferable to encourage Manley's return to office. Interviewed in June 1988, the Bank's Roger Robinson told the author:

> Five years ago, people were still thinking about 'meeting local needs', but not any more. Now the lawyers and others with access to resources are interested in external export investment. Once you have that ingrained in a population, you can't go back easily, even if the PNP and Michael Manley come in again.

'Michael Manley,' Robinson added with undisguised satisfaction, 'is making all the right noises' to reassure the Bank and potential foreign investors, and to spurn what Robinson called the 'irrational' self-reliance strategies of the 1970s. 'The PNP even gave support to Jamaican potato farmers, when it's well-known that potatoes coming in from Miami make better French fries!' he exclaimed.

Almost immediately after Manley's re-election in February, 1989, Jamaica government officials were again shuttling back and forth between Kingston and Washington, the site of World Bank headquarters and of many of the IMF negotiations. There, they met with a corps of callous, denationalized technocrats, accountable to no country, whose primary allegiance is to their own lucrative careers in the institutions they serve.

For three months, the government was locked in intense negotiations with the IMF for a new stand-by agreement to replace the US$106 million deal accepted by Seaga in September 1988. That agreement called for a limit on wage increases to 10 per cent (despite an anticipated inflation rate of 15 per cent that year), interest rate hikes, credit constriction and further government spending cuts. A new stand-by agreement for US$65 million IMF Special Drawing Rights was reached in May 1989, but Jamaica was only allowed to withdraw a quarter of that loan.

On 31 October 1989, the government announced the suspension of a new round of negotiations. Meanwhile, Bank of Jamaica officials searched for further sacrifices to placate the IMF and persuade its representatives to continue the current agreements and prepare the ground for new loans in the spring. Without an IMF agreement, further World Bank loans and other sources of credit would be hard to obtain. On 8 November, the government announced a further devaluation of the Jamaica dollar from J$6.31/US$1 to J$6.5/US$1. (The exchange rate of the Jamaica dollar was revised again months later to J$7/US$1, and then allowed to float, reaching J$10 to US$1 by June 1991.)

In addition, the government lowered food price subsidies designed to protect the poor. New price ceilings raised the legal maximum prices for bread, cooking oil, milk, flour, cornmeal, rice and other staples by amounts averaging 13 per cent. The government's importing agency announced that it would stop buying and reselling slated codfish, an important protein source and essential ingredient in Jamaica's most famous national dish. The devaluation and price hikes provoked outcries of anger and despair from the public and even from the right-leaning press. The conservative *Gleaner* newspaper calculated that a worker earning the standard minimum weekly wage of J$100 a week, after buying a minimal basket of food for a family of four, barely enough to last a few days, would be left with only J$32.50 to cover school costs, transportation, rent, utility bills and all other expenses. (Food prices in Jamaica are only slightly lower than those in the United States, where the minimum wage is 11.5 times as high. In November 1989, a pound of chicken in Jamaican markets cost the equivalent of US$106, a loaf of bread cost US$0.80, and a dozen eggs sold for US$2.32.) Seaga, in contrast, had managed to resist foreign creditors' demands for subsidy cuts and price increases during his second term, and had kept real food prices level from 1985 until 1989.

The United States showed little inclination to help the Manley government cope with the US$4.4 billion debt burden it inherited. In fiscal 1988/89, Jamaica paid a net amount of US$213 million to the IMF and US$75 million to the World Bank; its net outflow to all multilateral creditors was US$263 million, and the debt was reduced to US$3.95 billion. Manley reminded a US congressional delegation to Jamaica in November 1989 that the country would have to pay half of its export earnings and 40 per cent of all government revenues to continue covering debt service costs in the coming year. 'That means we're running a 50-cent dollar country,' he said.

The prime minister begged the congressmen to persuade multilateral lenders to bend their rules against debt rescheduling, not just for Jamaica but for other debtor nations. He reminded them that the US-sponsored Brady Plan, even if it were to offer substantial relief of debts owed by poor countries to commercial banks, would be of little help to Jamaica, whose external commercial debt is only 14 per cent of its total foreign debt.

Manley reassured the US representatives that, drastic as the crisis might be, he had no intention of approaching it 'in a confrontationist way. We had enough of that in the 1970s,' he said, dismissing the popular mobilizations and protests against IMF pressure during 1970s as an impolite 'hiccough' that would not be repeated. Manley then switched his topic to his Seven Point Plan for an international war against drugs. The congressional audience praised his anti-drug stance but, with the exception of the delegation's leader, Representative George Crockett, said almost nothing in response to Manley's pleas for debt relief.

Jamaica on the auction block

Faced with the debt crisis, credit cuts and intensified US, IMF and World Bank pressure, the PNP has tried to ride out the storm by postponing more drastic currency devaluation, while grasping every possible source of foreign exchange. An infamous example was the sale of US$80 million worth of bauxite and alumina in advance to the Alcan corporation and to US speculator Mark Rich. Jamaica got quick cash from the deal but the futures buyers will reap the profits of expected increases in alumina prices, perhaps as far into the future as 1995. The country's 20 per cent block of shares in the only national telephone company was sold to the British Cable and Wireless Ltd.

Other public land, rights and property are also on the auction block. The apparent conversion of Manley to a pro-capitalist privatizer allowed the *Enterprise*, voice of the Private Sector of Jamaica association, to gloat in an editorial:

> Schools can't find teachers. The entire system seems to be on the verge of collapse. Nurses are fleeing. . . . Everyone knows about the pressure on the dollar and the foreign exchange shortage. But underneath the bad news there is some movement like a tide beneath the waves that should give us some hope. The government has quietly dropped the nonsensical rhetoric of the recent past and is divesting state enterprises at an even faster rate than its predecessor. . . . The old gospel that government should be operated in the interests of the poor is being modified, even if not expressly rejected, by the dawning realization that the only way to help the poor is to operate the government in the interest of the productive!

There is scant evidence that the private sector is either efficient or inclined to invest substantially in productive activity in Jamaica. But as long as it seeks accommodation with the IMF, the government has little choice but to shift resources in its direction and away from social needs. The Fund's rules are so stringent that they require even profitable public enterprises to be sold and efficient services to be cut back.

The government was forced to swallow other onerous conditions to obtain new foreign loans from other sources. In November 1989, the government concluded a US$62 million agreement for a World Bank-designed Agricultural Sector Adjustment loan package. Its release was contingent upon conclusion of an agreement between Jamaica and the IMF. Among other conditionalities of the agriculture loan were the near-elimination of tariffs and quantitative restrictions on livestock imports. One government official said this would be likely to destroy local industries: US producers were already in the country proffering US beef to hotel managers before the ink on the agreement was dry. Another condition of the World Bank loan is the reduction of government participation in commodity marketing boards. A Jamaican economist observed:

> The Bank believes the government should have no say at all in what is bought and sold to whom and for how much. But the alternative of total privatization means one or a few big producers will monopolize every sector and manipulate it for their own benefit; this has already happened to our coffee [most of which now goes to Japan].[11]

The Bank also urged disbanding the Jamaica Commodity Trading Corporation, a step not even Seaga was willing to take because of the corporation's importance in enabling the state to stabilize food prices and capture revenue from the sale of foreign-donated surplus food. In addition, the Bank wanted the Jamaica Agricultural Credit Bank to raise its interest rates to, or close to, market rate levels, even though the source of the Credit Bank's funds is not the World Bank. Said a government official concerned with agriculture:

> We told the World Bank team that farmers can hardly afford credit now, and that higher rates would put them out of business. The Bank told us in response that this means 'The market is telling you that agriculture is not the way to go for Jamaica.' They're saying in effect that we should give up farming altogether.

A bizarre aspect of the agriculture loan agreement, the official reported, is that not one penny would go to aid Jamaica's farmers! Instead, he said, the funds would be converted into Bank of Jamaica certificates of deposit, to shore up the government's credit reserves in preparation for the next IMF test:

> The Bank is fully aware that we will have to use the money for other foreign exchange needs and not to add anything to our agriculture budget [another

government source explained]. But down the road, when more farmers go out of business, they'll tell us it's because we didn't use their loan money wisely.

During negotiations for a World Bank housing project loan, the Bank insisted on further increases in mortgage interest rates, even though the rates were already so far out of the reach of most Jamaicans that the National Housing Trust (NHT), paid for mainly by a tax on all Jamaican wage-earners and responsible for 80 per cent of the country's housing financing, was banking its money instead of building homes. Even higher interest rates, the Bank reportedly acknowledged, might mean even less construction of housing. More important, in the Bank's view, was the fact that the NHT's operations 'would become more profitable', a party to the negotiations reported. Similar criteria were expected to be applied by the Bank to a 'Trade and Finance Sector Adjustment'.

Said a Jamaican official:

The Bank's logic is that the less that goes into government, the more there will be for the private sector, and that the private sector, not government, should determine how resources are used. They tell us we should let the market determine the exchange rate, even if it means the Jamaica dollar falls to J$15/US$1. [Until the mid-1970s, the Jamaica dollar was worth more than the US dollar.] If that happens, they say, wages will drop further and we'll be flooded with free zone-type manufacturing. We'll reach the limit of our ability to import, so that way our foreign exchange 'problem' will be 'solved!'

The World Bank and the IMF don't have to worry about the farmers and local companies going out of business, or starvation wages, or the social upheaval that will result. They simply assume that it is our job to keep our national security forces strong enough to suppress any uprising.

He might have added that the creditors also know they can count on the US government to lend a hand.

The Resistance Continues

Jamaicans have fought in the past against overwhelming odds; they struggle today to survive increasing impoverishment with remarkable resilience and creativity. But the popular organizations that were encouraged, up to a point, by the PNP in the 1970s have been badly damaged by the economic pressures and political assaults of the 1980s. The new Manley government has shown little inclination to revive them. Workers in the country's cane fields, factories and export-processing sweatshops continue to organize, demonstrate and protest, but with little support from the party they put in power. The communist Jamaica Workers' Party, like other parties of the left in much of the

Caribbean, has lost ground. Even before the disintegration of the Eastern bloc, more than two-thirds of its members had resigned or become inactive although many remain politically involved.

Independent progressive organizations work valiantly to keep up with the demands from farmers, workers, unemployed youth and the urban poor for organizing assistance and logistical support, and important victories have been won. But more visible, at least in the mass media, is the frustration, despair and social dislocation that spews forth in the form of ghetto gunfights, politically manipulated violence, soaring cocaine use, drug wars, and a sense of near-panic among many in the middle classes. The level of popular consciousness in Jamaica, upon which the potential for an alternative development approach depends, remains relatively high. It is most evident in popular theater and music, which, at its best, combines righteous anger against poverty, pollution, sexual and other forms of violence, and foreign control with calls for African liberation, Caribbean unity, racial harmony and peace. But the Rastafarian-inspired, feminist and other artists who convey these messages face tough competition for the hearts and minds of Jamaicans from satellite TV's Dallas and Dynasty, evangelical fanaticism and the CNN news.

The achievement of Jamaica's sovereignty will necessitate an appeal to Jamaica's poor majority for continued struggle and sacrifice, guided by a clear vision of an alternative to the failed development-through-indebtedness strategy. It will also require greater economic leverage based on alliance with other Caribbean nations and the strengthening of ties with the region's Central American and South American neighbors, as well as with Cuba. Above all, the reconquest of Jamaica's freedom will require a mobilization of the Jamaican people, not by the blaring of any trumpets but by the careful heeding of their own voices, and by support of battles against exploitation in which they are already engaged. The path to Caribbean liberation is perilous indeed. But its dangers could hardly be greater than the immense human suffering, social disintegration, environmental destruction and political instability that Jamaica and most of her neighbors are now facing, or will soon inevitably encounter, if they are forced to continue on their present course.

Notes

1. Barry, Preusch and Wood, *The Other Side of Paradise*, Grove Press, New York, 1984.

2. Cited by Medea Benjamin and Kevin Danaher in 'Jamaica, Free Market Fiasco', *Food First News*, 1986.

3. Calculated from USAID, *Overseas Loans and Grants*, September 1986, and USAID *Congressional Presentation*.

4. Fitzroy Ambursley, 'Jamaica from Michael Manley to Edward Seaga', in Ambersley and Cohen (eds), *Crisis in the Caribbean*, Monthly Review Press, New York, 1983.

5. Government of Jamaica, 'Economic Performance', submission to the CGCED, Spring, 1988.

6. Interamerican Development Bank, Annual Report, 1984; Government of Jamaica, Labor Force Survey.

7. Norman Girvan, Ennio Rodriguez, Mario Arana Sevilla and Migueal Ceara Hatton, *The Debt Problem of Small Peripheral Economies: Case Studies from the Caribbean and Central America*, 1990.

8. Increased poverty in Jamaica is documented by Joan French in *Hope and Disillusion: The CBI and Jamaica*, ADA, Kingston, 1990.

9. Timothy Ashby, *Missed Opportunities: the Rise and Fall of Jamaica's Edward Seaga*, Hudson Institute, Indianapolis, 1989.

10. AID, *Country Development Strategy Statement for Fiscal Year 1989: Jamaica.*

11. Author interview, November 1989.

Part V:
The Price of Adjustment

10. The Downward Spiral

We export what we produce and import what we consume. There's nothing new in that; it started with colonialism and slavery. The US model we're being told to follow now — relying solely on a free market strategy and support for the private sector — leaves those structures in place. If we try to follow this model, the result will be more control from the outside, more extraction of wealth, more unemployment, and the sort of development that forgets about people. Real development has to start with people.

Adrian Fraser, Coordinator of the NGO network CARIPEDA

Structural adjustment is a means of maintaining the continued transfer of wealth from the poor nations of the world to the rich ones, and from the poor and working classes to elites worldwide. Structural adjustment ideology prolongs the myth that economic growth is just around the next bend, and will soon enable debtor nations to improve their balance sheets. In this way, it provides a rationale for the repeated refinancing of loans to countries which have little or no chance of ever repaying them in full. Rather than reducing foreign debts of impoverished countries, structural adjustment refinancing merely replaced their current debt bills with even larger ones due in the future. As long as these debt bills remain on the books, poor countries must continue to pay interest on them.

Cash subsidies given to debtor country governments in connection with structural adjustment programs, such as AID Structural Adjustment Support grants, help to postpone bankruptcy for favored governments but do not alter the underlying process of resources flow from the poor to the wealthy. These adjustment-related bail-outs by AID recycle money from taxpayers in the United States to indebted US allies, and back to commercial banks, multilateral lenders and corporations in the North.

Structural adjustment policies reinforce a global double standard for economic enterprise. Adjustment programs require indebted countries to drop or reduce their import quotas, export tariffs, corporate taxes, foreign exchange controls and other barriers to international free trade. This opens their markets and resources to corporations from Europe, Japan and North America, whose industries and agriculture already have the advantage of being subsidized and protected by the very sort of policies forbidden under the terms of structural adjustment programs to governments in the South.

The experts who concocted the structural adjustment remedy believed, at least in the beginning, that it would stimulate productive investment and economic growth in the South, enabling indebted nations to climb step by step up the economic hierarchy of nations. As they ascended, the adjustors said, the benefits of growth would gradually seep down to the poor within each developing nation. In reality, rather than establishing a sound basis for economic growth, structural adjustment is reducing both those nations' capacity to sustain their own populations and their chances of catching up with the world's industrialized economies. Far from helping poor nations to increase their export earnings, adjustment undermines their ability to obtain a fair price for their products by pitting nation against nation in a bitter struggle destructive to all.

In their desperation to obtain this hard currency from their exports in spite of lower commodity prices, the governments of poor countries in the Caribbean and elsewhere are inviting investors to fell more forests, mine more mountains, harvest more marine plants and animals from fragile reefs, drain more wetlands and replace local food crops with more export crops.[1] Thus, structural adjustment policies are also contributing to the environmental débâcle which threatens the entire planet. This destructive and seemingly irrational policy becomes understandable if we abandon the misconception that the purpose of AID, World Bank and IMF-sponsored adjustment programs is to aid the world's poor countries. Their actual, immediate aim is to stave off large-scale defaults by debtor nations; their longer-term goal is the global expansion of free trade.

In today's interdependent world, no nation or group of nations can control all the factors that influence its development. The United States, European countries and Japan all must adjust to economic forces they cannot easily alter and must make accommodations to one another. Within this context, however, most nations of the North determine both their own policies with regard to international trade, valuation of their currencies and the allocation of resources domestically, and the laws and principles which shape the roles and relations of government, private interests and the public sector.

Structural adjustment programs take control over many such policies away from Caribbean governments and people. They place policy-setting power in the hands of foreign governments and international agencies, the interests of which seldom coincide with those of the Caribbean majority. By enforcing a strategy of increasing extra-regional exports at any cost, structural adjustment conditionalities weaken, or rule out entirely, the possibility of building alternate strategies. The political requirements attached to adjustment loans and AID grants usurp the power of Caribbean governments and regional bodies to determine their own priorities and foreign policies.

Compensatory Programs: Cosmetics and Cooptation

The World Bank and the IMF have been forced to acknowledge that the burden of adjustment has indeed fallen disproportionately upon those least able to bear it. Both institutions have gone to great lengths to convince governments and policy-makers that the damage done to children, women and the poor in general by adjustment-related economic austerity can be mitigated, and that structural adjustment, by creating the conditions for growth and future prosperity, will benefit the poor in the long run.[2]

In addition, the World Bank has supported limited compensatory social welfare programs to cushion the impact of austerity, in the hope that governments in the North and private aid agencies will step in to clean up the social wreckage left in the wake of structural adjustment. At the 1988 meeting of the CGCED, the Bank and the Government of Jamaica unveiled a five-year, US$800 million Social Well-being Program to compensate Jamaicans partially for what the Bank described as 'the deterioration of publicly provided social services caused by fiscal stringency'. The Bank asked CGCED member governments and agencies to pick up the costs, and encouraged Jamaican and foreign development NGOs to lend a hand in bandaging the country's 'sociological problems'. Nowhere have such compensatory programs been implemented successfully. It is unlikely that they could be, since the intentional lowering of incomes is central to structural adjustment strategy. Adjustment mechanisms such as real wage reductions, food price increases and other measures are meant to force people to consume less; to succeed, they necessarily cause the immediate worsening of poverty.

In any case, the Bank is not about to relinquish its structural adjustment weapon voluntarily. A Bank economist told the author, in a remark that typifies the Bank's use of jargon to avoid talking about people, 'Structural adjustment is essential because it relieves tremendous aggregate demand pressure.' In plain language, the statement means that reducing people's real incomes and access to services saves money and thus props up fragile, debt-ridden economies. World Bank double-speak does not fool Caribbean leaders such as Peggy Antrobus, coordinator of the regional Caribbean women's organization Women and Development (WAND). Says Antrobus: 'No adjustment proposal is acceptable that sacrifices children to save financial structures.'

USAID, echoing the Bank, has recently begun to recognize that the structural adjustment measures it requires are harmful to the poor. 'AID's strategy,' states the agency's 1988 Congressional Presentation, 'is to encourage the necessary economic adjustments, and at the same time to moderate the negative impact of such adjustments, particularly on the poorest groups.' The AID funds allocated for the latter purpose, however, are a small proportion of the agency's budget and, as Chapter 4 has indicated, only a small percentage of AID money earmarked for the poor actually reaches them.

World Bank social programs and AID anti-poverty grants are intended as temporary, stop-gap measures to ease social tensions until market-driven growth produces prosperity that will trickle down to the poor. These programs do not signal a departure from the belief that the private sector can best take care of social needs. They are in no way intended to redistribute resources from the wealthy to the poor. In fact, a major goal of the World Bank's social programs is to reduce the cost to governments by trimming social services, by getting the poor to pay more of the costs of clinic visits, school books and other services, and by giving the private sector a piece of the social service business.

Social benefits, in the words of one World Bank official, 'are totally dependent on growth'. In the Bank's view, better education, health and community services will be possible in the future *if* the 'adjusted' economies grow fast enough to work their way out of debt, and *then* generate a surplus which can be tapped to address social needs. Thus, even if the short-term damage done by structural adjustment could be reduced by means of compensatory programs and the fine-tuning of adjustment measures, this would be to little avail if structural adjustment fails to foster economic growth in the long run. But adjustment policies, as we have seen, are doing more to undermine than to enhance the likelihood of growth.

The World Bank has become perversely adept at enforcing social services reductions while describing these cut-backs as if they were improvements. A Bank summary of Ghana's World Bank-sponsored Education Sector Adjustment Program asserts that the program 'is enabling all students to gain access to textbooks and other basic materials, and is improving teacher training, curriculum content and primary school enrollment'. These gains, says the Bank's report, are to be made at the same time that Ghana's spending on education is to be *reduced*. A closer reading of the report reveals that this seemingly impossible goal is to be achieved by shortening the duration of schooling, simplifying textbooks and requiring students to pay more for them, reducing the number of teaching posts and education department employees, and cutting funds for school food and boarding in half. Since the training period for teachers will be shortened and the qualification standards revised, the Bank reports with pride that 'by 1985, there will be no untrained teachers' in Ghana.[3]

The Blocked Alternative

As many Caribbean development workers and scholars point out, structural adjustment policies do not alter the underlying structures that keep Caribbean societies dependent and poor. Dr Neville Duncan of the University of the West Indies maintains that a different type of structural adjustment could generate genuine development:

> USAID should support structural adjustment, but not the World Bank version that gives balance of payments support and soft credit in exchange for cuts in social services. This kind of foreign assistance doesn't lead to development, because for real development we need a wide redistribution of assets, not short-term welfare. Real structural adjustment would help us increase our self-reliance and build the internal basic capabilities of our economies, starting with what we already have. It would allow us to identify new products and new uses for existing ones, such as sugar here in Barbados, while protecting existing jobs. It would help us develop energy-conserving technologies and new methods of processing and storage, and ways to link industry with agriculture within the region, not just between here and Miami.[4]

Throughout the Caribbean, scholars, community leaders and grassroots organizations are pursuing these and other ideas, for alternative approaches to structural change and development. But unless the current trend that subjects Caribbean governments and economies to increasing foreign control is reversed, their efforts could be in vain.

Much of the technical groundwork for developing a more self-reliant food system in the Caribbean has already been done by the CARICOM Secretariat, the University of the West Indies (UWI) and the Caribbean Food and Nutrition Institute, notes former CDB president William Demas:

> [The studies] indicate both the technical and economic feasibility of substantially increased food (including fish and meat as well as animal feedingstuffs) in the countries of the region. What is more, these studies also indicate that the increased local and regional food production can have a substantial impact in raising nutritional levels.[5]

The opportunity for food security in the English-speaking Caribbean is greater today, says Demas, as a result of the elimination of tariffs and other trade barriers among CARICOM member states in 1989. However:

> It is almost certain that such a system of free intra-regional trade will only be feasible if regional producers are protected to a reasonable extent from extra-regional imports. I am fully aware of the political and other difficulties that this 'protectionist' approach entails, but I am convinced that it is the only way regional agricultural development can proceed effectively. . . . The plain fact is that in nearly all developed countries there is massive government intervention both to subsidize agricultural exports and to protect the local market for agriculture production.[6]

Demas remarked during a December 1988 conversation at CDB headquarters that:

> Three-quarters of the European Economic Community budget goes into agricultural subsidies for their own products. They require free trade from us while they subsidize their own agricultural products. There can't be rational, effective price structures in the Caribbean unless we can protect our local markets.

A senior civil servant in the Government of Grenada, who asked not to be quoted by name, said that with World Bank experts, IMF economic inspectors and AID consultants looking over their shoulders, Grenadian officials are repeatedly forced to make decisions that violate CARICOM guidelines for regional cooperation, decisions that they know are detrimental to the economy of both their country and the region. For example, he said, officials are under pressure to waive regulations limiting the freedom of foreign firms to set up packaging and processing operations, even when the companies want to come to Grenada only temporarily, to take advantage of its cheap labor, subsidized facilities and tax holidays. In so doing, the official pointed out, many such companies do little to relieve unemployment but a lot to damage Caribbean economies. They put local or regional firms producing or packaging the same products out of business, and thus undermine efforts by countries in the region to coordinate their economic policies of regional self-reliance and long-term growth: 'Even when we know the operations or imports will probably destroy local industries, we're expected to let them in, because nobody wants to be accused of turning away anything that creates jobs, even bad jobs.'[7]

World Bank economist Roger Robinson scoffs at the notion that Caribbean countries ought to be permitted to nurture and protect their own food-producing capacity. 'Barriers to protect local food don't make sense for anybody,' he says.[8] A *Regional Food and Nutrition Plan Strategy*, for enhancing agricultural production, trade and self-reliance in the region was developed by CARICOM in the early 1980s. Neither Robinson nor Christian Delvoie, who was World Bank Program Director for the Caribbean when interviewed in 1988, had read the CARICOM plan. The World Bank, said Robinson, 'hasn't done studies on the potential for import substitution in the Caribbean'. Such studies are unnecessary, he says since:

> All the potential for growth is external and market-led. It might be okay to use some local materials for packaging, but they [the Caribbean countries] shouldn't be producing iron and steel, certainly. It's just not viable to produce tires or shoes [for local and regional markets] in the Caribbean, although maybe some of the surplus from the garments manufactured for export could be sold to the local market.

A Fundamental Choice

In the view of the World Bank, the Caribbean economy exists as a mere appendage of the Northern-dominated global capitalist system. The Caribbean economy can grow, says Christian Delvoie, only if Caribbean governments accept:

> the need to keep wages low and exchange rates realistic [by devaluing local currencies]. Otherwise, they'll destroy investor confidence. They need markets in the US, and so they can't restrict the repatriation of profits [by foreign corporations] and they have to keep up their incentives to investors.[9]

The role of the Bank, says Delvoie, is not to tell those investors what to produce: 'We have no idea of the particulars of what will sell in the US and other external markets. That's up to the individual businessman. The Bank's goal is to make sure the lines of credit, the incentives, and the pricing policies are right.' Caribbean governments, he added, have to pay closer heed to Northern consumer preferences and brand names, and keep an eye on 'whatever is selling in Miami'.

As a result of such Northern-determined development policies and structures geared to agro-exports, countries in the South that were self-sufficient in food production until recently are now net importers of food, Atherton Martin recently reminded US policymakers and development agencies. Martin, a development analyst and activist from Dominica, told participants in a Washington conference on sustainable development that:

> The Caribbean paid US$2 billion for food an agricultural imports in 1988. This externally imposed 'need' for food created the 'need, for borrowing. . . . It's easier to phone the United States and have a 40-foot trailer load of carrots delivered, because the infrastructure exists for that, but not for local production and distribution of carrots. The short-term economics may not appear to favor local food production. But expense of those imports and damage and dangers of the pesticides and herbicides used on export crops, make prohibitive the long-term costs of anything other than greater food self-reliance.[10]

Martin looks to people-centered Caribbean institutions — credit associations, trade unions, farmers' organizations, cooperatives, community groups and development NGO's — as the most important part of the solution to the economic crisis in the Caribbean and in the South. In his view:

> Our task is to broaden our horizons, and to widen our people's view of what is possible, and to expand our nations' visions of themselves. The role of USAID and the World Bank is just the opposite: to narrow our sense of what is possible, to convince us if we need a factory, we must pay a foreign company to build it; if we need flour, we must import it. That philosophy is what keeps us in debt and puts blinders on our people and on our Caribbean governments, which vacillate between the practical necessity of developing our own resources, and blind allegiance to the ideology of private enterprise.

The choice facing Caribbean people is not a choice between modernization and progress on the one hand, and a nostalgic retreat to an idealized agrarian past on the other. The conditions endured by Caribbean peasants and farm laborers have been far from ideal. Rather it is a question of who will determine the course of Caribbean development. Will the decisions that set the direction of the region's development course be made by foreign institutions, governments and corporations, or by organizations that represent the people of the Caribbean, particularly its working class and poor majority? Will the criteria on which those decisions are based be those of short-term profitability and competitiveness in the cut-throat international marketplace, or those which maximize the long-term security, sustainability and development of Caribbean economies and ecologies?

The dominant view among governments and institutions that hold power today *in* the Caribbean and *over* the Caribbean is that progress and improved living standards will arise as a by-produce of economic growth. But significant and sustained growth is unlikely as long as the uses of the region's land, labor and resources continue to be determined by those who hold no long-term stake in the development and well-being of Caribbean societies. To the extent that economic growth is possible under such conditions, it can only take place at the expense of the majority of Caribbean citizens. Most of those who remain in the region will have to work harder and longer for less, while the rest, quite possibly the majority of Caribbeans, will have little choice but to leave their homes to join the swelling ranks of displaced citizens of the South struggling to survive in the cold economic climate of the North.

Notes

1. Information on the environmental impacts of structural adjustment was presented by representatives of southern NGOs at the 4th and 5th conferences of the International NGO Forum on IMF and World Bank lending, held in September 1989 and September 1990 in Washington DC.

2. *Helping the Poor: the IMF's New Facilities for Structural Adjustment* (International Monetary Fund, Washington DC, 1988), and *Alleviating Poverty under Structural Adjustment* by Tony Addison and Lionel Demery (World Bank, Washington DC, 1987) are among numerous Bank and Fund publications that attempt to address this issue.

3. *World Bank News Special Report: Lending for Adjustment: An Update*, World Bank, Washington, April 1988.

4. Author interview, November 1987.

5. William G. Demas, 'Agricultural Diversification in the Caribbean Community', Grand Anse, Grenada, May 1987.

6. Ibid.

7. Author interview, March 1988.

8. Author interview, June 1988.

9. Author interview, June 1988.

10. Remarks at a US Congressional Symposium sponsored by the House of Representatives Subcommittee on Western Hemispheric Affairs, organized by The Development GAP, Washington DC, 7 February 1989.

11. Follow the NICs?

The NIC experience does have tremendous relevance for the third world, but this is not to be found in the World Bank–IMF injunctions. . . . Not only do these prescriptions distort the NIC experience, they lead to disaster in an increasingly protectionist world economy.

Walden Bello and Stephanie Rosenfeld, authors of
Dragons in Distress: Asia's Miracle Economies in Crisis
(Food First, San Francisco, 1990), p. 343

The structural adjustment development formula for the 1990s includes some new variations on an old theme. The sponsors of adjustment still view economic growth as the essence of development and increased exports as the key to growth. The adjustors continue to advocate increased production of raw materials and unprocessed commodities. Indebted countries, they believe, should be cutting more timber, digging up more minerals and planting more coffee, cocoa and cotton, while mechanizing their mining and agriculture to speed exports of these traditional commodities. But the failed adjustment programs of the early 1980s, and the continuing decline and instability of the prices of most of the South's food and raw materials, have convinced the economic experts that these exports will not be enough. Increasingly, they stress agricultural diversification, tourism and, above all, export-oriented industrialization.

The adjustors call for the production of more specialized, high-value export crops in addition to traditional ones. Mexico, Central America and many countries in Africa are being encouraged to grow more vegetables and fruit for sale to Europe and North America. USAID Caribbean agricultural projects are still primarily geared to traditional crops, but AID's publicity emphasizes production of new exports such as exotic fruits, vegetables and flowers for the US markets. Tourism is also receiving more attention in AID and World Bank development recommendations, particularly in the Caribbean. 'After all,' asked a Bank economist, 'what is the Caribbean's most valuable product? It's their climate, and their land and water.'

But more than any other strategy, the adjustors stress the expansion of light manufacturing export industries as the key to growth and their version of development. The US government, the World Bank and other lenders and donors all point to the export success of the NICs, particularly those in Asia, as a model for Caribbean and other indebted countries.

In the Eastern Caribbean, USAID, the World Bank and some island governments laud the examples of South Korea, Singapore, Hong Kong and Taiwan, dubbed the 'four tigers' or 'four dragons'. Technical assistance and demonstration projects have been established to reinforce the message that 'Taiwan is a small island, Taiwan has developed; follow its lead and you can develop, too'. Signs advertising the embassies and demonstration development projects of the Republic of China (Taiwan) are oddly prominent in these small island nations.

Why the Caribbean can't be another Taiwan

Is rapid economic growth based on increased manufactured exports a realistic scenario for the South? Certainly it is not a new strategy. During the time when the multilateral lenders' emphasis was on large dams and other infrastructure, their purpose was more to serve export industries than to bring power and light to rural villages. The attempts by some countries at import substitution — manufacturing goods for local needs instead of importing them — were tolerated but generally not encouraged by the big lenders.

After three decades of efforts by nations of the South to achieve major increases in their industrial export earnings, only a handful of countries has done so. Mexico, Brazil, South Korea, Taiwan, Hong Kong and Singapore have become major exporters of factory-made goods. Thailand and Malaysia have also attracted significant low-wage export assembly industries in recent years, although neither country can be described as industrialized. India's strong industrial sector makes products for Indian factories and consumers as well as for export.

None of these NICs, however, has succeeded in solving the problems of development. The majority of the populations of Mexico, India and Brazil are still burdened by crushing poverty and illiteracy, while most of the proceeds of industrialization have been absorbed by foreign corporations or by their countries' élites. Repressive and often dangerous working conditions, and high levels of poverty and homelessness, afflict the populations of South Korea and the Southeast Asian NICs. In nearly all the NICs, rapid industrialization and export competitivesness has been bought at the price of political instability, environmental disaster and great human suffering.

These problems, say proponents of structural adjustment, must be addressed sometime in the future. The more urgent priority, in their view, is for non-industrialized countries to implement policies necessary to increase their industrial export earnings as quickly as possible, so that they too can follow the path charted by the NICs. But even if the problems of poverty and environmental destruction are seen as temporary, or accepted as the inevitable price of economic progress, the question remains: can the poor nations of the South hope to repeat the industrial export success of the NICs?

An examination of the reasons for NIC export success and an understanding of the NICs' current role in the global economy make it abundantly clear that genuine development depends upon finding a path quite different from that taken thus far by Mexico, Brazil and the Asian exporters. The export achievements of the NICs do not provide the solution to the development dilemma facing the poor nations of the South. They certainly cannot serve as a model for the Caribbean.[1]

Taiwan, touted in the Caribbean as the NIC to be emulated, and other successful Asian exporters are very different from any Caribbean country. Taiwan and South Korea's much larger populations (20 million and 41 million respectively) and their single land masses are only the most obvious contrasts with the insular Caribbean. In Taiwan, and also in the other most successful Asian NIC, South Korea, the growth of industry has taken place in the context of food self-sufficiency and close linkages between farming and manufacturing. The Caribbean situation with respect to food and land — very high dependence on imported food and highly skewed distribution of land — is the opposite of that upon which Taiwan and South Korea's industrialization was based.

In neither Taiwan nor Korea did today's industrialization and relative prosperity derive from the sort of 'outward-oriented, market driven' development strategy advocated by the structural adjustors for the Caribbean. Development analyst Walden Bello writes in reference to the East Asian NICs.

> The NICs have achieved a high rate of growth precisely because they eschewed a *laissez-faire* approach to development in favor of active state planning. Moreover, the NICs' surge was facilitated by a unique set of historical circumstances, including massive US economic aid in the 1950s.[2]

In both Taiwan and South Korea, the strengthening of agriculture was a government priority under Japanese colonialism during the first half of this century and also in the years following World War II. The Japanese promoted increased farm productivity and modernized infrastructure in both Taiwan and Korea. Japan did so largely in order to serve its own needs for food, fiber and manufactured goods. Nevertheless, this emphasis on agriculture contrasts markedly with the neglect of agriculture, especially small farmers, in the Caribbean during most of the 20th century.

In both Taiwan and South Korea, the distribution of rural land and income during the period of industrialization has been relatively broad. Unlike in the Caribbean or the Philippines, the colonial masters of Taiwan and South Korea did not introduce an exploitative plantation system with an almost exclusive emphasis on export agriculture. The majority of farmers in both countries, although not wealthy, were comparatively secure. This was largely the result of extensive land reform carried out in the early 20th century and again in 1949–51 in Taiwan, and in the 1940s and 1950s in Korea. These land reform programs were much more far-reaching than those being recommended by the World Bank in the Caribbean.

Post-war South Korea has not abandoned agriculture geared to local consumption, as structural adjustment plans would have Caribbean countries do. During the process of industrialization, South Korea increased its food production for local use. Although Korea does import corn and wheat today, it is largely self-sufficient in its major staple food, rice, and has become more so as industrialization has progressed. According to World Bank figures, food constituted 15 per cent of South Korea's imports in 1965 and only 6 per cent in 1986.

Taiwan's and South Korea's ability to feed their own populations has meant that their resources are not drained by huge food import costs, as in the Caribbean today. And, because they have had access to land, plus government help in increasing their productivity and incomes, the small-scale farmers of Taiwan and South Korea constitute a large domestic market which has helped industrialization to get off the ground. At the same time, rural savings have helped to finance industrial development. In contrast, most impoverished rural families in the Caribbean could not afford to buy the goods produced in their countries' export manufacturing enclaves, even if those products were sold locally.

In addition, the governments of both Taiwan and South Korea played an active role in promoting farming and agro-industry as a basis for, and a complement to, manufacturing for local needs and for export. Government enterprises and state-sponsored investments in agricultural research and extension, transportation, communications and hydroelectric power helped to build economies in which agriculture and industry were integrated. Farmers produced fibers and other raw materials for export; factories produced fertilizer and other inputs for agriculture. As a result, proceeds from agriculture and manufacturing have not been cancelled out by the high cost of imported industrial parts and materials and farm inputs, as has happened in much of the Caribbean.

In Taiwan, post-war industrialization was subsidized by a huge influx of US assistance, averaging about US$100 million yearly for three decades. The United States financed an estimated 26 per cent of the value of Taiwan's capital formation in the post-war years, in addition to substantially reducing the country's trade deficit. US aid to South Korea totalled about US$6 billion between 1945 and 1978.[3] No comparable level of sustained support for Caribbean-owned industry or agriculture has been offered by the US or any other foreign donor to independent nations in the Caribbean.

Furthermore, during the early decades of industrialization, Taiwanese and Korean manufacturers were aided and protected by government subsidies, controls over the uses of foreign exchange and restrictions on the import of goods which might compete with those produced locally. The city-states of Hong Kong and Singapore, which have experienced similar success in export-oriented industrialization, have also relied heavily on government planning, protection and subsidies. These import substitution policies are the opposite of the open-market, free-trade development strategy endorsed by those who tell today's Caribbean nations to follow the Asian NICs. According to Walden Bello:

> Both the Taiwanese and South Korean Governments are interventionist states par excellence. In South Korea, the authoritarian state, working closely with huge monopolistic conglomerates called *chaebol*, targeted for development promising manufacturing industries like steel, electronics, and cars, and supported them with a variety of direct and indirect subsidies. The Economic Planning Board . . . channeled local and foreign capital into

favored industries using a variety of mechanisms, including preferential financing, protectionist barriers against competing exports, and tax incentives. But most attractive were the monopoly profits that awaited the conglomerates should they pioneer production in the industries favored by government planners.[4]

Most of the other low-income countries which have been trying to emulate the success of the Asian dragons are failing badly. The Philippines, for example, has been striving for export success under IMF and World Bank guidance for more than two decades. By 1987, it had received more than US$5 billion in World Bank loans, including US$2 billion for structural adjustment. All of this has brought to the Philippines not prosperity or even higher living standards, but rather increased poverty, malnutrition, landlessness, labor unrest and political instability.[5] Many other countries attempting to boost their net export earnings by offering generous incentives to foreign investors and establishing low-wage manufacturing enclaves and FTZs have not fared better than the Philippines.

Conditions in much of the Caribbean, particularly high levels of landlessness and rural poverty, resemble more closely those of the Philippines than Taiwan and South Korea at the time those countries began to industrialize. The Caribbean also lacks the Philippines' advantage, in the eyes of the adjustors, of extremely low wages compared with other would-be industrializing nations. The wages of workers in Philippines export industries are only one-fourth of those earned by export assembly workers in the Windward Islands, and only 45 per cent of factory wages in Haiti, the poorest country in the Caribbean.[6]

The Philippines' population of more than 50 million, although spread over 200 islands, is a potentially significant domestic market which could complement foreign markets as an outlet for the products of local industry. But the terms of its structural adjustment program, especially the orientation of agriculture and industry to external markets and the lowering of the wages, real incomes and purchasing power of the country's poor majority, ensure that this potential domestic market remains untapped. Meanwhile millions of Filipinos remain underfed, poorly clothed and badly sheltered.

Parallel structural adjustment policies are propelling poor nations worldwide into self-defeating, cut-throat competition. In their critique of the NIC development model, Robin Broad and John Cavanaugh note that during the 1980s, the World Bank:

> was helping to create a group of countries that would compete against each other in their crusade to become NICs. The result of all this were two vicious battles — the first, to offer cheaper, more docile labor forces and more alluring incentives to attract TNC [transnational corporation] assembly lines away from other countries; and, second, to win scarce export markets.[7]

In the Caribbean today, this competition pits nation against nation in an attempt to offer foreign investors cheaper labor and more attractive incentives. St Lucia promises 'up to a 15-year tax break' and wages approximately one-fifth of those in the US, located 'a mere 1,950 miles — a two-megabyte satellite feed — from Wall Street'. Antigua offers a labor force 'easily trainable, highly dextrous, reliable and loyal'. Haiti boasts of 'generous tax incentives', and 'the largest labor force and the lowest production costs' in the region.[8]

As they strive to undersell one another, many Caribbean countries are giving away to foreign corporations more than they gain from the short-lived export assembly operations that typically respond to these kinds of incentives. But even these give-away industrialization programs are not enough to make the Caribbean competitive with low-wage Asian exporters such as the Philippines, Sri Lanka, Thailand, and also China and Eastern Europe.

The market opportunities predicted by structural adjustment experts have failed to materialize for NICs in the Caribbean and elsewhere. The World Bank had predicted that NICs such as Taiwan and South Korea would shift their production toward more complex and profitable exports such as cars and computers. This, in theory, would have left openings for other NICs to take over the export of less sophisticated products such as clothing, textiles, shoes, toys and electronic components.

However, as Broad and Cavanaugh note, the Asian NICs have not abandoned light manufacturing, but have instead increased their world market share of these products. At the same time, they have improved the efficiency of their light manufacturing industries, making it more difficult for would-be industrializing nations to break into international markets for such goods. Rather than out-competing the Asian NICs in this field, Caribbean countries which have established industrial parks geared to exports have become hosts to Taiwanese- and Korean-owned assembly factories.

In addition, economic crisis in the United States is lowering wages and incomes in many rural and inner-city areas to the point that they have begun to resemble those of the Third World. Consequently, the United States, too, competes with Asian, Latin American, Caribbean and poor European countries such as Portugal, offering low wages and proximity to US markets to multinational investors. US Secretary of Housing and Urban Development Jack Kemp stated his intent in 1989 to revive a Nixon-era proposal for 'urban enterprise zones', similar in concept to EPZs. These zones would offer tax incentives or other subsidies to businesses interested in taking advantage of high unemployment and the desperate need for income in US urban centers. Claude Leach, director of St Vincent's government-sponsored business promotion agency, DEVCO, complained that 'Mayor Koch was trying to bring to the South Bronx the same business I try to attract to St Vincent'.[9]

The growth of the 'global assembly line' is making low-wage export industries even less dependable as sources of foreign exchange and employment for their host countries. Export-oriented investors today rarely establish complete manufacturing operations in industrializing countries in the South. Instead, new technology makes it possible for transnational corporations to divide the manufacture of cars, clothing and video recorders into separate stages. This enables them to shift those phases of production which require the least machinery and technical skills from one low-wage country to another, wherever production costs to the company are lower and incentives higher. Increasingly, service industries and utility companies in the North are adopting a similar strategy. They locate low-wage, labor-intensive data entry jobs in Caribbean and other poor countries and then beam the processed data by satellite to offices in the industrialized nations.

In these fragmented industries, the amount of value added to the products assembled by workers in Caribbean and other export processing enclaves is a small proportion of those products' total value. This is equally true in service industries, where the product may be a utility bill or an insurance policy. Reflecting this is the fact that the amount of income remaining in the host countries in the form of workers' earnings is small. Cary Harris, head of Dominica's Economic Planning Division, acknowledges that EPZs might cost their country more than they would contribute to its economy. They are desirable nevertheless, he says, because their 'demonstration effect' can prove that Dominica is a stable and profitable place to invest. 'Maybe we should apply free trade policies to the whole country,' he remarked.[10]

New technology is also reducing the value of many of the natural resources of the South as a factor in attracting investors in export-oriented industries. The development of synthetic substitutes for materials such as rubber, sugar, timber, tin, aluminum and natural fibers has already reduced the prices and the demand for these Southern exports in international markets. Among Caribbean nations, the sugar and mineral-exporting countries of Jamaica, Guyana and the Dominican Republic have felt the most severe impact of this trend, as their earnings from exports of these commodities have fallen dramatically. The use by international beverage, plastics and other industries of synthetic materials also reduced the potential advantage that countries of the South might otherwise have had in attracting investers by offering ample and accessible supplies of natural raw materials for manufacturing and food processing industries.

Countries striving to grow economically by increasing their exports today face the huge added hurdle of global economic stagnation. Continued low levels of growth in most countries of the North and the South during the 1980s resulted in decreased demand for nearly all commodity exports and even tighter competition among would-be industrial exporters for markets for their products. With glutted international markets, no combination of adjustment, austerity and efficiency can make export promotion the engine of successful economic growth and genuine development.

During 1981, just at the time when the World Bank and the US government began systematically to pressure impoverished countries to pursue structural adjustment and export-oriented growth strategies, total world trade actually shrank for the first time since 1958. As the decade wore on, economic recovery around the globe was partial, spotty and sluggish. Between 1981 and 1985, total world trade grew by only 2.8 per cent. Largely because of this, exports from the South declined by an average annual rate of 0.4 per cent from 1981 to 1986.[11]

Would-be industrializing countries today also face the barrier of the 'new protectionism'. During the 1980s, the United States has stepped up its criticism of protectionist practices by other nations. USAID Director Donald Woods told Congress in 1988: 'Many of the economic problems developing countries face can be traced to the propensity of governments to control economies, rather than give market forces and international enterprise a chance to generate growth.'[12] The US government, echoing the World Bank, has sharpened its insistence that countries of the South drop their remaining barriers to free trade, particularly any tariff or quota regulations that limit exports from the US.

But at the same time, the United States and other industrialized nations have been erecting even higher protectionist barriers against exports from the Caribbean and other nations of both the North and the South. Already by the end of the 1970s, half of all world trade was restricted by tariffs and quota systems. Since then, despite official endorsement of free trade as the fundamental basis of sound international economics, the United States, the European Common Market countries and Japan have all increased their own barriers against each other's exports and against exports from the South. The double standard under which the United States restricts its own imports from the Caribbean and Central America, while pressuring Caribbean Basin countries to purchase more US goods and services, has had a detrimental effect on CBI eligible countries.

The exploitation of female labor in export industries and agriculture creates severe social strain and undermines overall productivity in the host countries. The majority of workers in export assembly factories are women, particularly young women. Employers choose young women because they can get away with paying them less, hiring and firing them as suits their convenience, forcing them to work longer hours and otherwise denying them basic labor and human rights. The social costs are grave. New export industries do not take jobs away from men, but to the extent that they undermine local industries by competing for capital, infrastructure services and government support, they can contribute to increased overall unemployment. In some countries, such as Malaysia, hard-pressed peasant families sacrifice their daughters to the export industries where, in exchange for a few years of cash income, the young women frequently lose their health and their respectability. In other countries, such as Jamaica, many export zone workers are women who already have children and may be household heads. Their long working hours prevent them from doing other work on which they and their families depend, especially the care of the young, the sick and the elderly, and the creation of family life and recreation of traditions.

This is most certainly not to argue that women are better off not working outside the home. But when they are forced to do so in the context of gender-biased attitudes and institutions that fail to recognize and compensate for the loss of their important work in the household and informal economy, the entire society suffers. Their extreme exploitation not only saps the strength of women but also diminishes the health and productivity of current and future generations of Caribbean farmers and workers.

Sound economies cannot be erected on a base of bare subsistence wages, high dependence on imported food, and extreme indebtedness. No country in the world has succeeded in achieving genuine development by such means under such conditions. Some Southern countries, such as South Korea, have achieved success in industrialization geared to both domestic consumption and to exports. But, as we have seen, the reality facing most low-income nations today is very different from that encountered by the Asian NICs when they began their push towards rapid industrialization. There is little reason to expect that Caribbean or most other impoverished and indebted countries will be able to take off along the flight path followed by the Asian dragons.

'Capitalism and Democracy: A Terrible Mix'

Export success and economic growth, even if these goals were achievable through structural adjustment, are not the same as development. Even the fastest-growing NICs have not been able to address the problems of persistent and deepening poverty. In Mexico, Brazil, Thailand, Malaysia and the Dominican Republic, increases in manufactured exports in the past decade have been achieved against a background of worsening hunger, pollution, displacement of peasants from their lands, and spreading urban blight and homelessness. The 'successful' Asian NICs now share many of these problems.

Moreover, despite Reagan and Bush administration rhetoric, free enterprise-led development is not equivalent to democracy. Among the Latin American and Asian NICs are some of the world's worst violators of human rights. The country that has achieved the greatest success in export-oriented industrialization, South Korea, has done so at the price of severe political repression, including the massacre of as many as 2,000 people in the city of Kwangju in 1980, and the continuation of serious and widespread police state practices, such as mass arrests of peaceful protestors, political detentions and torture.

The chief of Dominica's Economic Planning Division and close advisor to Prime Minister Eugenia Charles, Cary Harris, compared Asia to the Caribbean in commenting on the obstacles to development: 'The United States is asking us to carry out policies under a democracy that really require dictatorship. Capitalism and democracy — it's a terrible mix.'

Notes

1. Parts of the following discussion draw upon the work of Robin Broad and John Cavanaugh. Their argument is summarized in 'No More NICs', *Foreign Policy* No. 72, Fall 1988. An excellent study of the costs and limits of industrialization in Taiwan, South Korea and Singapore is Waldon Bello and Stephanie Rosenfeld, *Dragons in Distress*, Food First, San Francisco, 1990.

2. Walden Bello, 'Asia's Miracle Economies: the First and Last of a Dying Breed', *Dollars and Sense*, January/February 1989, Somerville, Massachusetts.

3. *The Republic of China, 1987: A Reference Book*; Bello and Rosenfeld, *Dragons in Distress*.

4. Bello and Rosenfeld, *Dragons in Distress*.

5. World Bank, 'Lending for Adjustment', 1988; Walden Bello, Elaine Elinson and David Kinsey, *Development Débâcle: The World Bank and the Philippines*, Institute for Food and Development Policy, San Francisco, 1982.

6. World Bank, *Caribbean Exports*, 1988.

7. Broad and Cavanaugh, *No More NICs*, p. 85.

8. Government of Antigua and Barbuda, *Investment Guide*, December 1985; *Wall Street Journal* supplement, 'Caribbean Investment Opportunities', 4 November 1988.

9. Author interview, November 1987.

10. Author interview, December 1987.

11. Broad and Cavanaugh, *No More NICs*, World Bank, *Caribbean Exports: Preferential Markets and Performance*, May 1988.

12. USAID, *Congressional Presentation for Fiscal Year 1989*.

Part VI:
Toward Alternatives

12. Strategies for Greater Self-reliance

> The food crisis which is looming in the Third World, already raising its ugly head in Africa, will make the debt crisis and the oil crisis of the 1980s and 1990s look like a Sunday picnic. Thus, regardless of what CBIs or other measures are presented by officialdom, the Caribbean people *must* maintain the capability to grow and market the basic foods on which the bulk of their population can survive.
>
> Alan N. Williams, Association for Caribbean Transformation

Caribbean scholars, development workers, and union and community leaders are breaking free from long-dominant theories of development that have been weighted and warped by Northern-country standards and priorities. This is notably true in the realm of agriculture. Oscar Allen of St Vincent's Rural Transformation Collective points out, for example, that the statistics listed as 'agricultural production' in reports on his country's GDP are based on the amount of crops *exported*, as if that were the total of St Vincent's agriculture production. As a result, he says, 'We don't know how much we produce now for ourselves, much less what we would produce under different circumstances. New concepts of the economic interests and capabilities of our people must be created,' rather than assumed or taken as given from the textbooks of colonialism.[1]

'We need to break out of the plantation system and our existence as appendages of foreign economies,' says Osborne Riviere, who was director of Farm to Market, a small non-profit making regional food marketing company. Projects similar to Farm to Market have the potential to make the region more self-reliant in food while increasing farmers' incomes. However, colonial ties and current economic policies have thus far stifled that potential.

In order to pursue their own development course, Caribbean countries and regional bodies must be able to set their own internal and regional priorities, control their imports, protect their own markets and foster regional industries. Both access to external sources of capital and better terms of trade will be needed to help Caribbean people pursue these goals. Meanwhile, there is a great deal that they are already doing to enhance their own self-reliance. Even without greatly increasing their funding to the region, Northern governments and international aid and lending institutions could foster Caribbean development by recognizing the value of these regional efforts and by removing the external policy obstacles that now hinder them.

Many activities to increase food production and security are already being undertaken, for the most part on a small scale, by Caribbean farmers' associations, cooperative enterprises, regional institutions, private businesses and some government agencies. Many of the efforts by small farmers and co-ops are supported by Caribbean NGOs. The practical feasibility of carrying out such programs on a national and regional scale needs to be tested. But rather than encouraging and learning from these efforts, Northern governments and multilateral agencies, and some Caribbean governments as well, tend to ignore or discourage them. A closer look at some of these activities suggests the tremendous potential for the Caribbean. At the same time, it reveals the ways in which the priorities of USAID and the terms of structural adjustment undermine Caribbean efforts toward greater food security and more equitable and democratic development. Among the means proposed by Caribbean NGOs to promote greater self-reliance are:

- *increased food production for local sale and subsistence;*
- *agro-industries and other linkages between farming and non-farm sectors of the economy;*
- *a new approach to import substitution;*
- *a new type of tourism;* and
- *reversing the brain drain.*

Increased Food Production for Local Sale and Subsistence

Increasing the amount and quality of food produced in the Caribbean to meet Caribbean needs would not only foster the well-being of Caribbean citizens, it would also reduce the region's huge food import bill. This would go a long way toward reducing the balance of payments deficits that compel Caribbean countries to accept onerous, growth-stifling IMF and World Bank structural adjustment programs.

The decline of the subsistence farming which existed alongside export-oriented, plantation agriculture has left the region's poor majority more vulnerable to economic shocks and has increased the pressure upon them to emigrate. The reasons for this trend are complex, and include changing tastes and attitudes as well as direct economic factors. The solution is not to turn back the clock to the era of sub-poverty-level subsistence agriculture. But many Caribbean farmers today would like to grow both traditional and new food crops if they could earn a regular income from them. At the same time, many Caribbean consumers would purchase Caribbean-grown foods if they could get them for a reasonable price. The fact that Caribbean hucksters, most of them women, continue to make arduous and risky trips in wooden boats and small planes to carry produce from island to island attests to the strong regional demand for Caribbean produce as well as to the determined and enterprising spirit of the hucksters.

Standing between Caribbean food producers and consumers are policies that neglect the production and marketing of crops for local needs. With a few exceptions, government agricultural extension services and foreign aid to agriculture are geared to promoting extra-regional exports. Farmers can get technical assistance, fertilizer, land or loans to grow bananas or cocoa much more easily than they can get help in producing root crops, beans or green vegetables. Systems for storing, transporting and marketing local foods are haphazard or inadequate, while those for export crops and food imports are relatively well-developed. The result is that Caribbean produce reaching urban areas in the region is often scarce, expensive or of poor quality. Even in rural areas, it is often easier to buy imported macaroni, frozen chicken, canned beef or bottled soft drinks than traditional staples such as cassava, dasheen or yams, locally raised meat or fresh fruit juice. Meanwhile, Caribbean food import bills continue to climb.

This situation owes more to political priorities than to economic necessity. According to Dr Thomas Henderson, a highly respected agronomist who worked for 30 years with the agricultural research and extension programs of the UWI, the goal of greater food self-sufficiency subscribed to in principle by most Caribbean governments and some foreign donors is seldom matched by a commitment of resources. UWI research, Henderson says, has shown that local processing of Caribbean fruits is both technically and economically feasible:

The products are of excellent quality, and could compete with anything imported. But it's easier for our manufacturers to import and repackage fruit in barrels, and none of our governments have had the gumption to enforce the use of local produce.[2]

Despite what he calls the 'bombardment of the region with foreign cultural tastes', Henderson believes that policy changes could make the region much more self-sufficient in food, including protein-rich foods. The greatest potential in this area, he maintains, lies in the development of Caribbean fisheries, dairy industries and small livestock.

To be effective, foreign lenders and donors must shake off their assumptions of superiority and start learning from Caribbean farmers. Too frequently, says Henderson:

USAID programs are based on policies which have absolutely no bearing on the situation of the people they profess to assist. AID personnel have preconceived ideas of what they want to achieve, and are not sensitive to local physical, social, political, or psychological and cultural realities. People here have ideas, and AID needs to get these from the people. Our people don't have all the answers, but that is where you must start.

Multi-purpose NGOs such as People for Progress and the Social Action Center in Jamaica, the Small Projects Assistance Team and Development Alternatives in Dominica, Projects Promotion in St Vincent and the Grenadines, and the Agency for Rural Transformation and the Grenada People's Development Agency in Grenada give organizing and technical assistance to rural cooperatives, and women's and farmers' groups involved in food production, processing and other economic activities.

A Jamaican NGO, Projects for People, is helping farmers to organize themselves to produce food crops for local and regional consumption. The Hillside Farmers Association in Clarendon Parish is a cooperative of exlaborers, formed with help from Projects for People, which has leased 740 acres of land on the Monymusk sugar estate from the Jamaican government. With support from Northern NGOs, the association is installing irrigation equipment to make the former sugar lands more productive.

In St Lucia, an NGO known as the Staff Cooperative has helped farmers to organize themselves in buyers' and producers' cooperatives. They began producing eggs, chicken and pork at a time when St Lucia was importing half its eggs and 13 million pounds of chicken yearly. The cooperative was able to take over and rehabilitate an abandoned feed-mill to produce feed grain and to establish its own slaughterhouse. By the late 1980s, all of the country's eggs and 93 per cent of its premium pork were being provided locally. Essential to the project's success was the organization of the farmers themselves and the development of a close working relationship with the government ministries of agriculture and trade, which at the time helped to protect the local egg producers from foreign competition.

Fishing is another type of food production that has been badly neglected in the Caribbean. Although environmental problems threaten stocks, the waters off the shores of most Caribbean territories are rich in fish. Local demand for this excellent source of protein usually exceeds the supply. Most Caribbean fishermen cannot afford radios, radar or strong and reliable engines. Many venture into the rough Atlantic seas in small wooden schooners or dugout canoes, and many lose their lives in rough weather. French, Japanese and other trawlers and fish-factory ships reap much of the ocean's harvest, while many Caribbean people eat canned herring or salted cod imported from the North. The Agency for Rural Transformation in Grenada, Development Alternatives in Dominica, Projects Promotion in St Vincent and the Grenadines, and the National Research and Development Foundation in St Lucia are among the Caribbean NGOs that support fishing co-ops, helping the members pool and expand their resources to obtain better equipment.

These and other NGOs support similar projects to increase the production of small livestock, including poultry, goats, pigs and agouti. A regional policy to build on these local efforts and develop storage and processing facilities for fish, meat and eggs could contribute to food self-reliance. According to George Huggins, director of Oxfam America's Latin America Program and himself a native of Trinidad:

> What is needed are incentives provided by the public sector to help small and medium-scale producers and investors to get involved in food production, processing and regional trade. That's a policy choice, but a choice that is in the opposite direction of current policy.[3]

A system for regional food security will not spring full-grown from the minds of officials or NGOs but must be developed through what Huggins calls a 'pragmatic dynamic', in which Caribbean and Northern NGOs, Caribbean producers' associations, cooperatives, governments, regional institutions and the private sector all have roles to play.

Agro-industries and Other Linkages between Agriculture and Non-farm Sectors of the Economy

More local processing and packaging of local crops would have many benefits. Food-processing plants could provide more reliable markets for farmers and badly-needed jobs for other people. Fruit and other crops that now go to waste could be utilized and, as agro-processing industries become larger and more efficient, at lower cost than imported foods.

Linkages between agro-processing and other economic sectors in the Caribbean could reduce import costs, provide jobs and stimulate other economic activities. The possibilities include: providing Caribbean food, furniture and other products to the region's tourist industry, which now imports more than 60 per cent of its inputs; producing fuel from agricultural by-products, including ethanol from sugar cane and methane from manure; using local fibers and woods to produce packaging materials; and incorporating agricultural by-products, such as coconut meal, surplus bananas and sugar cane, and citrus wastes as components of animal feeds to replace imported feed ingredients.

Processing, preserving and packaging Caribbean crops

There are agro-processing plants in the Caribbean but many of them mainly reprocess or repackage imported foods. Imported wheat is milled into flour and imported feedgrains are mixed into animal feed. Diamond Dairies in St Vincent processes milk from England and juice from the United States and packages them in boxes sold under Caribbean labels but made in the United States. Even juices made from fruits that can be grown in abundance in the Caribbean, such as grapefruit and oranges, are typically imported from the US or England, already canned or in the form of concentrate. Most of the proceeds go to foreign processing and shipping companies, while Caribbean citrus and other fruit crops go to waste.

Some Caribbean factories, for example in Trinidad, do make use of local crops. Their products include bottled sauces and syrups, canned fruit, frozen juice concentrates, and soap and cosmetics made from coconut oil and aloe vera. Such operations add value to Caribbean crops and increase the national income. But they do not figure prominently in the development plans urged upon Caribbean countries in the name of structural adjustment. Moreover, many private Caribbean industries, including food-processing plants, have reduced their operations or have gone out of business due to the reduced purchasing power of Caribbean consumers, competition from foreign investors and exporters, lack of credit, limited foreign exchanges available to import parts and machines, and privatization measures, all of which are related to structural adjustment policies and the burden of debt payments.

It is all the more remarkable, then, that low-income Caribbean people persist in their efforts to sustain small-scale agro-industries. Farmers in central Jamaica provide one example. A 1981 survey showed that many Jamaican dairy farmers could not sell their milk because of the rising cost of transportation and the decline of the Jamaica Milk Products marketing company. At the same time, the country was spending US$250 million yearly to import food, including 85 per cent of the dairy products its people were consuming. A cooperative cheese-producing plant was constructed under the guidance of Projects for People and with grants from Northern NGOs and a loan from the Interamerican Foundation, a US government-funded agency not related to AID. By 1987, the 3M Dairy Project was selling 2,000 pounds of cheese a week. The project includes revolving funds for dairy herd development and extension services and training for farmers and cheese factory workers. As part of its effort to raise awareness of environmental issues and to make cheese production ecologically sustainable, Projects for People is helping project participants establish a fuel forest to provide a renewable source of energy for the cheese factory. Plans for other cheese factories have been developed.

Throughout the Caribbean, cooperatives and private enterprises, many of them backed by Caribbean NGOs, are processing locally grown fruits, herbs, teas and spices, mainly for local and regional markets but also for export. Members of the Grenfruit Cooperative, mainly rural women who might otherwise be unemployed, produce ground spices, dried and candied fruits, and bottled sauces. Grenfruit receives support from GRENCODA. The Banana Bunch cooperative, which makes packaged banana chips, gets assistance from a Dominican NGO, the Small Projects Assistance Team. Also in Dominica, Blow's Agro-Industrial Cooperative produces herbal teas and spices and a cooperative supported by a Canadian NGO, Plenty, produces high quality tofu, flour and other soy products for the local market (where demand still exceeds supply) and for export to neighboring islands.

Alternative uses of traditional crops

Caribbean researchers have carried out promising studies of alternative agricultural technologies and new uses for traditional crops. Among the potential new banana products are wine, dried chips, vinegar and other processed foods from the fruit, and rope, paper and other products from the banana plant. Ambrose George, director of Coconut Rehabilitation project in Dominica, reports that as many as 360 potential uses for coconut oil, meal, husks and wood have been proposed. The multinational corporation Tate and Lyle identified 135 products other than sugar, molasses and rum that might be produced from sugar cane.

The Caribbean Food and Nutrition Institute has demonstrated that flours made from Caribbean root crops can be combined, with or without imported wheat flour, to make nutritious and less costly bread, pasta and other products. Far from being applied, the lessons of these experiences and studies are gathering dust on the shelves of universities and research institutions. Instead, AID's vision is of new, exotic export crops for specialized 'market niches' in North America and Europe. But such niches are generally small and unreliable.

The development of new, more productive, nutritious and weather-hardy varieties, and the revival of valuable old varieties of staple food crops is another area neglected by donors and policymakers. Some funding for the introduction of new varieties of tree crops and other food crops has been available from British and other donor agencies but it has been directed almost entirely toward products for extra-regional export. Research suggests that Eastern Caribbean varieties of cassava can produce better flour and starch than the kind grown in Jamaica, but adequate resources are not available to grow and test the more productive varieties at the Goshen Cassava plant in Jamaica.

The neglect of traditional crops in favor of new ones has another disadvantage overlooked by AID. Caribbean communities are already organized around the production of crops such as bananas and sugar. The skills and infrastructure for producing and transporting these crops are already in place. Switching abruptly to entirely different crops would involve greater social dislocation and waste of resources than would a planned and gradual transition to new crops and new, more value-adding uses for old ones. 'Development has to be connected to what we've done in that past, while we quietly but firmly transform it, first by developing alternative uses for the crops we are already organized to produce,' Neville Duncan points out.[4]

Alternative technologies in agriculture

Increasing the limited food productivity of small plots is urgently needed. Development of food-producing technology that does not rely on expensive, imported machinery, chemical fertilizers and hazardous pesticides is another important but under-funded area.

Oscar Allen of St Vincent points out that land-holding patterns and farming technology in his country remained virtually unchanged from the era of slavery until the early 1970s. In the past two decades, however, expensive agricultural machinery and chemical inputs, rising land and farming costs, and slumps in farm earnings have hit the country's poor majority very hard. They have contributed to rural unemployment rates of 40 per cent or more, the breakdown of family and community support systems, serious social problems, and the out-migration of many of the society's most productive members. To cope with such problems, Allen says:

> We need to place a priority on developing options other than the old, exploitative systems and technologies and the new, even more damaging ones. What other technology can we use instead of the old cutlass and hoe, on the one hand, and expensive, imported machinery, on the other? Planning and financing of these types of activities should be coordinated by the public sector.[5]

Research in food production technology is not a current priority of most Caribbean governments, or of foreign donors and lenders. USAID has given some support to research and extension services. The results, however, particularly in the area of food production for local and regional needs, have not reached the majority of farmers. The former agriculture laboratory in St Vincent has been closed for years. Agricultural ministry planners reported in 1988 that the government planned to reopen it. The primary emphasis, however, would be on meeting standards, such as those of the US Department of Agriculture, for food exports to foreign countries, not food for malnourished Vincentians or for markets on neighboring islands. Meanwhile, the country's main agricultural experiment station has been squeezed out of existence by the expansion of the Camden industrial park, where young women assemble electronic parts, garments and sporting goods for export. The demise of the experimental farm is both a real and a symbolic reflection of the shift in attention away from agriculture, even though farming is still the economic mainstay of the nation and the main source of income for the majority of its citizens.

A similar trend can be seen in other Caribbean countries. The Mirabeau Agricultural Research and Training Center in Grenada was revived by the PRG in 1979. In the mid-1980s, the center's director reported, the school had to cut back its programs because of reduced funding, and was unable to take students for its two-year training course in 1987. According to the director, interviewed in March of 1988, 'Farmers in Grenada are suffering immensely,' while services to help them have decreased.

Many Caribbean NGOs are working to reverse this trend. Many of the projects involve small-scale technology using local inputs, such as solar driers for fruit, and windmills to power generators. Biogas digesters are using pig, sheep and goat manure to produce fuel for cooking and refrigeration. The potential for these and other affordable technologies and decentralized energy sources, such as small-scale hydropower projects, has barely begun to be tapped.

A New Approach to Import Substitution

The high cost of imported non-food products also drains Caribbean economies. Imports of essential consumer goods such as clothing and cookware, agricultural tools and fertilizers, as well as vehicles, fuel, machinery and parts for industry and construction, all absorb scarce foreign exchange. At issue is the question of how imports should be reduced and whether the types of goods imported should be regulated, and by whom.

The IMF and the World Bank advocate reductions of imports in order to reduce the trade deficits of Caribbean and other countries of the South. The most effective way to do this, in the adjustors' view, is by means of macro-economic policy mechanisms such as currency devaluation. (If a country's unit of money is made less valuable in relation to the US dollar, spending on imports will drop, since the Trinidad dollar, for example, will buy a smaller amount of imports than it did before it was devalued.) Devaluation lessens the purchasing power not only of individual consumers but also of Caribbean governments and businesses. Some manufacturing plants producing for local markets have been forced to shut down, hurt by the higher, post-devaluation costs of imported parts and materials or because their products cannot compete with cheaper imports.

What is to be imported, say World Bank economists, should be determined by the market, and not by governments or regional organizations. Caribbean governments 'should be holding open auctions of foreign exchange', said the Bank's senior economist for Jamaica.[6] Under such a system, those who can muster the most cash can import what they choose, be it spare parts for factories or luxury goods for the upper crust. Those citizens with the lowest incomes and, thus, the least purchasing power — the poor majority of farmers and workers and the unemployed — must increasingly do without. Such an approach leaves Caribbean workers, consumers and even governments with little or no say in how their countries' resources will be used and which sectors of the economy will be developed.

Some Caribbean development analysts advocate a regionally planned method of deciding what should or should not be imported and how scarce foreign exchange should be spent. They argue that unless Caribbean industries meet more of the needs of the region, Caribbean nations will have to continue to sell cheap and buy dear, and will remain perpetually vulnerable to economic shocks when the costs of imported goods they depend upon exceed their incomes. Some maintain that Caribbean manufacturing and service industries must be developed to produce higher quality and more complex goods, both for regional needs and for export, with more value added to their products by Caribbean materials, machinery, labor and know-how.[7]

Enhancing self-reliance and productive capacity in Caribbean industry, as in agriculture, will require economic policies to support fledgling industries and to insulate Caribbean markets from international competition. Such policies would probably include limiting imports by quotas or tariffs and providing services and resources to those enterprises and economic sectors most essential to increased regional self-reliance. Caribbean scholars such as Clive Y. Thomas have identified two main categories of industry that should have first priority: enterprises that produce goods to meet the basic needs of the people of the Caribbean for food, clothing and shelter; and industries that provide materials and supplies needed to produce those basic goods, such as tools and fertilizer for farming and construction materials for housing.

To the extent to which such industries make use of indigenous materials and local skills, their prospects for economic success and their stimulating effect on other sectors of the economy will be enhanced. In addition, if these priority industries could produce goods in sufficient quantity and of adequate quality for export, the impact on the region's economy would be that much more positive. Earnings from the export of well-made furniture, ready-to-eat chocolate and smelted aluminum would be greater than those now earned from exports of timber, cocoa beans and bauxite (aluminum ore).

Protection of Caribbean food markets and farming
But policies to insulate Caribbean farming and agro-industries from the global market, even temporarily, are considered by advocates of structural adjustment to be an unacceptable form of protectionism. In their view, protectionism rewards inefficiency and smacks of what USAID has called

'statism' or 'socialism'. According to Errol Berkeley, a Chief Project Officer at the Caribbean Development Bank:

> Since most of our agro-processing is still in the infant stage, we need to give some closely monitored economic protection to local agro-industries. Our governments shy away from giving protections to our industries because to do so might generate an adverse reaction from other countries, such as retaliation against our exports, or loss of credit, or being labeled 'socialist.'[8]

Adding to the barriers against more self-reliant food systems are public preferences generated by colonialism for many higher-status, imported, brand-name foods. These tastes are reinforced today by advertising, especially on satellite television. Because of this, says Berkeley, 'We need to educate and sensitize people to the importance of using local products.'

The policy obstacles to greater Caribbean food security are summarized by Vincentian agronomist Glenroy Browne:

> There is vast information on ways to utilize local products and by-products, including on how to develop instant, convenience foods from crops such as yams, sweet potatoes, and cassava, and on alternative uses of what are now waste products of agriculture. A lot of the research and testing has been done, but no funds are available for commercialization. It takes a patient and slow process to develop new commodities and to convince people to use them. Even US brand names took many years to become well known.[9]

Little assistance is available to promote Caribbean consumption of Caribbean foods, Browne says. 'To put money and resources into commercializing our own products is considered "subsidizing", and the thrust of development policy today is *not* to subsidize'.[10]

An irony not lost on Caribbean observers is that the types of policies to support indigenous agriculture and industry that are discouraged or forbidden to Caribbean governments by the terms of foreign assistance and structural adjustment conditionalities are the very policies which the United States, Europe and Japan have been using effectively to protect their own markets and promote their own exports. Had Northern country governments not employed such policies — import quotas, tariff barriers, reciprocal trade agreements, agricultural subsidies, price supports, use of public resources, investment insurance and other government services — to strengthen their own economies and foreign trade, Caribbean and other Southern countries would not be as dependent upon them as they are today.

The myth of the free market

The theory of market-driven development holds that economic activities that require government support or protection are, by definition, inefficient. Structural adjustment proponents content that the free market, unhindered by political intervention, should be allowed to weed out such inefficient enterprises, so that each country will specialize in the type of economic activity at which it is best. According to a former World Bank Caribbean program officer, 'It's just not economically viable for Caribbean countries to attempt to produce tires or shoes. . . . They certainly should not be producing iron and steel.'[11]

Such a policy would base the development strategies of most Caribbean and other nations of the South on their supposed comparative economic advantages, mainly their abundance of unemployed workers and unprocessed minerals and crops. The Caribbean's role in the global economy, if determined mainly by market forces as the World Bank recommends, would remain primarily that of a source of cheap, unskilled labor, unremunerative and environmentally devastating agro-export industries, and undervalued, soon-to-be-exhausted supplies of metal ores, lumber and oil. Nilsa Medina of the League of Puerto Rican cooperatives told visiting members of the US Congress: 'We have totally free trade with the United States, and one result is that we import 80 per cent of what we consume. That is one of the greatest barriers to rural and national development in Puerto Rico.'[12]

The free market development model ignores the fact that the current global economic hierarchy, with the nations of the North at the top, has been shaped by political and military actions. It is no more the result of market forces or of some natural law of economic development than of cultural or ethnic superiority. Governments of the colonial powers promoted their own industries while suppressing the traditional industries and exploiting the resources of the South. Moreover, the present international pecking order is maintained by a system of double standards; the industrial powers of the North continue to subsidize and protect their own agriculture and industries, while Asian, African and Latin American countries are pressured not to protect or to subsidize theirs.

This double standard stifles the growth of Southern economies and widens the gap between poor and wealthy nations. But most governments in the South are under constant pressure to come up with cash as quickly as possible to pay their foreign debts, also a product of unequal political relations and military power, and to avert a cut-off of credit for imports of essential goods. This contributes to a crisis-response mode, in which short-term priorities, mainly the meeting of structural adjustment criteria in order to refinance debts and continue imports, take precedence over long-range planning for sustainable development.

Learning from experience
The reluctance of many Caribbean governments in the 1980s to protect and coordinate their industries stems in part from the perception that similar efforts in the recent past have failed. A number of Caribbean countries, including Trinidad and Tobago, Jamaica and Guyana, tried to implement import substitution policies in the 1960s and 1970s by producing goods locally that would otherwise be imported. For the most part, these policies did not meet expectations. In many cases, import substitution industries cost more than the

value of the goods they produced. Among the reasons were that these industries relied heavily on imported raw materials, machinery and management systems, so that only a small part of the process of producing formerly imported goods, for example, cars assembled in Trinidad, took place in the Caribbean. Foreign corporations, which in many cases supplied the technology and inputs and controlled licenses and patents, often got most of the proceeds.[13]

The choice of which goods would be produced was based largely on the list of goods already imported and sold to those who could afford foreign products. These were not necessarily the goods most needed by the majority of the population or, most important, as inputs for other local or regional industries. Rather, they were largely the sorts of goods needed to reproduce structures of production and consumption similar to those of Europe or the United States. This industrialization by imitation proved impossible to sustain. With these lessons in mind, some advocates of strengthened Caribbean self-reliance call for a renewed but revised effort at import substitution, in which decisions about which products should be produced would be based upon:

- the basic needs of Caribbean people;
- the inputs, skills and services needed to maximize backward and forward linkages with other economic sectors, provide employment, stimulate productive activity and foster more broad-based and sustainable growth;
- the availability of inputs, such as energy sources and minerals, fibers and other raw materials, which can be produced locally or obtained through equitable trade or barter, especially with other nations in the greater Caribbean region;
- the potential of the goods to be traded within the region; and
- the potential of the goods to be sold at good prices outside the region.[14]

NGOs throughout the Caribbean are developing small-scale industries that meet these criteria, including furniture-making, metal-working, printing, manufacture of school uniforms and machine-knitted clothing, concrete block-making, housing construction and a wide range of handicraft production. Many of these projects have been designed to provide skills training and employment for unemployed women and young people, and some have been quite successful. But most face hurdles of scarce credit and supplies, high duties and taxes, lack of marketing channels, competition from imported goods advertised on radio and television, and the refusal of some governments to license cooperative enterprises.

In the market-driven development model, the alleviation of poverty is, at best, a distant, hoped-for by-product of the prosperity which is expected to trickle down from export earnings, foreign investment and tourism. In contrast, the approach outlined here aims to foster development by addressing directly the wide gap between what the Caribbean produces and what it consumes, which is the fundamental basis of its continuing poverty and economic vulnerability.

Access to credit

Enterprises specifically geared to increasing regional food production and marketing, whether private, public or cooperative, also need start-up capital, particularly in view of the lack of marketing infrastructure. However, commercial banks prefer to lend money to established, large-scale import and export companies, to those with land holdings and other forms of collateral, and to members of the élite with whom they have family or political ties. Business people and well-paid public servants can obtain loans to buy imported cars or other goods which drain the country's foreign exchange without contributing to its production. But loans to small-scale farmers and cooperatives to buy land or transport their crops, or for regional produce marketing, are commonly considered too risky by the banks.

To leave decisions about credit and investment entirely to private enterprise is to reinforce existing patterns of import dependency and extremely unequal distribution of land and wealth. USAID credit and investment projects which favor foreign and large-scale export enterprises, such as HIAMP, have the same effect. Alan Williams of the Association for Caribbean Transformation (ACT) observes that:

> As much as international capital can come in and invest in the Caribbean, local capital can also move out and be consumed or invested in other parts of the world. So the decision of the private sector is not a nationalist one of serving and building one's country. It is simply where, in the short-term interest of the owners of capital, they can best utilize their surplus value to fulfill their *personal* ambitions.[15]

There are many possible alternatives, some of which are already functioning. Governments or regional bodies can establish loan funds specifically geared to financing the production and marketing of foods and other local products within the Caribbean. ACT has proposed that a portion of foreign aid be set aside for the informal sector. Development initiatives should specify that a fixed percentage of the resources be channeled through and used directly by institutions other than the official ones. Some loan funds have been established to funnel credit to small-scale farmers, fishermen or artisans. But in practice, these funds generally require ownership of land or some other form of collateral, which is precisely what the marginal producers do not have and why they need the credit so badly.

Women in particular face discrimination. Although they are responsible for a large proportion of agricultural labor and often handle farm as well as household finances, they typically lack title to the land they farm. Said a woman farmer in Dominica, 'I can't walk into the bank with my five healthy children and tell the credit man, "Here! This is where my profits from 20 years of food and banana farming have gone. Now give me a loan." '[16] Creative solutions to such problems have been tried in other parts of the world. One method has been offering credit to groups of producers, small-scale traders and women's credit cooperatives. Since each member of the group stands to lose if another member does not or cannot repay a loan, mutual aid and peer group pressure generally result in low default rates.

In addition, more resources could be channeled to credit unions, which accumulate substantial funds and are often the only way small farmers can obtain loans. NGOs, cooperatives and producers' associations have established revolving loan funds to benefit their members. Such means of providing credit are a logical extension of the tradition of saving and careful spending by Caribbean farmers and workers. This tradition is still evident in the myriad of small, informal saving groups, whose members contribute equal amounts weekly or monthly and withdraw larger amounts when their turn comes or when the need arises.

A New Type of Tourism

Tourism has become the leading source of foreign exchange for many Caribbean countries but, unless the industry's current structure is radically altered, it will continue to be of limited economic benefit to Caribbean economies and damaging to Caribbean societies. Visitors to the Caribbean today are transported into a fantasy world, much of it constructed and furnished with imported materials and according to foreign design. The travel services, ships, planes and hotels used by tourists to the region are, for the most part, owned by Northern-based companies. A large proportion of the food visitors eat is imported.

When the tourist industry does consume Caribbean resources, it often does so at the expense of Caribbean people and their environment: hotels and golf courses have displaced farms and homes from fertile and accessible land, especially in small Caribbean countries where flat areas are rare; vacation villas frequently command the finest views and exclude local residents from the best beaches; luxury yachts claim the safest mooring places from local fishing boats. Uncontrolled tourism development speeds the industry's own demise by destroying the natural beauty exalted in tourism brochures. In St Lucia, for example, construction of a tourism complex by Iranian developers threatens flora and fauna, including rare turtles, in the region of the island's best-known natural attraction, Two Pitons. Throughout the Caribbean, speculation, spurred in part by tourism and retirement home development, has caused land prices in many areas to soar beyond the reach of all except wealthy foreigners and the Caribbean upper crust. Along with the expansion of tourism has come increased traffic in hard drugs, gambling and prostitution.

Most tourists experience local culture only in the form of night club shows and interactions with waiters, maids, tour guides, vendors and beggars. The packaged entertainment presented as Caribbean is frequently a product of Northern sensibility, a stereotyped and distorted vision fashioned to reflect what tourists supposedly want or expect to see. Government campaigns exhort Caribbean citizens to be friendly and smile for the tourists. Many manage to do so while retaining their dignity and pride in their work; but a tourist industry based upon exploitation, servility and hypocrisy is bound to foster hostility among those required to serve and smile for poverty-level wages.

The Caribbean cannot afford to reject tourism as one of its economic options. Moreover, the intermingling of people from different cultures and climes is valuable and essential to development globally. In the long run, however, the only sound basis for genuine hospitality and people-to-people exchange is the elimination of Caribbean poverty and the creation of greater equity between North and South and within the Caribbean itself.

In the meantime, and as a contribution to the establishment of equity, the Caribbean tourism industry could be transformed in the direction of greater self-reliance. As in the cases of agriculture and manufacturing, the keys to such a transformation include linkages among various sectors of the local and regional economy, more value-added in the Caribbean, and greater local ownership and control. Among the most obvious possibilities are the use of local materials and skills in the construction and furnishing of tourism facilities and the use of locally produced and processed food and beverages. Some NGOs, such as the Grenada Handicraft Cooperative, have already demonstrated the feasibility of producing furnishings for tourist facilities. Equally important are the skills and services involved in tourism planning and management: architecture, construction and artisanry; food brokering, processing and gastronomy; entertainment and the arts. The greater the proportion of Caribbean inputs, skills and control, the greater are the potential benefits to the region.

Caribbean analysts also urge diversifying the region's tourism to include not just sun, sand and escape from reality, but also 'eco-tourism' and 'heritage tourism'. The industry as now structured offers limited opportunities for visitors to be exposed to and learn about the region's rich but vulnerable ecology, its history, the daily life and struggles of its people, and culture as Caribbeans experience it. Some coalitions of Caribbean and Northern NGOs sponsor study tours and exchanges between Caribbean farmers, workers, students and artists and their counterparts from Europe and North America. There is also potential for South–South tourism and for tourism less oriented than at present to the upscale end of the market.

As is true with regard to the export of food products and factory goods, a more diversified tourism can be economically successful and socially valuable if it is built upon a base of greater local self-reliance and regional coordination. The higher the level of environmental awareness and sustainability in the Caribbean, the better are the prospects for ecologically attractive and sensitive tourism. The sharing of culture with visitors will be possible and positive only to the extent that the region's varied cultural heritage is preserved, revived and valued in the lives of Caribbean people.

Reversing the Brain Drain

The export-oriented, market-driven development strategy is draining the

Caribbean of another vital resource: knowledge. Most Caribbean countries have relatively high levels of literacy and significant numbers of university graduates and skilled professionals in comparison to other regions of the South. But education systems in the Caribbean are suffering from economic crisis, austerity policies and neglect.

Dilapidated buildings, teachers' salaries that barely support an individual, reduction of government scholarships and declining academic standards are among the effects. In addition, the development strategy based on assembly industries and unprocessed exports requires relatively few highly skilled employees. Many of the few professional positions that do exist are filled by foreign nationals and consultants hired by foreign investors and aid agencies. In the words of a Grenadian teacher: 'In the type of development that's being fostered now, the managers are imported and all we are supposed to do is the menial work.'[17]

As a result, many Caribbean scientists, technicians, managers and other professionals must work abroad, depriving the region of badly needed skills. At a time of social crisis, when the skills of nurses are especially needed, US hospitals use aggressive advertising to recruit nursing staff trained at the expense of Caribbean governments. In the context of deteriorating Caribbean health services, the promises of better pay and working conditions are hard to resist.

Under a development plan for greater Caribbean self-reliance, the skills of educated and of experienced Caribbean citizens would be needed in the region. The training of educators and health workers would be a vital component of such a strategy, rather than merely a drain on government resources, as such training tends to be viewed by structural adjustment planners and some Caribbean governments today. The skills of farmers, fishers, household workers and practitioners of traditional healing arts would be a rich source of knowledge to be tapped and developed in conjunction with more modern information and technology, rather than a backward, irrelevant vestige of the past to be uprooted and discarded.

A division of labor in which different territories take responsibility for different education programs, types of technology development and health specializations could make such schemes more effective and efficient. Services and technologies developed in the Caribbean are in themselves a potentially valuable exportable resource so long as they remain under Caribbean ownership and control. This is an area in which the Caribbean, by virtue of its cultural and linguistic diversity and its position as an international crossroads, has a potentially great advantage. Among the many areas in which Caribbeans already have some expertise are banking, insurance and reinsurance, food brokering, research in tropical agriculture and aquaculture, art, music and design, the academic disciplines, social services, and non-traditional methodologies for popular and adult education and literacy training.

Foreign expertise is another form of expensive import on which the Caribbean cannot afford to depend, particularly when the specialized knowledge of outsiders is so often inapplicable to regional conditions. But the market-driven development model, especially export-oriented industrialization, relies upon imported, prepackaged knowledge. At the same time, it discourages Caribbean states from investing in Caribbean human resource development, which could ultimately reduce the region's dependency and add value to its industries.

Notes

1. Statement to US visitors, March 1988, Kingstown, St Vincent and the Grenadines.

2. Author interview, April 1989.

3. Author interview, October 1990.

4. Author interview, February 1988.

5. Author interview, March 1988.

6. Roger Robinson, June 1988.

7. In *The Poor and the Powerless* (Latin America Bureau/Monthly Review Press, New York and London, 1988), Guyanese economist Clive Thomas proposes a set of criteria for development-enhancing trade and industrialization for the Caribbean. An alternative economic and social policy for Jamaica, developed through a nationwide consultative process during 1977, was published as *Pathways to Progress, the People's Plan for Socialist Transformation* ('by the Jamaican People with the assistance of George Beckford, Norman Girvan, Louis Lindsay and Michael Witter', Maroon Publishing House, Morant Bay, Jamaica, 1985). In 1989, economist Dennis Pantin put forward 'an alternative path to the IMF/World Bank road' for Trinidad and Tobago in *Into the Valley of Debt* (Ferguson, Port-of-Spain, Trinidad and Tobago).

8. Author interview, December 1987.

9. Author interview, March 1988.

10. Ibid.

11. Author interview, June 1988.

12. Statement to US Congressional delegation, November 1989, Montego Bay, Jamaica.

13. Clive Y. Thomas, *The Poor and the Powerless*, Latin America Bureau/Monthly Review Press, New York and London, 1988.

14. Ibid.

15. Excerpt from correspondence, July 1990.

16. Reported by investigators in the Women in Caribbean Agriculture project of the Caribbean Association for Feminist Research and Action (CAFRA), Tunapuna, Trinidad and Tobago, 1990.

17. Michael 'Senator' Mitchell, interview by the author of members of the Grenada Popular Theatre Organization, December 1987.

13. Toward One Caribbean

Only structural transformation of economies can rescue peoples from old and new debt and continuing servitude. . . . The challenge? To turn the geographic, historical, and cultural commonalities of the region to economic and political advantage and unity. No country can ignore the current of globalization now sweeping the world. The countries of our region must negotiate together and firmly and we need to push our governments to do this, since they are failing to do so. Regional integration is the only way to insert ourselves into global trends from a position of independence and with the power to resist domination.

Joan Ross-Frankson and Horace Levy, development activists from Jamaica

The road to Caribbean unity has never been smooth, as the history of CARICOM and its predecessors shows, but unity is no less essential for that. Among the roadblocks to unity today are bilateral aid with strings attached and structural adjustment programs that pit nation against nation and undermine the sovereignty of Caribbean states.

Genuine economic and political sovereignty would enable governments and NGOs to explore a wider range of development options. In such a context, Caribbean states could pursue greater regional economic cooperation and integration. More unified regional policies and organizations could strengthen the ability of Caribbean territories to break free of today's impoverishing patterns of trade and the stranglehold of foreign debt.

Strengthened regional cooperation could enhance the Caribbean's self-reliance and productive capacity. Exchanges of skills and technology, and a division of labor among Caribbean states in the production of various commodities and specialized services, could increase economic efficiency and the quality, range and value of what the region produces, both for local consumption and for export. Perhaps most important, genuine Caribbean sovereignty could democratize the development process through broader and more direct participation by Caribbean citizens and popular organizations.

Some Caribbean countries have sought to overcome the disadvantages of size and geography by coordinating their trade and economic development policies. In the English-speaking Caribbean, efforts at political federation have failed thus far. The continuing ties of many Caribbean nations and ruling élites to their former colonial masters, and the go-it-alone attitudes of some Caribbean governments, have made it easier for multinational agencies and foreign governments to succeed in their divide-and-rule approach.

However, CARICOM, established in 1973, has adopted measures to increase trade and enhance development within the sub-region by eliminating tariff barriers and pooling information and expertise. CARICOM countries have agreed upon a planned economic division of labor that encourages specialization in particular crops and industries by different Caribbean territories in order to maximize the size of the regional market for each

CARICOM country's exports and to reduce destructive forms of competition between member states. But these and other Caribbean efforts at regional coordination are often treated with disdain by multilateral agencies and foreign governments, particularly when Caribbean goals do not reflect the lenders' priorities. The CARICOM Regional Food and Nutrition Strategy issued in 1983, a comprehensive plan aimed at reducing the region's dependence on imported food, increasing commodity exports and reducing malnutrition, is a prime example. After years of mostly fruitless efforts by CARICOM officials, agriculture ministers and others to obtain support for the plan, it became obvious that foreign lenders preferred to provide grants and loans for particular projects on a country-by-country basis.

Structural adjustment policies increase competition and undermine cooperation within the Caribbean region. By the late 1980s, IMF-required currency devaluations pressed by the multilateral agencies on Jamaica, the Dominican Republic, Guyana, and Trinidad and Tobago were pushing other Caribbean nations to follow suit, risking acceleration of the downward spiral of competition to offer the region's cheapest labor and lowest export commodity prices.

Greater bilateral dependency on the United States fostered by the CBI has further undermined regional efforts at economic coordination and development cooperation. CARICOM Director for Trade and Agriculture, Hayden Blades, told US legislators in 1988:

> The process of regional integration was highjacked by the United States by means of the CBI. All the pressure from the US has been for closer bilateral ties, and this has undermined regional integration plans. . . . Adding to this has been the bypassing of Caribbean regional institutions by USAID.[1]

Economically sustainable development will require the expansion and democratization of existing Caribbean regional institutions such as the OECS, the CDB and CARICOM. Especially important is the development of genuinely representative and inclusive pan-Caribbean organizations that surmount language and political barriers. Government-associated structures need to be complemented by non-government networks and structures. Among the existing non-government regional structures that could be strengthened are the Institute for Social and Economic Research (ISER), based in the University of the West Indies and with links to the Coordinadora Regional de Investigaciones Economicas y Sociales (CRIES), with offices in Panama and Nicaragua; the Barbados-based WAND; CAFRA; the Caribbean Conference of Churches; ACE; the Caribbean Network for Integrated Rural Development (CNIRD); CARIPEDA; the Puerto Rico-based Projecto Caribeno de Justicia y Paz (PCJP); and the Windward Islands Farmers' Association (WINFA).

Among the means proposed by Caribbean NGOs to foster greater regional integration are:

- *increased food production and marketing for regional trade;*

- *regional planning and coordination of agricultural development and diversification;*

- *greater Caribbean control of regional and external trade;* and

- *ending the quarantine of Cuba.*

Increased Food Production and Marketing for Regional Trade

Caribbean NGOs and grassroots organizations are working in a wide variety of ways to foster food production for regional trade. In Trinidad and Dominica, ACT compiles information for farmers about the prices, credit sources and marketing prospects for root crops, vegetables and other produce. ACT's director, Alan Williams, explains:

> ACT believes that in helping small farmers and other producers to produce and successfully market their produce, the issue is one of sustainability. But the periphery is never sustainable. . . . Therefore, we not only assist farmers who are currently on the periphery, but also plan out strategies so that they can move into the mainstream. One important part of any strategy of changing one's position in the economic sphere is to have information and to utilize information.[2]

Farmers' organizations such as the National Farmers Union in St Vincent, the Dominica Farmers Union, the Grenada Productive Farmers Union, the Staff Cooperative in St Lucia, and WINFA have helped farmers to organize. They provide their members with information on the banana industry and on ways to diversify their crops and increase their harvests, as well as services such as vegetable seeds sold at low cost and low-interest loans. The Dominica Hucksters Association (DHA) has received support from Northern NGOs. But changes in policy and attitudes are needed even more than aid to recognize and build upon the valuable contributions of the hucksters. Peggy Antrobus of WAND told a US Congressional delegation in Jamaica: 'The ones most in need of training are those that women hucksters have to deal with: the customs officials, immigration people, stevedores, transport workers and government officials.'[3]

Organizations of small-scale traders, such as the DHA, are working to systematize and expand the lively, informal inter-island trade in food and consumer goods. By providing training in packaging and accounting skills, information on visa and tariff regulations, and small loans, the DHA improves produce quality and helps its more than 400 members get better prices for what they sell. It draws attention to the difficulties faced by the hucksters, including dangerous, over-loaded boats, the lack of navigational equipment and storage facilities, inadequate sources of credit and of marketing information, and the need for a regional organization of hucksters. St Vincent now has a huckster's organization; another is being formed in Grenada.

The CARICOM-sponsored CFC already exports about US$2 million worth of farm produce, much of it grown by small-scale farmers from seven English-speaking Eastern Caribbean countries, mainly to Europe and Canada but also to Caribbean markets. This is done through the joint private/public sector enterprise CATCO. CFC/CATCO's goal is to be self-sustaining, with no need for foreign aid. But with no transport facilities of its own, it must depend for now on airplanes and on Geest corporation boats to carry produce to Europe. Given the very high cost of this type of transport, CATCO can cover its costs only if it pays relatively low prices to local farmers. This underscores the futility of dependence on extra-regional unprocessed agricultural exports as a means of earning foreign exchange and capital for development.

Other NGOs working on regional food marketing include the Interamerican Institute for Cooperative Agriculture (IICA) and a coalition effort by ACT and Development Alternatives (DAI) in Dominica. ACT and DAI are seeking to establish the Kanoua project to transport food crops within the region in refrigerated containers. But most small-scale Caribbean marketing enterprises lack facilities to get Caribbean staple foods from farms to ports and from one country to another. There are few buildings where produce can be graded, washed, packed and stored until shipment, and almost no refrigerated boats to carry it. By the time the small wooden schooners operated by the hucksters reach Trinidad from St Vincent or Grenada, much of their cargo is spoiled. Under these conditions, as Neville Duncan points out, 'It's easier for store owners and traders and hotels to buy goods from Miami than from within the region.'[4]

For small and medium-scale Caribbean farmers and traders to increase substantially their capacity to meet regional food demands, they need more access to credit, better organization, and facilities for collecting, packaging, storing, transporting, advertising and distribution. The lack of this type of intraregional marketing infrastructure further increases the region's external dependency. But, as we have seen, assistance for intraregional food trade is a low priority for most aid and lending agencies. Programs to promote public, cooperative or private investment in production of Caribbean food for Caribbean needs contradict AID's policy of deregulation and the export-oriented thrust of structural adjustment. In fact, by requiring governments to spend their tax and aid revenues on infrastructure to assist foreign agribusiness and shipping companies, these policies have the effect of shifting resources away from smaller-scale Caribbean producers and traders. The USAID SEA project did provide credit, via National Development Foundations, which in some countries was accessible to a number of small-scale farmers but in amounts too small and for too short a time to have a significant impact.

Regional Planning and Coordination of Agricultural Development and Diversification

The danger of dependence on one or two crops is widely recognized. Dividing the endorsers of diversification are some controversial issues. Should more varied crops be produced mainly for exports to the North, or primarily for local and regional needs? Should regional bodies and governments play a strong role in the planning, production and marketing of more varied crops, or should the major decisions be left to private investors? Should Caribbean governments and regional institutions adopt policies to protect Caribbean farming and agro-industries by insulating them from the global market?

Thoughtful Caribbean agriculturalists point out that, while the region can grow a greater variety of crops, its geography and limited land will continue to put unprocessed Caribbean export crops at a disadvantage in world markets. 'Almost anything we grow for export can be grown and transported more cheaply from West Africa or Central and South American countries,' comments Andreas Wickham, a planner in the Ministry of Agriculture in St Vincent and the Grenadines.[5] Moreover, in the name of diversification, international agencies and consultants are encouraging many indebted Third World countries to grow the same non-traditional export crops. That this will contribute to decreased world prices and insecure foreign markets for the new crops is obvious. However, foreign consultants are usually engaged to make recommendations for one country at a time. Government planners, in the Caribbean as in Northern countries, typically are asked to provide short-term solutions to meet annual fiscal goals or to improve appearances for the governing party. As a result, the longer-term consequences of competition among diversified exports are often not taken into account.

Many Caribbean people share the view that the region's export markets and agro-industries should be developed as an outgrowth of agricultural production and processing for local and regional markets. 'Any plan to develop exports has to include not just production, but also plans for processing, packaging, the use of by-products, and marketing,' says Neville Graham of ACT. According to Wallace Joefied-Napier, senior economist for Grenada at the CDB:

> At present we in the Caribbean don't process and export our agricultural products *after* we have fed ourselves and have produced a surplus. That's what the US did in developing its agriculture and industry, and that's what we have to do.[6]

Under pressure to open their economies to foreign investors and to cope with rising unemployment, individual Caribbean states have allowed companies to set up export operations with virtually no linkages to other economic sectors and often in competition with local industries. In the absence of effective regional planning, existing agro-industries are also weakened by competition with each other for a relatively small regional market. The ability of regional institutions, particularly CARICOM, to build a stronger regional economy has been reduced as some member nations have opted to go it alone in their struggles to meet debt payments and carry out structural adjustment directives. For example, according to Theo Shallow of St Vincent's Central Planning Division, 'So many flour mills have been opened, all privately owned, even though according to CARICOM, responsibility for different industries is supposed to be distributed among different countries.'[7]

Because of these trends, many Caribbean observers have concluded that the region needs more, not less, direction of economic policies by Caribbean governments and regional bodies:

> Our priorities have to be developing agro-industries, so that more value is added to our exports, and marketing, to generate demand in our *own* economies. If we look at our regional food import bill, it's clear that we need to do this, and that we need a total, planned programmatic approach

says John Elwin, an agricultural specialist at the CDB.[8]

Economic planning does not necessarily mean that governments should replace the private sector. According to Oscar Allen, 'We need ways to guide the employment of land, capital and resources. We should have a planned program for the state sector, the private sector and the cooperative sector.' Nor does it mean that foreign investment is entirely unwelcome: 'We do need investment, preferably joint ventures, and possibly with US businesses. But if we're going to benefit, we have to tackle the problem of feeding ourselves at the same time,' says Neville Graham of ACT.[9]

Greater Caribbean Control of Regional and External Trade

As an aspect of planned regional development, increased Caribbean control, and share in the benefits of trade could strengthen Caribbean food production and agro-processing industries. As the example of Geest Industries illustrates, profits from exporting Caribbean crops mainly accrue to Northern-based shipping companies. Until Caribbean countries acquire a greater share of these earnings, foreign trade will remain a losing proposition for most Caribbean producers.

Reliance on high-cost shippers for export not only of bananas but also of non-traditional crops leaves Caribbean farmers vulnerable to the sudden loss of markets if the company finds a more profitable use for its ships and warehouses. According to Dr Thomas Henderson:

> As long as you're dependent on companies like Geest, you can't have control. You may develop a program for new exports, but if your thing competes with what Geest wants, Geest can say they don't have space on their boat, and that's the end of your program.[10]

AID strategy for Caribbean export diversification, as demonstrated in HIAMP and the Windward Island Tropical Produce project, would repeat the pattern of dependence on foreign shipping companies. AID proposals assume that US companies with established marketing channels and transport facilities, such as Hershey's chocolate company, will purchase, process and distribute cocoa and other products. If such companies do find it profitable to buy Caribbean agricultural exports, it will be they, not Caribbean farmers, who will reap the greatest benefits from any funds made available through AID. If at any point such companies decide that Caribbean crop exports are not their most profitable option, for example, if high-quality cocoa can be obtained more cheaply from West Africa, Caribbean farmers will again be left in the lurch.

USAID could support regional institutions in their efforts to play a stronger role in planning a transition to agricultural diversification and greater food security, for example, by means of the CARICOM Food and Nutrition Strategy. But this would be the opposite of AID's current policy, which insists that decisions about production, lending and investment must be left to the private sector. Even within the private sector, AID is missing important opportunities for assistance. For example, small-scale private traders operating in the so-called informal economy are helping to keep Caribbean economies from collapse. The majority of non-formal traders in the Caribbean are women, including those who share or barter produce among neighbors or carry food from the countryside to sell in towns. Especially important is the role of the hucksters or higglers who transport and sell produce from rural areas and food and manufactured items from abroad. Women hucksters, even many who are illiterate, have developed sophisticated business skills, such as the ability to calculate exchange rates, duties, shipping costs, prices and profits with great speed and accuracy. In spite of their crucial economic role, they are more often harassed and taxed than aided, and are ignored by most official sources of foreign assistance.

The potential for regional prosperity

Caribbean advocates of more self-reliant development do not propose economic isolation nor regression to a more primitive type of economy in which nothing is bought or consumed which is not produced locally. On the contrary, it will require a sophisticated combination of traditional knowledge with new information and technologies designed to make the most of the Caribbean climate, resources, skills and social structures.

This development will require investment in research and experimentation, infrastructure, education and training. Such investment will not be profitable in the short term. Consequently, it is not the sort of investment that individual entrepreneurs, foreign or Caribbean, are likely to make. Nor does the short life-span of national governments encourage the long-range planning and investment necessary for greater self-reliance. Furthermore, no individual Caribbean country has the material or human resources to pursue this approach alone.

The prospects for Caribbean-determined development depend upon regional coordination. The Caribbean as a whole has substantial resources which, if combined and developed in an integrated fashion, could be the basis for building more modern and efficient industries, agriculture and services. While the populations of many Caribbean countries are too small to absorb the products of, for example, a fruit and vegetable processing plant, the 35 million people of the Caribbean region could constitute a significant market. The potential market in the greater Caribbean, including Central America and nearby regions of South America, is much larger.

To tap such markets and establish such industries will require planning by Caribbean governments and regional institutions. It will necessitate a division of labor and allocation of responsibilities among Caribbean states similar to that already proposed and partially implemented by CARICOM. It will also entail some degree of protection for local and regional markets, at least in the short and medium term.

The Caribbean region as a whole also has considerable mineral and energy resources that could be combined to produce both inputs for Caribbean industries and also more valuable export commodities. For example, Jamaica, Guyana and Surinam have significant amounts of bauxite that can be refined to make alumina and smelted to produce aluminum. Guyana also has substantial deposits of silica and bauxite. Some countries in the region have sources of energy needed for refining and smelting, especially Trinidad, which has oil and natural gas, and Guyana, where large rivers are a potential source of hydroelectric power.

Attempts were made in the 1970s to link these resources in order to establish smelters to produce aluminum in Jamaica and Guyana. The effort failed because the producing countries could get relatively high prices outside the Caribbean at that time for their bauxite, and Trinidad and Tobago could earn more in the short term by using its petroleum resources to produce ammonia and fertilizer. The multinational aluminum companies, which now control the use of Caribbean bauxite, find it more profitable to use refining sites and sources of energy outside the Caribbean in the production of aluminum. Today, the need for indebted and impoverished Caribbean countries to produce more valuable commodities is greater than ever, but the lack of genuine sovereignty of Caribbean states rules out serious investigation of these and other options.

The pressures to meet debt payment schedules, to match IMF economic targets and to maintain credit ratings in order to continue imports foster short-term planning and penny-wise, pound-foolish policies on the part of indebted country governments. Structural adjustment programs establish externally imposed economic priorities, allow little scope for planning and discourage regional coordination. (Only in the Eastern Caribbean have the World Bank and the EEC encouraged the political unification of small states, both because it would be more efficient for the multilateral agencies to deal with the OECS states as a group than individually and because it would facilitate the use of structural adjustment policy tools, especially currency devaluation, in the Eastern Caribbean.)

US government programs have also undermined economic cooperation and planning for greater self-reliance in the Caribbean. The CBI left Caribbean countries worse off than before in terms of their balance of trade with the US, but by creating *expectations* of benefits for those countries which followed US guidelines, the CBI encouraged Caribbean states to look to the United States rather than to each other. It required favored treatment of US businesses in CBI countries without providing significant numbers of jobs or transfers of technology. It threatened loss of CBI eligibility to any country which adopted policies not satisfactory to the United States. 'We in the Caribbean have to take some of the blame ourselves,' says Arnhim Eustace who headed an agricultural diversification project at the CDB. But, he adds:

> US aid and trade policies are a large part of the reason for CARICOM's problems. Their bilateral approach reinforces differences among the members. When countries all have fiscal deficits, and all are financed by borrowing, a powerful bilateral agency can be a very divisive and destructive force for regional integration.[11]

Similar conditions attached to USAID project grants also foster bilateral ties to the United States at the expense of regional economic integration. Many AID grants require recipient countries to purchase dollar amounts of US goods equivalent to the grant totals. These clauses prevent the recipients from seeking the most appropriate and least expensive sources of needed goods, and leave them dependent on US sources of spare parts. Such policies discourage planning for production and trade, undermine the ability of Caribbean countries to diversify the outlets for their goods and sources for their imports, and increase their vulnerability to politically motivated economic pressure. Patrick Thompson, head of the USAID-backed Caribbean Association for Industry and Commerce (CAIC) notes that: 'We haven't been able to get USAID to fund regional economic projects on any substantial scale. This gives the United States greater leverage over our governments, especially since we lack a regional body such as Europe's.'[12] The main obstacle to sound intra-regional development is the strategic interest of the United States,' says professor Neville Duncan.

Ending the Quarantine of Cuba

US policy deprives Caribbean nations of the opportunity to trade goods and services with the region's most populous, industrialized and economically developed independent country, Cuba. Caribbean nations, such as Jamaica in the 1970s and Grenada in the 1980s, that have pursued diplomatic relations and cultural and service exchanges with Cuba have suffered US criticism and economic reprisals as a result.

Cuba has not solved the problem of export dependency; sugar still accounts for more than 80 per cent of its export earnings. The US-sponsored economic boycott has contributed to this problem by depriving Cuba of potential trading partners for other goods in the region. But, within the confines of an economy which is still largely agrarian, indebted and poor, Cuba has achieved a great deal that is worth sharing with its Caribbean neighbors.

It has a significant foreign debt to the West of more than US$7 billion, most of which it owes to foreign commercial lenders, in addition to an even larger debt to the Soviet Union.[13] But Cuba in the 1970s and 1980s managed to avoid the kind of ballooning of its debt bills that have suffocated many of its neighbors, and has maintained a slow but steady rate of growth.

It has developed education and health systems that are effective and also more equitable, in terms of access to services by all sectors of the population, than those of any other Latin American country. Cuba's infant mortality rate (IMR), one of the best indicators of a population's health and well-being, is only 13.6 (fewer than 14 babies die among every 1,000 born), the lowest IMR in Latin America. The country's rates of school and college enrollments and numbers of physicians per capita are also outstanding in the region.

Cuban advances in the mechanization of sugar production, utilization of sugar by-products, citrus cultivation and processing, pharmaceutical and medical equipment production, and the dairy industry are among the many fields in which a sharing of knowledge by Cuba with its neighbors could contribute to regional food productivity and security. The Cuban government wants to break out of its economic and political isolation from the rest of the region. But most Caribbean governments have kept their distance, for political reasons of their own in some cases, and out of fear of US reprisals.

Cuba has offered scholarships to thousands of students from other Caribbean countries, many of whom would not otherwise have been able to afford professional training. Some Caribbean governments have hired Cuban-trained physicians, agronomists, veterinarians, engineers, architects and other professionals, and technicians. Those governments most closely allied with the United States, particularly those of Grenada and Dominica, refuse to recognize Cuban qualifications. They either refuse to hire Cuban-trained professionals, even when there are vacancies for which other qualified applicants cannot be found, or they place them in positions of lower responsibility and status than those for which they are qualified.

The disintegration of the Eastern bloc deprives Cuba of trading partners and sources of technology on which it had been forced to depend. Already by 1990, the prospect of being required to trade in US dollars, rather than Soviet roubles, and the disruption of trade with Eastern Europe were worsening the strain on Cuba's economy. The thaw in the East–West Cold War offers an opportunity for Caribbean nations to build new and mutually beneficial relations with their quarantined neighbor.

Notes

1. Testimony before the Congressional Subcommittee on Western Hemispheric Affairs, 6 February 1988, Bridgetown, Barbados.

2. Correspondence with author July, 1990.

3. November 1989, Montego Bay, Jamaica.

4. Author interview, February 1988.

5. Author interview, February 1988.

6. Author interview, December 1987.

7. Author interview, March 1988.

8. Author interview, December 1987.

9. Author interview, April 1989.

10. Ibid.

11. Author interview, February 1988.

12. Author interview, February 1988.

13. Statistical Appendix B, Phillip Brenner *et al.*, *The Cuba Reader*, Grove Press, New York, 1988.

14. Elements of a Holistic Alternative: I

> We are looking at a continuing struggle between two competing approaches
> to development: one which places economic growth before all else; the other
> addressing issues of structural inequality (including gender inequality), and
> understanding that the model for development must be holistic, paying
> attention to the social, cultural and political needs of the majority of the
> people. One is profit-oriented, the other is people-oriented.
>
> Peggy Antrobus, Women and Development (WAND)

The objectives outlined in chapters 12 and 13 — increased economic self-
reliance and greater regional integration — are part of the foundation of
sustainable development. But the vision of an alternative model of Caribbean
development that is emerging from the work of many Caribbean NGOs
transcends the traditional methods and measures of development that stress
economic criteria at the expense of the social, cultural and psychological.

The emerging vision of Caribbean-centered development calls for:

- *development that re-defines growth;*
- *development that is ecologically sustainable;*
- *development that is economically sustainable;*
- *development that is psychologically and socially sustainable;*
- *development in which women play a central, active and guiding role;*
- *development that rescues and revitalizes Caribbean culture and identity;*
- *development that permits a spectrum of political and economic options and experiments;* and
- *development that empowers the region's poor majority and, in so doing, builds a basis for more genuine democracy.*

The first four of these points are discussed in the present chapter and the others
in Chapter 15.

Development that redefines growth

Most proponents of structural adjustment assess development primarily by the
growth of a country's formal economy, measured by its GDP. In setting goals
and assessing progress, the World Bank and its sister institutions tend to equate
development with such growth. But, as organizations working with the
Caribbean poor are keenly aware, increases in GDP can occur side by side with
worsening unemployment and poverty and sharpened inequality. Where
commercial and land-holding élites and foreign-owned firms control the bulk
of any country's resources, a correspondingly disproportionate share of the
material benefits of GDP growth accrues to them.

Nor is GDP necessarily an accurate reflection of the level or trend of material well-being of any social sector or class. A landowner may receive unpaid services from tenants, for example, or the families of working women may receive child care services from family members or neighbours who provide them voluntarily or in exchange for other unpaid services. The families receiving the child care benefit in an immediate, material way that is not reflected in standard economic production or growth statistics.

Furthermore, in calculations of GDP or GNP, the exchange of goods and services for money, and the sale of natural resources as commodities, are recorded as positive contributions to a country's economy. But what appears positive on paper and in the short term may have disastrous consequences for development in the medium and long term. If a country were to cut its entire forested land and sell the timber, the sales would be counted as part of GDP growth, even though they would clear the ground for environmental and economic débâcle.

A better criterion of development-promoting growth might be the expansion of the productive capacity of the population, accompanied by increased access to material and other resources to meet individual and community needs, and to ease and enhance living, whether or not all such changes are reflected in GDP growth. This definition of development-promoting growth focuses on the elimination of poverty and improvement of the quality of life for the majority as a goal in itself, rather than as a hoped-for by-product of growth. Says Joan French of the Caribbean Policy Unit:

> An alternative development model growing out of the needs expressed by Caribbean people right now would not be one which focuses exclusively on economics. Our people have made it clear that they want not just to survive but to *live*, and that life is much more than just eating and drinking. Life is also developing a sense of self-worth, creating, building community, socializing, recreating, deepening the understanding of oneself and of others, developing local, regional, and international structures for communication and participation, and much more.

Organizations that are based in the grassroots — community associations, small-scale producers' and traders' associations, the rank-and-file of trade unions and NGOs accountable to such organizations — are better able to identify these hard-to-quantify aspects of living standards and quality than are most urban-based professionals, government officials, or foreign consultants. Even these organizations cannot easily assess genuine development criteria in advance of the development process. New goals, and better ways of achieving and measuring them, can only emerge through praxis, from the experience of people understanding and changing themselves. These goals and criteria will change repeatedly as new levels of awareness and of material development are achieved.

Caribbean NGOs, especially those with a high level of women's participation and leadership, are already promoting and analysing development in partnership with village groups and other popular organizations. An outstanding example of a cooperative, holistic, pro-active and empowering approach to development is the Women in Caribbean Agriculture (WICA) project sponsored by CAFRA.

In the first phase of the project, researchers with professional experience trained non-professional women from several countries in survey methodology. Together, they developed questionnaires to ascertain the overlooked contributions of rural women to Caribbean economies, their access, or lack of access, to land, and the complex of problems that impede them. The project's coordinator reports:

> Researchers spent time living in the communities with the women, observing day-to-day activities and sharing life stories and concerns with the women. The women and other members of the community came together to discuss the issues and clarify the information.
>
> A really intimate relationship was developed over time between the researchers and the women who were sharing their lives. The results were shared in the communities, at the national level, and with regional organizations. Recommendations for action were made at all these levels and developed into programs for follow-up action.[1]

These actions are now being carried out with the women in the communities involved, and in cooperation with local and national NGOs. The WICA project shows the value of a participatory approach that links learning to action, recognizes women's leadership capacity and fosters cooperative interaction among NGOs. The knowledge, confidence and organizing ability created among both the researchers and the researched are vital preconditions for genuine development and for gains that can be measured in terms of improved standards and quality of life.

Development that is Ecologically Sustainable

The market-driven, private sector-led development model is also not sustainable environmentally. The competitive export production cycle in the Caribbean has already propelled increased cultivation of watershed areas, erosion-prone slopes and other marginal lands. It has led to the widespread and often indiscriminate use of damaging pesticides, and to quick-result farming methods that depend on high-cost chemical fertilizers and deplete soil fertility.

Pressure to offer the least-cost opportunities to industrial exporters is causing Southern governments and international agencies to turn a blind eye to extensive chemical pollution. Desperate to earn foreign exchange, some indebted governments offer their lands and waters as dumping grounds for the toxic wastes of the industrialized world. The efforts of more farsighted government officials to curb environmental destruction are stifled by funding cuts or overruled by governments for which maximizing short-term foreign exchange earnings has become the overpowering priority.

Even the threat of environmental blight to potential tourism earnings has not stemmed the trend of sacrificing the environment for short-term gains.

Environmental constraints limit the potential of tourism as it is now organized. Yves Renard of the St Lucia-based Caribbean Natural Resources Institute (CANARI) notes:

> It's an example of how we are cutting off the very branch that we are sitting on by allowing destruction of the resources on which the industry is based, while at the same time other resources for a more sustainable and socially and economically integrated tourism are underused or overlooked entirely.

Among the perpetrators of environmentally destructive practices are agribusiness firms that promote the use of unsafe chemicals, including many banned in the United States. Other firms contribute to ecological damage by employing unsustainable methods on their own plantations, which they abandon or sell when fertility, production or profits decline, as did Gulf & Western with its vast sugar holdings in the Dominican Republic. Some purchasers of export crops, such as Geest, require farmers to use costly and hazardous chemicals and inputs, some of which are intended mainly to improve the appearance of export produce. Structural adjustment requirements that restrict the regulation of foreign-owned corporations by Caribbean governments make it harder to prevent such practices.

Many small-scale Caribbean farmers have come to depend upon damaging methods of cultivation, such as the clearing and tilling of rainforest slopes. It would be futile to outlaw such practices unless alternative, more reliable and less destructive means of earning a living are developed. Caribbean advocates of alternative development recognize that this will not be an easy transition. However, a more regionally integrated and self-reliant Caribbean economy, in which extreme export and import dependency is lessened, would allow more scope for exploring solutions to environmental problems. In such an economy there would be a closer connection between those who own or control land and other productive resources, those who do the producing and those who use or consume the products and live in the affected environment. Producers and consumers in all corners of the globe can understand better their interdependency, the long-term impacts of technological choices, and their common interests in environmentally sustainable farming and manufacturing. This understanding is the first step toward gaining the power to determine those choices.

Environmental issues have been taken up by Caribbean NGOs in their education and organizing work with Caribbean farmers, low-income communities and consumers. Their approach to the issues links the economic, environmental and social aspects of the problem. 'I don't think our country has ever counted the real costs of growing bananas,' says Earlene Horne, general secretary of the National Farmers' Union of St Vincent and the Grenadines:

We think about the cash costs of chemical inputs, but not about their other effects, such as degradation of the soil, the animals and other organisms that the pesticides kill, and the additional pests that we have as a result. From what I've seen, I believe the chemicals used in bananas are causing serious illnesses.

There are also social costs that are unrecognized, such as the labor of children five years and up in deflowering and toting bananas. There's the cost of having to buy more rice and flour when farmers don't have time to grow vegetables and beans. When some farmers are more successful than others because their land is more suited for bananas, it creates social divisions. And when the banana industry goes down, as we know it will, there's a whole range of problems we'll have to deal with.[2]

Unlike some conservationists who see the issue as one of people versus the environment, these Caribbean NGOs view people as potentially the most effective guardians of the lands and waters they depend upon for their living. Those who live and farm and fish in ecologically fragile areas are likely to have more incentive to conserve than either governments under pressure to boost short-term export earnings or footloose transnational corporations seeking quick profits. This is true, of course, only if the people are confident that their continued ownership of, or access to, the land and water is secure.

In St Lucia, the regional NGO, CANARI, has been testing and disseminating participatory approaches to conservation and environmental management. CANARI's Southeast Coast Project involves the traditional users of the environment — fishers, charcoal producers and farmers — in research and planning, and placing some of the project's legal and managerial responsibility in the hands of community organizations. CANARI's Yves Renard says the project demonstrates:

> positive linkages between conservation and development. With the promotion of nature tourism in a protected area, a seaweed mariculture program, improved sea urchin and lobster management, or with the establishment of fast-growing fuelwood plantations, these projects show that conservation can and should contribute to immediate and long-term community needs.

Even with more sustainable technology, farmers and rural residents can preserve their environment only if they have adequate information and support, reliable markets and prices or other sources of income, and if they know that they can remain in their homes and pass on their land, forestry and fishing rights to their children. Solutions to environmental problems therefore must address social and political issues as well as economic and technological ones. Of these, thoroughgoing land reform that results in secure land tenure for farmers, whether as individuals, cooperative members or holders of long-term leases on public lands, is probably the most urgent. Caribbean NGOs are helping small-scale farmers gain or retain access to farm land. They face government policy and World Bank and AID pressure to divide and sell communal or publicly owned lands to individuals at prices the majority of farmers cannot afford.

Development that is Economically Sustainable

Decisions about aid and local resources are frequently based on short-term criteria, such as rapid generation of funds to pay debt bills or completion of showcase projects before elections. Such criteria cannot be applied indefinitely; the continuing escalation of external debts to unpayable levels is one reason why. The development strategy that relies on cheap factory labor and unprocessed commodity exports to the North leads into a downward spiral. World markets for Southern exports become glutted and prices of Southern commodity and industrial assembly exports fall still lower, especially in relation to prices of Northern-country manufactured goods. The impoverished commodity-exporting countries receive lower instead of higher earnings. The economic consequences of the export-led development cure are worse than the debt disease.

Structural adjustment strategies postulate that, at some future point, benefits will create the basis for self-sustaining development. But this vision remains a distant, ever-receding mirage on the economic horizon. To break out of this debilitating cycle, say critics of the current strategy, Caribbean countries must adopt strategies that add more to regional economies than they remove from them, beginning now, not at some future time. The goal is not economic isolation or autarchy; import–export trade with the rest of the world will still be important in a more self-reliant Caribbean. But exports contribute to development only to the extent that the process of producing them and the earnings from selling them increase the productive capacity of the exporting countries.

As argued in the preceding chapter, development-enhancing agricuture and industry must entail:

- *Reduced exploitation.* Caribbean workers must earn more than it costs them and their families for them to work, in terms of transportation, child care, the loss of the employed workers' contributions to subsistence and household economies, and the toll of the work on physical and mental health.
- *Technology transfer and development.* Caribbean employees and joint venture partners need to acquire skills and access to methods and equipment applicable to building Caribbean-owned industries.
- *Import substitution that increases self-reliance.* Industries must produce a greater portion of the essential goods consumed in the region's markets and the inputs necessary for more productive Caribbean agriculture and manufacturing.
- *More linkages to local economies and greater Caribbean value-added to*

exports. Industries producing goods or services for extra-regional markets must utilize a much higher proportion of Caribbean skills and expertise, Caribbean-made components and renewable or carefully managed Caribbean resources than export assembly industries now use.

These criteria for development-enhancing manufacturing and agriculture are generally not the least-cost, most profitable uses of capital in the intensely competitive global market. Private investors responding to market incentives are not likely to initiate them. Under an externally directed, market-driven, private sector-led strategy, they simply will not take place. Nor will such investments provide the quickest return in the form of foreign exchange earnings to the countries that host them. Structural adjustment programs geared toward reducing deficits as quickly as possible make investments in long-term development practically impossible.

Cancellation of the region's heaviest debt burdens, expansion of South–South trade and more managed, equitable trade with the North are also critical components of any plan for self-reliant development. Within the context of such a plan, and with greater control over the terms and forms of assistance by the recipients of foreign aid, development aid from the North could certainly support genuine development. With the lifting of the debt burden, the amount of aid required might be far less than the sums now being channeled in the form of grants and loans to the South and recycled back to Northern banks.

Development that is Psychologically and Socially Sustainable

The drive to maximize export production is disrupting rural communities and speeding migration to urban areas at the same time that it is absorbing the already-scarce resources needed to maintain those cities and their swelling populations. As self-provisioning economies disappear, the need to earn cash contributes to the pressure to produce crops for export (however low the price), to take manufacturing jobs (however poor the wages) or to accept demeaning jobs in the tourism industry (however degrading the conditions). It impels many to resort to drug-selling, violence and prostitution in its many forms, and thus increases social fragmentation and instability.

Advertising, movies and especially satellite television promote North American foods, fashions and consumption-centered lifestyles in the Caribbean. This mass media influence contributes to the decline of local food production and consumption and to the weakening of traditions of mutual aid within families and communities. Television glamorizes macho individualism, violence and crime, and further erodes such traditional values as self-reliance and respect for elders. Oscar Allen observes: 'Intergenerational communications are breaking down, first between different peer groups, and within families. Television is becoming the peer group of everyone.'[3]

Electronic mass media create desires and build markets for industrial country exports. Adrian Fraser notes: 'Where there was once an attempt to make us carbon copies of the British, there's now an effort to make us carbon copies of the Americans.' To acquire the goods needed to pursue a US lifestyle, or just to survive in the cities or in rural areas where subsistence and support systems are breaking down, requires money, and money is getting harder to obtain. According to Fraser:

> We're exposed to the market economy at the same time that it's more difficult to find employment than it was even 10 years ago. . . . People are being bombarded on both sides: the economic squeeze on the one hand and TV values on the other. The ideas we get from the media of 'the good life' are not the life we live. The result is a sort of 'collective split personality'.

Just as their forebears endured and eventually overcame slavery and indentureship, Caribbeans today are struggling to survive, and survive with dignity. To do so they draw not only upon their physical stamina and economic resourcefulness but also upon their inner psychological strength, their collective pride, and their humanistic and spiritual values. Many leaders and members of Caribbean churches, including Roman Catholic, Protestant, Rastafari and others, play a leading role in holistic development efforts. These religious movements, however, face strong competition from fast-growing conservative fundamentalist sects, which encourage submission to the status quo and an individual path to salvation. Most of these are imported from North America via satellite TV and gospel missions.

The social, psychological and spiritual dimensions of development are not reflected in standard statistical measures of poverty or progress. But guidelines for development success must not be confined to the strictly quantifiable. New, more holistic and multi-dimensional development goals and criteria of efficiency must be defined and applied. A Jamaican NGO, Projects for People, (PFP) describes its mandate as that of a holistic approach to development:

> A holistic approach . . . requires not only that each individual should receive an income, but more fundamentally, that the life and character of the individual should be enhanced by the process and that his/her self-esteem should be developed; he or she should acquire marketable skills; his/her environment should be enhanced and his/her life chances improved. . . . PFP defines development as '. . . empowering people to continuously improve their abilities to satisfy their basic physiological and psychological needs. These include food, shelter, clothing, relevant education, mentally stimulating employment, dignity, and a feeling of adequacy'.[4]

Evaluation of development projects — for example, a hydropower plan — must not only compare the wattage that can be produced to the construction costs and projected energy demands. It must also take into account the environmental, social and psychological impacts. What are the cultural costs of the flooding of an inhabited valley if its residents are displaced, unique traditional arts of the region lost and species of animals and plants made extinct as a result? What may be the social and psychological effects on families and communities that for the first time have access to electric power, machines that replace certain forms of wage labor, television, and also electricity bills to pay? To what extent is a power plant or new road a priority that arises from the real needs of the majority of people affected? Is it proposed because it attempts to replicate the pattern of Northern-country industrialization or because foreign funds for it happen to be available? What are possible alternative uses of the project funds?

If a new industry is established, will the job-creation benefits outweigh the economic, environmental and social costs? What standards of health and safety will be set and how will they be enforced? Will new machines and products replace traditonal jobs and services, especially work once done by women? Will those displaced be better off because of labor saved, worse off because of income lost, or both? How can work be organized to maximize group interaction, the learning and sharing of skills, and self-esteem and respect for workers? Should the project perhaps be postponed until such issues are dealt with? The object of such considerations is not to stop the clock but rather to achieve a more farsighted and realistic understanding of the consequences of development choices.

Such understanding can be enhanced by relevant education, including non-formal education and adult literacy, education and skills training tied to economic production projects, and education that draws upon and preserves local and traditional knowledge. The adult education programe of the St Vincent Union of Teachers provides an example.

Education for empowerment

Every weekday afternoon, groups of young women and men gather in a school building in Kingstown, St Vincent, after regular classes have been dismissed. At 4:30, classes begin in basic reading, writing, mathematics, bookkeeping, typing and other skills, taught by tutors who receive only a small stipend for their work. The classes of the Adult Education Program of the St Vincent Union of Teachers offer no academic credits; students come because they want and need to learn. For many, the classes are their best hope of escaping the cycle of poverty, illiteracy and unemployment that plagues their nation.

'Education is as ticklish a subject here as politics or religion,' explained Camelita Williams of the literacy project staff. 'Education officially ends at 15, but a lot of people don't get that far.' She added:

> The powers that be prefer to keep the population illiterate. A few big names have most of the land, while the poor people get cheated and don't think they can do anything about it. We produce fresh foods that are sent out of the country and eat expensive things that are brought back in tins; a lot of people think foreign food is more prestigious. These are the kinds of attitudes that a relevant education could change.[5]

'Illiteracy is a class problem,' say Project Director Mike Browne. 'It's not the rich who are suffering from this. It's a problem perpetuated from generation to generation that we are only going to solve by taking it on ourselves.'[6] 'When we started this project,' Williams adds, 'A lot of people told us that "those people" from the poor neighborhoods wouldn't come to classes, and that they were nothing but prostitutes and thieves. But they did come, even when they had to come in bare feet.'

The Adult Education Project quickly outgrew its initial phase and facilities and was extended into the smaller towns and villages of St Vincent's rugged countryside. Out of this has grown an island-wide organization, the National Association for Mass Education (NAME). NAME works to devise a new, more relevant curriculum and participatory teaching methods that draw upon the learners' knowledge and encourage them to help plan classes. Says Williams:

> Our educational system has been so colonized that it's not meaningful to our people. We're taught about heroes from England and North America, but nothing about our own history and culture. We're actually taught that Columbus discovered St Vincent, as if there were no people living here already! Those who make it to secondary school read Shakespeare, and there's nothing wrong with that, but what about our Caribbean writers? When all we receive is this imported 'canned culture', people have no way to release what they learn. We try to teach appreciation of local things, and also to make education practical.

The program also attempts to deal with problems that cause many students to drop out of school. Women in the project have established a day-care center where young mothers can leave their children during classes. Nurse Gertrude Ferguson does basic physical checkups and nutrition counseling:

> When a young mother comes in with no way for her baby's father to support her or for her to support herself, we know she needs just about everything. We can help with some baby blankets or a box of detergent, but that doesn't really solve the problem as long as there are not enough jobs and no government programs for child support or medical care.[7]

For this reason, project staff encourage the formation and strengthening of community organizations to tackle problems of health, housing and the lack of productive local enterprises. Leadership training in the context of adult education is helping participants build the confidence to address these issues.

Adult education in St Vincent is only one example of the movement for popular education in the Caribbean. For many of the movement's leaders, the goal transcends the objectives of skills development and community-based development. It is a means by which Caribbean citizens can build the basis for meaningful democracy and strengthen their ability to confront the daunting economic and political challenges that face them. Says a popular educator from St Lucia, Didacus Jules:

You can't use literacy classes as a way to get people to line up with a particular political party or point of view. If you're committed to the people, they will see you for what you are. The most important aspect of popular education is to develop people's capacity to think for themselves and to think critically about the problems they are facing.

Notes

1. *CAFRA News*, August 1990.
2. Author interview, March 1988.
3. Ibid.
4. *Projects for People: An Overview* (n.d.), Kingston, Jamaica.
5. Author interview, November 1987.
6. Ibid.
7. Ibid.

15.   Elements of a Holistic Alternative: II

In the perspective of the Western notion of development, . . . the good life is based on the availability of material products, the more technologically recent, the better. . . . Underlying this 'old' economics is the pandering to human greeds. . . . The 'new' economics recognizes the critical importance of women to the economy, and the unpaid labor in villages, urban areas, and families which under the present crisis of capitalism has saved millions of people from total devastation. We also need to explicitly recognize non-material human needs — mutual respect, dignity, meaningful work and life, tenderness, caring, nurture, human relations — as important to development.

Neville Duncan

Somewhere between, or beyond, the model of contemporary industrial capitalism, with its regimentation, individualism, rigid separation of work from pleasure, polarization of wealth and power, and wasteful misuse of human beings and of the natural environment, on the one hand, and the varied forms of traditional agrarian society on the other, must lie alternatives that are humane, achievable, and sustainable. The search for alternatives is no less urgent for the industrial world, where current patterns of consumption, environmental destruction and social breakdown cannot long be sustained, than it is for the South, where economies are collapsing and human misery is approaching the point of explosion. The new ways of understanding the roles of gender and culture in development and the meaning of democracy that are evolving in the Caribbean can contribute to the creation of such alternatives.

Development in which Women Play a Central, Active and Guiding Role

As those who have suffered most from structural adjustment-related austerity, women are in the forefront of the struggle for economic survival and restructuring. In the process, women and women's organizations are redefining the concept of development.

Mainly as a result of scholarship and activism by women, it is now widely recognized that development policies and practices in recent decades have frequently marginalized women and damaged their health, social status and overall well-being. The shift toward export crop production and cash-based economies has reduced the economic importance and social value of many types of work traditionally done by women, including tasks central to the production, preserving and trade of food crops. The introduction of machinery and agrochemicals, which typically have been channeled to men, and the trend toward the commodification of land tenure have reduced women's access to food-producing resources and diminished their influence over the allocation of resources within households and communities.

The expansion and relocation to the global South of low-wage export assembly industries have drawn women in the paid labor force under exploitative and unhealthy conditions, without providing female workers with the support they need to carry out this work, and without providing compensation for the loss of their non-paid work in households and communities. Urbanization and emigration have speeded the disruption of extended family and community-based networks which women traditionally have maintained and on which they and their families have depended.

The importance of women's unpaid labor in both cash and subsistence agriculture has been overlooked by development theorists, governments and most aid agencies. The economic importance of activities often not recognized as work, such as the nurturing and education of the next generation of female and male workers, has also been undervalued. These activities are essential to the well-being and productivity of any society. To the extent that industrialization, urbanization and gender-biased policies and practices have undermined support systems and reduced the ability of women to perform these tasks, the productive capacity of the entire population is diminished.

During the 1970s and 1980s, feminist activists and scholars put forward penetrating analyses of institutionalized sexism and the gender-based division of labor in modern industrialized societies, as well as critiques of the failure of liberal, populist and Marxist movements to come to grips with sexism and its links with racism and class. Women in the South have been developing their own analyses of sexism and the relation of gender issues to racism, imperialism, class oppression and underdevelopment. Thousands of women are contributing to this understanding through practical development work and by sharing the results of their experiences in women's exchanges and publications, and in international networks such as Development Alternatives for Women in a New Era (DAWN). Urbanization and industrialization, while placing extra burdens on women, have also created openings for new economic and political roles and increased awareness among women. Women worldwide are striving to overcome these setbacks and to transform obstacles into opportunities.

Caribbean women have been remarkably creative in their responses to economic crisis and the results that affect them directly: falling incomes, rising unemployment, social service cuts, increased malnutrition, and more widespread violence against women. These processes and women's responses to them have been analysed by (among others) Joan French (*The CBI and Jamaica: Hope and Disillusion*, Association of Development Agencies, Kingston, 1990) and Peggy Antrobus ('Gender Implications of the Development Crisis, in Beckford, Girvan, Senior and Wedderburn (eds), *Development in Suspense*, Association of Caribbean Economists/FES, Kingston, Jamaica, 1989).

Caribbean women's organizations such as Women's Media Watch and the Sistren women's collective and theatre organization in Jamaica have drawn attention to these issues. The majority of Sistren's members are women who have themselves been victims of poverty, social marginalization and violence. Sistren was formed in 1978 when a group of Jamaican women met through a government work programme in Kingston. With the support of a drama instructor, the group learned the power of self-expression. Beginning with their own life stories, they dramatized the lives of women and women's place in Jamaican society. Sistren is both educator and catalyst, working through drama, workshops, music, games and video to help women express their concerns and find solutions. The collective have become a powerful voice in Jamaica and region-wide, increasing awareness of the myriad ways in which all members of society are damaged by the attitudes, practices and institutions that hurt women.

Caribbean women have preserved support systems that evolved in rural areas and within extended families, and have adapted them to the challenging conditions of urban existence. They have carefully nurtured systems of mutal aid, such as the sharing of child care and household labor, in order to stretch meagre incomes beyond seemingly impossible limits. They consciously maintain contact with their rural roots and with relatives abroad, and carry out the exchange of goods and services between city and countryside and from nation to nation.

Village-based cooperatives and women's associations are performing productive tasks which build upon and extend the traditional women's activities in production, processing and exchange of food and other products. Women's groups in rural and urban areas are working to develop collective solutions to needs such as child care, which have been made more urgent by the dispersal of extended families. At the national level in many Caribbean countries, women's organizations are calling attention to issues such as wage inequality, violence against women, unequal access to skills training, and the impact of social service reductions on women and children. While women are still badly under-represented in the official leadership of most Caribbean trades unions, they are among the most active shop-floor and branch organizers.

National and regional womens' organizations in the Caribbean have been in the forefront of the fight for labor rights in export assembly industries and for the unionization of workers in EPZs. Even where they are not unionized, Caribbean female export assembly workers often put up strong individual and group resistance to the humiliating treatment and unhealthy working conditions they often face. Female nurses and teachers have fought bravely to save their jobs, to stop the erosion of health care and education, and to oppose laws that discriminate against female professionals, such as the mandatory dismissal of teachers who become pregnant and do not marry.

The most profound and far-reaching critique of structural adjustment and growth-measured criteria of development in the Caribbean has emerged from women's regional organizations, particularly WAND, CAFRA, and Women for Caribbean Liberation. While many progressive political parties and spokespeople have accepted the need for World Bank-style structural adjustment as an unfortunate but necessary step, some Caribbean women's organizations have been particularly outspoken in challenging the notion that such forms of adjustment are in the interests of the Caribbean majority.

The feminist critique of growth-measured development has drawn attention to the contributions of activities performed by both women and men that have not been recognized as work by orthodox theorists of development. This includes not only household labor and subsistence agriculture, but also activities such as the preserving and passing on of knowledge from one generation to the next, and the maintenance of cultural traditions and values. The feminist vision begins to bridge the conceptual gap between the formal and non-formal sectors of the economy, between the spheres of economic production and economic/social reproduction, between household work and agriculture and other labor for subsistence and local exchange, on the one hand, and paid labor to produce commodities and services for sale, on the other. In so doing, it uncovers potential sources of creativity and productivity unrecognized by standard development theory and practice, which generally takes for granted the contributions of women's, children's and other people's unpaid labor.

The women's movement in the Caribbean and other parts of the South recognizes that many of the most important activities that sustain life and make life worth living do not come with a high school or university degree and are not saleable in the labor market. Until development strategists and popular organizations also recognize and take into account the essential role of these activities, many of which are carried out by women, development that is sustainable and socially and pyschologically healthy will not be possible. Development of structures of support for these non-formal and other non-quantifiable activities could release a great deal of productive energy that is now drained or suppressed. As one starting point, the channeling of development resources directly to women could result in the liberation of women's creativity and productive power.

Understanding the relationship of the productive and reproductive spheres of life is central to the search for viable, holistic alternatives. The feminist vision suggests the closer integration of these spheres, as well as suggesting that forms of collective consumption such as communal laundries, kitchens and child care facilities may be a more efficient and feasible means of meeting certain needs than raising incomes to enable individuals to purchase washing machines, refrigerators and television sets. Such an approach to raising living standards and enhancing the quality of life may be desirable for societies in the North as well as the South. Desirable or not, it may be necessary: the earth's damaged ecosystems and limited mineral resources cannot indefinitely sustain the present industrial-country patterns of consumption, pollution and waste, much less extend such living styles and standards worldwide.

Development that Rescues and Revitalizes Caribbean Culture and Identity

The Caribbean masses brought from their African and Asian homelands an immense diversity of cultural traditions. To cope with conditions in the new world, they preserved and transformed their inherited forms of social organization, religion and artistic expression. They created a rich and varied repertoire of rituals, games, songs, dances and stories to express and ease the pain of loss and oppression, accompany work, reinforce community solidarity, mark life's transitions and celebrate its joys. The strong influence of Caribbean rhythms, from rumba to reggae, on the music of North and South America and 20th-century Africa is just one reflection of the Caribbean's artistic vitality and influence. In addition, many of the Caribbean's surviving indigenous people have maintained their languages, crafts, religions, rituals, and land tenure and self-government systems, particularly in Belize and the South American mainland. In St Vincent and Dominica, very few remember their Karifuna (Carib) language, but their traditional crafts of canoe-making and basketry are still important in the islands' economies and cultural groups such as Dominica's Karifuna are working to revive rituals, songs and other elements of indigenous culture.

Music and drama has been a powerful force in shaping popular consciousness and in mobilizing movements for change in the Caribbean. Participants in pre-Lenten carnival have used parody and pantomime since the era of slavery to mock and rebuke their rivals and oppressors, a practice that at times has spilled over into revenge. As recently as 1974 in Dominica, celebrators used the cover of carnival celerations to set fire to plantation buildings owned by the island's most prominent merchant-landlord. The barbed social commentary of calypso singers has cut short many a political career. Cultural creativity has ebbed and flowed with the strength of popular movements. Jamaica during the 1970s and Grenada during the 1979–83 revolution saw a flowering of drama, poetry and other creative arts.

Caribbean popular radio and dance-hall music today, especially in Jamaica, reflects the reality of rapidly worsening poverty and unemployment. Young poets and musicians, standing on the shoulders of predecessors including Louise Bennett and Bob Marley, present razor-sharp images of racism, street violence, hard drugs, pollution, militarization and the exploitation of women. The most insightful and uncompromising among them, such as dub poets Mutabaruka and the brilliant Jean Breeze, place the blame squarely on the 'big time thieves' of transnational capitalism and the small-time ghetto hustlers who imitate their dehumanizing pursuit of wealth. Calypso in Trinidad and the Eastern Caribbean has been a means of expressing racial and national identity and focusing popular discontent. But the increasing monopolization of the entertainment industry marginalizes the most socially conscious artists. By standardizing and homogenizing popular music and cutting it from its traditional roots, it blunts the edge of its social critique.

Even as it continues to evolve, much of the Caribbean's creative tradition is threatened with extinction. With the spread of economic individualism and the loss of common lands has come the decline of collective work traditions and the songs and dances that were an integral part of work. The drum rhythms and chants that used to accompany the clearing of fields or the grinding of cassava in village mills are now remembered mainly by the old. The spread of electronic media, especially television, is speeding the demise of traditional music, stories and rituals, such as the special games and social and religious ceremonies that marked nights of the full moon in many rural communities.

Caribbean NGOs are making imaginative and innovative use of cultural traditions and arts in their education and organizing work. Dance, drama, non-formal video, and performance poetry in vernacular language convey messages in ways that can cut across class divisions. The use of these forms, by encouraging participation and enabling people with little formal education to interpret their experience and express their views, has an equalizing and democratizing, and so an empowering effect.

For example, a weekend workshop may begin not with formal speeches and introductions but with group exercises based on traditional games, in which people laugh and relax while getting to know each other. At a meeting of community credit committees, groups from different parishes may present their problems and successes in the form of skits in which every member takes a part, instead of formal reports from official group leaders. When the issues are dramatized through real-life examples, patterns that might otherwise remain unrecognized are more easily brought to light. When problems are discussed in everyday language, people who might otherwise hold back – women, teens, the elderly, or those who cannot read or write – are more likely to get involved in debates and decision making.

Popular theater is a particularly powerful tool in consciousness-raising and community organizing. Groups such as the Groundworks Theatre Company and Sistren in Jamaica, the Movement for Cultural Awareness in Dominica, the Grenada, Antigua and Barbados Popular Theatre Organizations, St Lucia's Folk Research Center, and Naked Roots in St Vincent work closely with grassroots and non-government development organizations. They adapt theater exercises and traditional songs and games to help groups of workers, villagers or co-op members analyse problems and clarify goals. When a rural group, for example, identifies a problem such as the lack of safe water or access to land, theater is used as a way to investigate the problem's causes and get the community involved in a plan for collective action to solve it.

In this kind of theater, a finished script is an end product, not the starting point. To write the play, village theater group members must gather information from neighbors and officials. Community members, especially elders, are invited to criticize and contribute to the play as it evolves. To put on an exciting production, members learn and adapt traditional drumming, dance and song. In the final stages, village troups may tour neighboring communities facing similar problems. Networks such as the Eastern Caribbean Popular Theatre Organization (ECPTO) sponsor island-to-island and international exchanges.

Caribbean popular theater is more than an organizing tool; it is part of an effort to rescue national culture, language and pride from inundation by foreign fashions and media. Says Lana Finnikin of Sistren:

> National TV is almost all pure foreign, but the people are crying out for local stuff. In Jamaica, our real culture is not foreign, like an opera. It's things like reggae music, that the majority can control, that can get out the message of

the oppressed. It can help individuals who are suffering to express themselves in a way that asks for change.

In Sistren theatre we use the culture of Jamaica, like African/Caribbean rhythms that people still experience in Dinkimini and Kumina (religious movements with strong African roots). It's another kind of teaching than the classroom kind. Even people who can't read or write can feel relaxed and express themselves. In that kind of theatre people can look for solutions and take action. One drama workshop resulted in a group of women to go demonstrate in front of their Councillors to get water and lights in a poor neighborhood. They were more comfortable than they could have been with a petition or a formal chat. They expressed their needs exactly as they themselves felt them. They felt good about it, and they got results.

St Lucians face pressure for a process of cultural assimilation that would reduce the island to an appendage of North America. St Lucia's Folk Research Center works against that pressure, to uncover, remember, document, diffuse and dignify the country's rich and complex culture. While English is the language of government, business and schools, it is a French- and African-derived Creole (Kweyol) that most St Lucians speak first, and often best.

In the early 1980s, a group of cultural workers decided to take Kweyol seriously, and so to imbue the people who speak it with greater pride in their identity. They standardized the written form of the rich spoken language, improving communication among the region's Kweyol speakers in Dominica, Haiti, Guadaloupe, Martinique and St Lucia. They began to publish in Kweyol and promote literacy training in the people's own language. At the same time they began to document folk culture, recording the recollections of elders and tracing the history of music and instruments from all the myriad traditions of the island. They researched folk medicines and healing practices which were fast being replaced by imports.

Teaming up with academic researchers, they established the Folk Research Center in 1982. They implemented a programme of community popular theater, radio and video which drew upon all these forms while addressing local problems, and offered courses in St Lucian language and folk history. The Folk Research Center proposes to develop an authentic 'cultural industry' which can sustain St Lucian artists and give tourists a glimpse of the real St Lucia.[2]

Renowned Barbadian novelist George Lamming told an audience of Caribbean cultural workers and activists: 'There is a direct connection between the activity known as politics and the forms of expression you call culture.' According to Lamming:

Cultural autonomy is the basis for any genuine development. Development is the capacity to define and redefine our reality, with all levels of society sharing in that definition. Development is the capacity to see what are the collective needs of a society and to apply intellect and imagination to address those needs within the limits of our resources. . . . Development does not mean having more than the next person or the next territory. That definition leads toward barbarism. A materially prosperous society may be more underdeveloped than one that is materially poor. Large areas of the United States, where people have no means of participating in their development or defining their reality except by consuming, are perfect examples of underdevelopment.[3]

Caribbean culture is under foreign attack, Lamming says. 'No other region of the world receives so much television programming in its own language from outside. . . . For the Caribbean, the question of cultural resistance is urgent. Will we have the resources to resist?' he asks. NGOs and popular culture organizations in the region are working hard to make sure that the answer is yes.

Development that Permits a Spectrum of Political and Economic Options and Experiments

The experience of the past three decades shows that there is no single or simple blueprint for development. Governments in the South with widely differing ideologies have all faced tremendous difficulties; countries following disparate development strategies have found themselves facing many of the same problems of indebtedness, inflation, declining food production and social dislocation. At the root of many of these problems is the continuation of systems, albeit in modified form, which perpetuate the withdrawal of resources from the South and which concentrate power over global economic structures in institutions and corporations based in the North.

There is no easy way for any Southern country to break out of this pattern of disempowerment and dependency but there are promising possibilities, some of which have been outlined in this chapter. It is vital that impoverished countries have the freedom to explore these options, both individually and in cooperation with each other. Instead of encouraging this, the US and other Northern governments, commercial banks and the multilateral lenders are imposing a single, strict and stringent development strategy on the nations of the South. This strategy is based on a series of premises which have already proved false in practice and which primarily serve the interests of the wealthy and powerful of the North. In the name of promoting global free trade, privatization and deregulation, the United States and other aid donors and lenders discourage or forbid an alternative range of policy options, including:

- land reform and redistribution, except so-called versions of land reform based on privatization and market mechanisms;
- nurturing of Caribbean agriculture and agro-industries by means of quotas, tariffs or government subsidies and services;
- planning by governments and regional bodies of the allocation of resources and responsibility for agriculture, agro-industries and trade within the region;

- support for public and cooperative enterprises in addition to private ones; and
- diversification of export markets and import sources through trade agreements (until recently) with Eastern as well as Western bloc countries, including the largest and most developed nation in the insular Caribbean, Cuba, with certain Middle Eastern nations, and with the relatively prosperous French Caribbean colonies, Guadeloupe and Martinique.

The World Bank and USAID argue that governments in Southern economies need to cede more of their powers and resources to the private sector. But the governments of industrialized countries in fact play a greater role in setting economic policies and redistributing resources than many Southern country governments. The proportion of government spending in relation to the economy as a whole (GDP) is significantly greater in the countries classified as 'high income' than in 'less developed' countries.[4]

Many Caribbean proponents of alternative development contend that a stronger government role in economic planning is essential to overcoming the disadvantages stemming from the region's size, geography and colonial inheritance. Neville Graham of ACT notes that the decline of agriculture in Dominica and many of its neighbors is in large part attributable to government neglect. Says Graham, 'Planning, when it happens, is piecemeal, and as a result, resources are not used effectively. . . . A lot of the best flat, alluvial soils are given to housing instead of agriculture,' while small farmers responding to market incentives are 'cutting down citrus and coffee trees, and planting bananas on erosion-prone slopes', a trend that can only damage the country's agricultural potential.

> Agriculture is the basis of our economies, but it hasn't been a focus of government. There's no comparison in agriculture to the incentives and concessions given to foreign export manufacturers. There's no strong government work on diversification or development of banana by-products, and we're not serious about import substitution; even though there has been a lot of lip service to these things. Agricultural estates that were once very productive are being divided and sold. It's not that the farmers shouldn't have their own land, but the people who have worked the lands for years will not be able to afford it. Even from a private sector point of view, government isn't doing enough for agriculture.[5]

To develop, says Graham, 'we have to be able to look at an entire range of alternatives', including private, public and joint enterprises as well as cooperatives. But cooperative forms of land tenure are strongly discouraged by USAID and by the World Bank in favor of individual land ownership. 'This cutting up of the land undermines economies of scale. Individual ownership might work if there were a real emphasis on being able to feed ourselves first, by setting aside certain lands for staple crops, and attention to agro-industry,' Graham says, but this is not the case.

The Castle Bruce cooperative is one of those being broken up by the Government of Dominica. According to spokesperson Amos Wiltshire, the former Castle Bruce estate contained 1,118 acres:

> All this land was worked by the peasants, the poor people, to build up the estate. My great grandparents worked here. Because of the foreign estate owners, the people had to live and grow their food way up in the hills and work down here for pennies a day.[6]

Since 1972, the estate workers have been attempting to remain on the land and work it as a cooperative. According to Wiltshire:

> There is the tradition of people in this area of koudmen [helping hand] to gather and work together. . . . The Charles government said it would not deal with any co-op. We sent a letter [to the Freedom Party government] saying that we want to continue as a co-op, but we were told that the co-op was dissolved anyway, and the farmers hadn't been told anything about it.

Cooperative leader Helena Gaspar adds:

> The majority have been working this land for 40 or 50 years, and their parents before them, but very few will be able to afford to buy the land at the high prices the government has set. The people feel the government wants to sell the best land in a block to some big person. . . . What we want is to continue as a group, and get some concession from the government on the land price. We'd also like to get some help from government with the roads and with marketing, since we don't have a way to transport our tannias or grapefruits.[7]

For many farmers, cooperatives are a favored form of ownership because they have a social as well as an economic value. Says Gaspar:

> Some people would rather work as a co-op and others as individuals. But with a co-op, people work better. If we're side-by-side digging, and we're talking together, that eases the burden of the work for me. In a co-op, there is strength. We can group together and get some attention from government. But this government says this model of working together is a communistic type of co-op.

Another example of the contrast between the adjustors' private sector-led model and a publicly planned alternative is the role of marketing boards. AID, the IMF and the World Bank have pressed for a policy of placing marketing boards solely in the hands of the private sector. This means that the large-scale landowners and traders dominate the boards, while small-scale farmers get little or no representation. The result is that the large growers are in a position to get favored treatment with regard to decisions over where roads are built, whose crops are bought and who gets access to credit and agro-chemicals.

The structural adjustment goal of privatizing marketing boards has received some support in the region, in part because government-dominated marketing boards have often been inefficient and, in some cases, corrupt. In many cases, marketing boards have been more responsive to the interests of commercial and land-holding élites, who have dominated most governments, than to the needs of the minority. But to replace their functions entirely with free market mechanisms will not ensure that agricultural import–export trade is structured and developed to meet the needs of the majority. Rather, it tends to shift power to a higher level of the global hierarchy, toward greater control by the multinational food processing and shipping conglomerates that already dominate world food trade.

Encouraging the self-organization of small-scale farmers and traders, particularly women, and ensuring their representation on marketing boards may be the best way to ensure that such boards work in the interests of more than a narrow stratum of large-scale farmers and merchants. Representatives of Caribbean NGOs working with the poor contend that the solution to this problem, like many others, lies in the kind of grassroots organizations and empowerment that can make governments, banks, marketing boards and other institutions accountable to the majority of citizens.

Development that Empowers the Region's Poor Majority, and in so Doing, Builds a Basis for Genuine Democracy

The achievement of political and economic sovereignty requires changes within Caribbean societies, particularly empowerment of the poor. Says Cecil Ryan of Projects Promotion, a leading NGO in St Vincent and the Grenadines: 'Our current lack of control over resources on a Caribbean regional level is a reflection of unequal structures in our own individual countries. These structures, too, must be reoriented, so that the poor can have more of a say.'[8]

In working toward empowerment of the poor, Caribbean NGOs and popular organizations are creating the basis for a form of democracy more meaningful and profound than that reflected in European or US-style elections. According to Adrian Fraser of CARIPEDA: 'The Westminster type of political structure handed down to us is usually little more than an every-five-year merry-go-round, in which one party replaces another, while the basic, top-down structures remain in place.' Substitution of political institutions more like those of the United States will not solve the problem, Fraser says, 'We need democracy, but elections alone do not equal democracy.'[9]

A useful definition of democracy might be: the opportunity for individuals and the communities to have a significant degree of control over decisions that affect their lives, particularly decisions about the allocation of resources. Such a form of democracy depends upon the guarantee of civil liberties and of the freedom to form organizations without harassment, and to act in an organized manner to affect political policies and change economic conditions. It requires freedom from government or paramilitary repression and from the actuality or threat of overt or covert intervention from foreign political powers.

Genuine democracy also can thrive only in the absence of coercion and constraint resulting from hunger, poverty, illiteracy and lack of information. No woman or man whose immediate concern is where the next meal or day's wage will come from can be an active, responsible citizen of a democracy. That is why equitable development and empowerment of the poor is vital to the creation of real democracy.

Empowerment is used here to mean the creation of the capacity by groups and individuals, particularly the poor and disenfranchised, to survive; to understand their relation to the natural, cultural, economic and political forces that affect them; to organize, plan, implement and evaluate activities to protect their interests and improve their situation at the local level; and to enhance their ability to affect change on the regional, national and international level. Says Jeff James, Director of Vinsave:

> Community development is limited if it doesn't evolve beyond the local level to challenge what's happening at the national and regional levels. Now, our 'democratic process' ends when we leave the polling booth every five years. Our governments bring in experts from the outside, and the people have no real say. Empowerment through community organizing could allow a more truly democratic approach. This could help us achieve a more equitable distribution of resources, especially land, income, and access to finances. Currently, we have tremendous inequality in these areas, which perpetuates our dependency as a region and holds back development.[10]

Cecil Ryan explains how one multipurpose NGO, of which he is programme coordinator, works to promote empowerment:

> In St Vincent, Projects Promotion works through dialogue with farmers' organizations, trade unions, community associations, local non-government agencies, and political parties. We help local groups to establish projects, such as farming cooperatives, that enable farmers to gain access to resources they cannot obtain as individuals. Our model is to encourage projects that not only help people economically, but also enable them to prepare themselves and to create structures through which they can advocate for their own beliefs and participate in shaping government and other policies that affect them.

No alternative system can work, cautions Glenroy Browne, if it ignores local traditions or is imposed from above. The priority now, he says:

> is for Caribbeans seeking genuine development to help our people strengthen their ability to organize themselves, to see that they are important, that they can demand their just due, and that they have the capacity to lead. From this, an alternative system can arise, with people who

know how to make their leaders accountable, and with the ability to plan and to utilize our Caribbean resources in our own best interests.[11]

Joan French points out that during the Grenada revolution, 'despite its derailment by a few madmen, there was the beginning of a process of genuine consultation'. Today, says French, 'There is a sense of despair among political leaders, who have lost sight of our people's potential for defining and achieving their own goals. We know from experience that community, farmers, and women's groups can cut across political barriers.' The process of empowerment, French warns, cannot be separated from the problems of debt and poverty:

In Europe, the provision of basic services provided the jump-off point for new, more democratic processes and institutions, which will have to be developed further. But in Jamaica, in the Caribbean, in the South, we're being asked to jump off from a point of having absolutely nothing.[12]

Small projects, such as those supported by Oxfam America, can play a crucial role in this process. According to Joey Peltier, director of the Small Projects Assistance Team in Dominica:

Small projects can have a significant impact on a community's economic well-being. But they are even more important as a means of education, as a means of getting people to feel that they belong together and have a common purpose. When people come together to deal with common problems, they begin to ask questions like 'Why do we have these problems in the community?' and 'What are our links with other communities, and to other countries, and the world?' As their understanding increases, people in these small projects will become the leaders and the foundation for change and for genuine development.[13]

Notes

1. Author interview, November 1989.
2. Summer 1990 issue of the *Bulletin* of the Canadian NGO InterPares.
3. Address to culture and media workers, Roseau, Dominica, January 1990.
4. World Bank, *World Development Report*, Washington, 1988.
5. Author interview, December 1987.
6. Author interview, April 1988.
7. Statement to a visiting US citizens' delegation, April 1988, Castle Bruce, Dominica.
8. Author interview, November 1987.
9. Statement to US citizens' delegation, March 1988.
10. Author interview, November 1987.
11. Ibid.
12. Statement to US congressional delegation, February 1988, Barbados.
13. Author interview, April 1988.

Part VII:
New Roles for NGOs

16. Caribbean and Northern NGOs: Toward Equality and Partnership

In the context of the oppressive living conditions associated with the debt burden, small farmers (both women and men), higglers [small-scale traders], teachers, and community workers continually design and deploy methods of survival which have a valid place in the search for an alternative path of national development. A challenge for the NGOs is to involve the people with whom we work in this process in such a way that they become confident in themselves and in the contributions they have to make to the process of seeking solutions.

> Judith Wedderburn,
> Association of Development Agencies (ADA), Jamaica

The work toward development alternatives supported by Caribbean NGOs, working with the poor prefigures an alternative development strategy for the region. In parallel fashion, the changing relationship between Southern development NGOs and their partner NGOs in the North suggests a new model for restructuring economic and power relationships between the North and the South.

Caribbean NGOs are seeking a proactive rather than a reactive role, in which Caribbean people determine the agendas for development aid and action. The extent to which they can do so depends in part on the willingness of Northern NGOs to cede some of their power. It also depends on the clarity of Caribbean NGOs' analysis of development dilemmas and strategies and, most importantly, on their abilty to involve the poor in the development process.

Ultimately, it is the organized strength of popular movements that will determine whether the poverty-creating mechanisms analysed in this book, imposed by external powers, will prevail. NGOs have a crucial role in building those popular movements. At this time in the Caribbean and elsewhere in the South, most grassroots groups are motivated by demands for access to land, for less exploitative working conditions, and against threats to their survival from big dams and deforestation. Most lack the luxuries, which are really necessities for effecting change, of funds and time to travel, computerized communications, or even access to information about projects and processes that affect them directly.

At the same time, illiterate peasants, forest dwellers and residents of urban shantytowns may understand more profoundly than formally educated experts the true nature of the destructive projects and policies imposed in the name of development. Because their very survival is at stake, they may have greater determination to oppose them. As a representative of a small producers' cooperative told a recent NGO forum:

The IMF and World Bank already have an integrated strategy. We small farmers have to be unified, too. If we leave it just to the NGOs to confront the World Bank, it's mostly a confrontation of intellectuals. Without the support of groups at the base, it doesn't achieve anything, because there isn't enough power or resolve to really change the situation.[1]

NGO's in the South, with support from their counterparts in the North, can supply the information that grassroots groups need about official plans and policies, and about parallel processes unfolding in other parts of the world. They can link grassroots organizations in different countries and continents. They can decode development jargon. With help from supporters in the North, they can demystify the dogma of 'Bankthink' and challenge the legitimacy of the multilateral mega-agencies as global debt brokers on behalf of the powerful. They can help clarify the outlines of alternative development methods that are emerging out of the struggles for survival by the poor, and make those alternatives the focus of open, democratic debate at all levels of society.

Why NGOs?

NGOs in Asia, Africa, Latin America and the Caribbean are frequently more effective than foreign aid agencies, government institutions or political parties in reaching, mobilizing and representing the poor and marginalized. The Caribbean poor must be central to the creation of development alternatives. It is they who have suffered the most adverse effects of impoverishing 'development' policies, particularly structural adjustment. Thus, it is they who have the least to lose from the difficult but essential transition to a development strategy that places the needs of Caribbean people first. In addition, women and men farmers, workers and their children are the ultimate creators and providers of the region's wealth. To succeed, any development strategy must address their needs, enhance their well-being and productive capacity, draw upon their knowledge and skills, and carry their wholehearted and active support.

The importance of NGOs in the South is now widely recognized by Northern private aid organizations, governments and multilateral agencies, all of which are trying to influence the agendas of Southern NGOs. Many Southern governments also are aware of the potential power of NGOs. These governments have responded in a variety of ways, sometimes seeking to suppress them, sometimes to control them, and in many cases, to press them to take on functions that debt-burdened states can no longer perform.

NGOs have come to play this pivotal role in part because their variety and flexibility enable them to respond to rapidly changing conditions in ways that more formal and established institutions cannot. In the Caribbean, economic crisis and social dislocation have weakened community cohesion, especially the extended family, religious institutions and traditions of voluntary collective labor, sharing of harvests, and other forms of mutual aid.

Meanwhile, the majority of Caribbean political parties and trade unions have been unable to address the new needs arising from economic crisis. In contrast, many Caribbean NGOs have developed directly in response to the worsening problems of hard-pressed farmers, indigenous people losing access to their lands, immigrants to urban areas who lack housing and jobs, exploited factory workers, and women who suffer most from structural adjustment.

It would be misleading to suggest that these NGOs have sprung up purely spontaneously. Many are the outgrowth of the movements for Caribbean nationalism, Black Power and socialism, which reached their zenith in the 1970s. Some have evolved from charitable and service associations whose gains and contributions to social welfare were swept away by the swelling tide of poverty. Others have been quite consciously founded by activist intellectuals or churches, charitable societies, credit unions, Girl Scouts, sports leagues, cultural survival can only be built from the bottom up. Caribbean regional women's organizations such as WAND and CAFRA have acted as catalysts in the formation of community and women's organizations. Some Caribbean grassroots NGOs have been formed at the initiative of the poor themselves; by small-scale traders and farmers and by unemployed youth.

Circumstances particular to the English-speaking Caribbean help explain the rapid growth and proliferation of NGOs there. The achievement of independence by most of these territories in the 1960s and 1970s was accompanied by high hopes for regional federation and rapid progress in the direction of Northern standards of living. The sub-region's comparatively high per capita incomes and levels of literacy seemed a sound foundation for such hopes. But regionalism foundered, and significant and equitable economic growth failed to occur. Instead, economic crisis, exacerbated by structural adjustment, eroded the region's relative advantages and prompted an accelerated wave of emigration. It also led many of those who remained to search for different development paths.

The spectrum of NGOs

To describe an organization as 'non-government' does not explain much. NGOs include not only development organizations but also trade unions, churches, charitable societies, credit unions, Girl Scouts, sports leagues, cooperatives, chambers of commerce and many others. The Southern NGOs described in this book are change-oriented development organizations which are based among, or have strong links to, the poor and disenfranchised, and which are committed to improving the quality of life of their members.

Within this definition of development NGOs falls a range of organizations. Among them are organizations of the poor themselves, which may be called 'grassroots', 'popular' or 'mass-based' organizations. Examples include village development and community betterment committees, associations of farmers and other small-scale producers, cooperatives (based on production, purchasing or marketing), associations of small-scale traders or self-employed workers or artisans, grassroots-based women's organizations, and others. To the extent that they are composed of and accountable to the poor, and are oriented toward social change, this definition may also include trade unions, religious groups, cultural associations, structures representing ethnic groups, and other institutions not usually thought of as development organizations.

Another category of development NGOs is the intermediary organizations which provide services to, or function as a link among and catalyst for, the organizations of the poor. These Southern NGOs may operate at the local, national, regional or international level, and often serve as liaisons between grassroots groups, on the one hand, and local or foreign governments and Northern NGOs, on the other.

There is also much variety among intermediary NGOs. In the Caribbean, as elsewhere, some see their purpose as primarily one of charity or the direct provision of material aid, social services or disaster relief. Others are development NGOs. While these may provide similar services, they seek primarily to empower the poor and work toward structural and policy change to eliminate the causes of poverty. Most of Oxfam America's project partners in the Caribbean are intermediary development organizations of this type. Some are linked to a particular social sector, such as women, farmers or indigenous people. Others are specialized by their function, such as literacy training, marketing assistance or popular theater.

Other Caribbean intermediary NGOs are more multi-purpose, working with a variety of sectoral and grassroots constituencies. For example, Projects Promotion in St Vincent and the Grenadines works with village development committees; helps grassroots groups to establish cooperatives, pre-schools, and income-generating and material development projects such as concrete block-making; supports sports teams, steel drum orchestras, and calypso workshops; carries out surveys on the status of sectors such as indigenous people and women's organizations; sponsors symposia on issues of national importance; provides library and reprint services; carries out joint program planning with other Vincentian NGOs; promotes exchanges between grassroots groups in St Vincent and other countries; or organizes education and action on international issues such as apartheid; sends representatives to national and Caribbean regional organization meetings; hosts foreign visitors; carries out organizational and project evaluations; and produces the paperwork necessary to receive and monitor the use of funds from Northern NGOs.

Other Caribbean intermediary NGOs are national-level umbrella organizations, such as ADA in Jamaica, which help with fundraising, project planning and evaluation, and the education programs of their member NGOs. Still others are Caribbean regional organizations, such as CARIPEDA and CNIRD, which do the same things at the regional level and also participate in international exchanges. Other regional NGOs active in the English-speaking Caribbean include the Caribbean Conference of Churches, WAND, CAFRA, WINFA and ECPTO. These and other Caribbean NGOs are also forming ties with counterpart NGOs in Africa, Latin America and Asia, and with organizations of farmers, fishers, workers and community activists in the countries of the North.

Contradictions of NGOs

The unique importance of NGOs in the development process derives largely from their strong ties to the poor. Because they have either evolved from grassroots organizations or work directly with the poor, they are often better able than foreign-based agencies or local governments to reach the most oppressed or isolated sectors of the population. For example, after Hurricane Gilbert struck Jamaica in 1988, official relief funds and supplies were sent for the repair of devastated homes and infrastructure. Sistren and other member NGOs of Jamaica's ADA were able to respond effectively, working with community residents to ensure that roofing materials were distributed quickly and fairly to those most in need of them. In contrast, some of the relief supplies distributed through official channels were diverted, stolen or left to pile up in warehouses for months.

The special relationship of change-oriented intermediary NGOs to the people they serve poses certain dangers. In the words of Horace Levy, director of the Social Action Center in Jamaica:

> The NGO role is one of service to the popular movement by building participatory democracy and empowerment. NGOs . . . have therein a task uniquely their own. It requires resistance to a number of temptations: the temptation to become the representative of the popular movement; the temptation to become or to function as a political party; and the temptation to be an agent of government.[2]

As the capabilities of Southern NGOs have grown, so has the danger of being co-opted or used by local or foreign governments or by multilateral agencies for purposes that are counter to the interests of the poor. Governments, pressed by economic constraints and structural adjustment conditionalities to reduce health, education and other social services, frequently encourage NGOs to take over these functions.

Development NGOs can help impoverished communities to define their own needs, to develop more effective mechanisms for providing services and to make demands upon the state and the private sector. What they cannot do alone is to solve problems that arise from poverty-creating economic structures and trade relations. By taking over major responsibility for providing social services, NGOs risk drawing attention away from the need for more fundamental structural change. This can make it easier for states to abdicate their responsibility for the well-being of their citizens, and allow elites and private interests to continue with impunity activities which harm the poor and the environment.

This is precisely the role advocated for NGOs by the World Bank. According to a 1990 report by the Bank: 'There is a growing recognition that the public sector is limited in what it can do. Many look to citizens' organizations and non-profit groups to assume a greater role.'[3] Bank officials want NGOs to function as pacification teams or emergency rescue squads, which douse the fires of social discontent and act as buffers between the poor and the institutions — governments, multilateral agencies and corporations — most responsible for their poverty. By treating the most obvious symptoms of the global epidemic of poverty, NGOs may unwittingly help to disguise the true nature and virulence of the disease.

The World Bank notes with approval in the same report that, 'Some governments have turned to NGOs for help with social programs associated with structural adjustment or, in a few cases, for their views on the design of adjustment policies.' But by no means does the Bank contemplate a role for development NGOs in deciding whether or not structural adjustment of the kind required by the World Bank and IMF should be implemented.

Even less does the Bank envision any role in the policy-setting process for those most directly and adversely affected by the adjustment process. Asked whether small farmers, for example, have any say in the 'policy dialogue' between the Bank and Caribbean governments, a senior official in charge of the Bank's Caribbean Program replied, 'We don't know of any role for them.' However, he added, NGOs, 'should help with sociological problems, such as households with many children'. Another World Bank official remarked that the role of Caribbean NGOs should be limited to social services and, possibly, help with export production. 'Expatriate NGOs,' he added, 'might be able to help with technical assistance to farmers for growing and packing things like mangos for export.'[4]

Few governments see a role for either intermediary or grassroots NGOs in helping to define and direct development policies. Staff members from Jamaican NGOs were invited, as individuals, to participate in task forces set up by the PNP government in late 1989 to provide suggestions for the government's five-year development plan. One observer commented:

> It was very noticeable that the NGO input was very much confined to the social. In other words, the 'planners' and 'powers that be' are the ones to deal with the macro aspects of the plan, i.e., the economics, while NGOs get to help out with the 'micro' part. . . . How much room is there to maneuver when policy has already been set by the IMF, World Bank, etc.?[5]

Another development worker proposed that Jamaican NGOs 'need to build ourselves into a mighty phalanx or be subjected to the government's massive demands with little support in return'. ADA coordinator Peta-Anne Baker reported to the NGO coalition's members that, 'if ADA is to be clear in its goal of increasing the impact of NGOs on the development process, we will have to focus more of our energies on policy formulation and implementation.'[6]

Not many NGOs elsewhere in the Caribbean have opportunities for even token input into national planning. Governments such as those in Haiti before 1990 and Guyana have sought less to include or co-opt NGOs than to regulate and repress them. As the region's economic crisis deepens, Caribbean intermediary NGOs may find themselves, along with the grassroots organizations they support, facing repression and violence similar to that already faced by their counterparts in Central America.

The direct funding dilemma

The recent discovery of NGOs by official funding sources (governments and multilateral agencies) requires NGOs to face some thorny issues. Caribbean NGOs have long been receiving support from independent Northern development agencies. Some of those private agencies act as conduits for government funds channeled through sources such as USAID and the Canadian International Development Agency (CIDA). Others, including Oxfam America, do not accept government funds, but raise the money they send abroad from the public.

Official aid agencies, as well as branches of the UN, are increasingly making funds available directly to Caribbean NGOs, bypassing both Northern NGOs and Southern governments. The World Bank has done relatively little direct funding of NGOs, but strongly encourages governments to do so. Direct funding has some advantages: NGOs can get access to larger amounts of money, often more quickly, than they can when the aid flows through private Northern NGOs or Southern governments.

Direct funding also poses a number of perils. In some cases, official donors try to use local NGOs to circumvent Southern governments. The activities may provide immediate benefits to some, but such funding procedures can further undermine the sovereignty of Southern nations and make participating NGOs beholden to foreign interests and less accountable to the poor. Some 'debt for nature' swaps brokered by Northern creditors and NGOs have had this effect. In many cases, the acceptance by Southern NGOs of official foreign direct funding requires local government approval. Either way, the autonomy of the recipient NGOs is compromised.

Northern governments and multilateral donors will naturally use whatever means they have to pursue their own interests. Perhaps the greatest danger of direct funding is that these foreign institutions may call the tune to which NGOs must dance. This can distort Southern NGO priorities by making funds available for one sort of activity and not others. Official foreign funding can create a clientele of NGOs that is dependent upon it and thus more vulnerable to manipulation, and cause rifts among intermediary NGOs and between them and grassroots groups. 'NGOs today are divided between those that work with governments and the World Bank and those that work with the people and their organizations,' observed a Central American NGO delegate to the 1990 International NGO Forum for Ecodevelopment in Washington DC.

The same problem arises whatever the source of funds; private aid agencies in the North also promote their own institutional self-interests and strategies for effecting development. All decisions about what types and amounts of resources are offered, to which groups and for what purposes are inevitably political decisions. But because direct official funding is given on terms set by Northern governments and multilateral mega-agencies, and because the amounts of money involved are often large, the risks of co-optation and of the subordination of locally determined priorities to foreign agendas are proportionately greater.

Recipient NGOs may find their budgets tripled or quadrupled overnight by an influx of funds to provide a particular service in a way specified by the terms of a direct funding grant. This can divert NGOs from their locally determined programs. External criteria for project success can undermine local priorities and definitions of development in subtle ways. Large grants can overburden fledgling NGOs with new administrative tasks and paperwork and cause competition among local NGOs. Direct funding can also exacerbate problems of grant dependency, with staff so busy completing paperwork required for the last grant and applying for the next that there is little time and energy left for evaluation and interaction with the NGOs' own grassroots bases and the supposed beneficiaries of the funds. Nor are Southern NGOs immune from the temptations of higher salaries, prestige, power-brokering and other perquisites of the international development jet set.

Even without direct official funding, NGOs can become self-perpetuating bureaucracies. When the continued existence and growth of the organization becomes an end in itself, the goals of fostering empowerment can be forgotten. This can be a problem for any change-oriented organization, as the history of many trade unions, political parties and cooperative associations attests. The problem is magnified by access, even if temporary, to sizeable sums from official sources. The very availability of substantial funds sometimes leads to the creation of NGOs for the purpose of receiving those funds and carrying out the activities specified by the grantor. As official aid to Caribbean governments from sources such as AID has declined, some governments are working to foster local NGOs as a means of acquiring access to foreign funds. Naturally, they encourage the establishment of local NGOs that will not challenge their policies. Such organizations have been dubbed GONGOs (government-organized NGOs) by some development activists.

Joint Advocacy and Action for Policy Change

Many Southern NGOs now see their mandate as extending beyond the small-scale project level, to include action to bring about policy change. Among them are the Malaysia-based Third World Network, and DAWN. These and other Southern NGO networks are calling on Northern agencies to provide more support for direct South–South communication, for exchanges of resources and personnel between Southern NGOs, for direct links between grassroots groups in different regions in the South, and for support of Southern-based networks and organizations.

The more farsighted among Northern development NGOs have come to recognize, with some prodding by their Southern partners, that the root causes of the problems they have sought to address through international aid have their origins in the wealthy industrialized nations. Some are responding to the request from NGOs in the South that they take greater responsibility for public education about these issues and take action to bring about policy change within their own countries.

Finally, Southern NGOs are urging their Northern counterparts to pay more heed to marginalized and exploited people within their own societies, and to the need for social justice and structural change within the North. Many NGOs are becoming more acutely aware that problems once thought of as typical of 'underdeveloped' societies — poverty, illiteracy, pandemic disease, high unemployment, poor social services, decaying infrastructure and the lack of effective democracy — are increasingly characteristic of Northern industrialized societies. The environmental crisis, first recognized by many in the North as a threat to the quality of life in the wealthier countries, is now widely perceived as a global catastrophe that can only be addressed by a massive international movement that unites the majorities in the South and the North.

It is therefore urgent that the representatives and allies of the poor and the exploited of both the North and the South forge a new, more equitable relationship. Together we must create a common agenda and a joint strategy for confronting structural problems that are essentially the same in the North and the South.

New Relations between Southern and Northern NGOs

Many Northern and Southern NGOs are taking practical steps toward greater equality and genuine partnership. For example, representatives of the Caribbean regional NGO coalition, CARIPEDA, participate in meetings to plan the Caribbean programs of the Interagency Working Group, a Canadian NGO coalition. Oxfam America is discussing with its Caribbean partners the development of a structure in which Caribbean organizations will have the main responsibility for planning programs and disbursing and monitoring funds. Oxfam America has also joined The Development GAP, the Caribbean Conference of Churches, and the Ford Foundation in providing assistance to the Caribbean Policy Unit, recently established by many of the region's NGOs to assume responsibility from their Northern partners for injecting local-level Caribbean input into the economic policymaking process.

Similar steps are being taken in other parts of the world. The London-based European/Canadian consortium, ACORD, originally funded disaster relief and technical assistance by expatriate experts in regions of Africa suffering from wars, natural disasters, and rapid social change. ACORD is now working toward decentralization and the transfer of funds and decision-making power to African NGOs.

Southern development NGOs are growing rapidly in their capacity to plan projects and evaluate their programs. This lessens the need for placing Northern experts and expatriate staff in the field. The Canadian University Service Organization (CUSO), which used to give stipends mainly to Canadian volunteers in the Caribbean, now supports Caribbean nationals working under the guidance of Caribbean NGOs. This is becoming more generally the case.

Another trend among Northern NGOs is toward support for the longer-term programs of Southern NGOs and away from a focus on short-term projects. Criteria for project evaluation are also evolving. Project success was once, and still is among charity-oriented agencies, measured in terms of the delivery of material aid or services to disaster victims and to the poor. In the 1970s and 1980s, the ability of projects such as poultry cooperatives and handicraft enterprises to generate income for project participants, and thus to become financially self-sustaining, became a common measure of success.

Today, change-oriented NGOs in the South, and to a lesser extent in the North, are aware that while the financial success of grassroots projects is usually quite important, the achievement of self-reliance over a two- or three-year time span is often not a realistic goal. It is impossible for some projects to become economically independent from external NGO aid when the human and material wealth of a nation is continually being drained. Often other criteria are more important, such as development of skills in production, management, and planning by project participants, and their increased confidence, leadership capacity and understanding of the underlying causes of their problems and their relationship to the international economy.

It is incumbent upon Northern NGOs to transfer power to, and eliminate unnecesary burdens on, Southern NGOs. Specific measures include better coordination of Northern NGO programming (with Southern consultation) and reduction of the competition among Northern NGOs for funds, publicity and ownership of Southern partner organizations and projects. Oxfam UK, Oxfam Canada, Oxfam Quebec and Oxfam America all support development work in the Caribbean and in Central America. The four agencies have begun in recent years to work more closely with each other in planning, coordinating and evaluating their programs in both regions. Further steps might be the development of common procedures for reporting on the use of funds by project partners, common criteria and formats for evaluation, and coordinated timetables for visits by Northern NGO staff to Southern NGOs. Perhaps most important is the establishment of mechanisms for the direct participation of Southern NGO representatives in program planning and evaluation.

In order to increase their effectiveness and to avoid being manipulated by aid-givers, Caribbean intermediary NGOs have come up with a series of recommendations. These include: collecting information about the procedures and agendas of foreign donors; sharing information with NGOs in other parts of the South; developing a pool of Caribbean resource people with technical, administrative and evaluation skills; solidifying pan-Caribbean NGO networks that can negotiate the terms of foreign assistance collectively and from a position of strength; insisting on forms of funding that involve beneficiaries in decision-making and that respect local culture. ADA member Judith Wedderburn has noted that:

In the absence of a regional response to the debt [crisis] through formal or official CARICOM or government institutions, the networking process which has gathered momentum in the Caribbean NGO community needs to be fully explored and utilized, not only to widen public education about the debt, but to stimulate public discussion about realistic approaches to solving the problem of the debt. . . . Sitting down with government planners is important for NGOs, but we must be clear on our own agenda, confident in the value of our expertise, and not be afraid to demand respect and recognition. . . . Local NGOs cannot afford to become just branch plants of overseas NGOs.[7]

NGOs and the World Bank: Hard Lessons from the 1980s

Can NGOs foster policy change that is more than merely cosmetic? Can they help the movements of the poor to achieve structural transformation, rather than simply adjusting to adjustment? How can NGOs avoid falling into the trap of being used by the powerful to promote their own agendas? Is it possible for both Southern and Northern intermediary NGOs to ensure that they themselves, in seeking to pursue the interests of the poor, do not use or exploit the grassroots groups they serve?

These questions were explored when representatives of NGOs from 53 countries met in September 1990 at the Fifth International NGO Forum on World Bank and IMF Lending in Washington DC. Participants found some inspiring success stories in the experiences of NGOs and popular movements in opposing environmentally and socially destructive large-scale projects sponsored by the World Bank and other multilateral funders. In assessing the net results of efforts to reform the policies of the World Bank, however, they drew sobering conclusions.

The delegates agreed that organized North–South NGO coalitions have been able to stop some World Bank-funded mega-projects or, at least, to ameliorate the negative impact on people in the South and on the ecosystems of which they are a part. They found, however, that these coalitions have succeeded only when efforts to pressure the Bank by 'working within the system' — by means of dialogue with officials, pressing the Bank to heed its own rhetoric, insisting on environmental impact studies, issuing appeals via the mass media, lobbying legislators — have been accompanied by the mobilization of popular movements of the potential victims of huge hydropower, logging, mining, and oil extraction schemes. Witoon Permongsacharoen of a Thai NGO, Project for Ecological Recovery, told the forum:

At first we thought that the push for economic growth could go together with preservation of the environment, but all the energy projects built by the World Bank have led to environmental destruction. We were able to stop one big project opposed by NGOs and by local people, but not another, where the people were not mobilized. Our experience confirms that reform of World Bank policy is impossible. Our strategy is to strengthen our peoples' movements to promote our own solutions. That's the only way to affect World Bank activities that are destroying the environment.

Walden Bello, a development analyst from the Philippines and director of Food First in San Francisco, noted that NGOs have attempted three main types of interventions against international financial institutions: broad national coalitions, grassroots movements and international campaigns. NGOs need to use all these tactics, he said, but stressed that 'NGOs can only be effective to the extent that they are linked to popular organizations.' The victories resulting from these efforts have been outweighed by losses, added a Brazilian delegate:

> The international lenders have never had an ecosystemic approach. The World Bank selects small islands of unproductive lands to highlight as 'environmental' projects, while all around those islands, destructive 'development' continues. The productive and environmental potential of the lands and people being destroyed in never considered.

The World Bank has become adept at dodging its opponents, said Doug Hellinger of Development Group for Alternative Policy:

> Despite all of our resistance and organizing, the situation is worse than ten years ago. Bank reorganization to recycle money out of the South even faster has shortened the project cycle. The job of many of the Bank's staff now is damage control. They are there to blunt the impact of what we do by shifting conditionalities from project loans to sectoral adjustment loans; by setting up women's and environmental and NGO divisions to make us feel important; by devising compensatory programs to target troublemakers; by drawn-out negotiations for insignificant reforms; and by turning up their policy rhetoric without any impact on bank operations.

Barbara Bramble of the National Wildlife Federation noted that, in response to its critics, the World Bank frequently changes the titles of a project to call it a 'Natural Resources Management' plan without altering the project's resource-destructive content: 'The Bank's Policy Section produes a blizzard of paper about environmental concerns, but the Operations Section, where the real power lies, doesn't have to pay any attention.' A Senegalese delegate from the African NGO coalition FAVDO, said that in West Africa:

> The Bank works with NGOs only for its own interests. It has learned to bring in NGOs during the project pre-approval stage, but once a project has been approved by the government, NGOs are pushed out of the process. Then, when things go wrong, the Bank tells us 'go complain to your government'.

Maximo Kalaw Jr, of the Haribon Institute in the Philippines, summarized the consensus of the forum's session on the impact of the World Bank on people and their environments:

The World Bank reflects the interests of the beneficiaries of the industrial paradigm; its model of economic efficiency is the antithesis of ecologically sound development. The World Bank, which has been a debt manager, is now positioning itself to be a global resource manager. But the World Bank is fundamentally a poverty-creating and environment-destroying institution.

The campaigns of resistance against it have been pressed most strongly by its victims, especially women and indigenous people. The resistance has been successful in stopping some projects, but the bank has merely retreated to pursue the same aim at a higher level, that of adjustment policy. To deal with that, cooperation of NGOs internationally is crucial. We have to repudiate the Bank's claims of eco-legitimacy and sovereignty and challenge the right of the World Bank to control our resources.

The delegates analysed the rapid realignment of political forces from East–West confrontation to a competitive and uneasy tri-polar alliance of the United States, Europe and Japan. The wealthy and powerful within each pole, and transnationally, are seeking greater scope for exploitation of the people and resources of the South, with the aid of Southern-country élites. The US élite looks Southward, especially to Latin America and the Middle East, for the means to maintain its global hegemonic power, attempting to press its advantage by the use of tied foreign aid, structural adjustment conditionalities, and US-sponsored extension and revision of the Global Agreement on Tariffs and Trade (GATT). As returns from these mechanisms diminish, the United States is likely to turn increasingly to military force, many predicted. (Four months later, the United States launched its war against Iraq.)

The global confrontation is no longer one of nationalist and revolutionary movements against colonialism, but rather 'a resistance to recolonization and the loss of our sovereignty in the name of free trade,' said Chee Yoke Ling of Sahabat Alam/Friends of the Earth in Malaysia. If NGOs are to aid in that resistance, 'Our accountability must be to the people,' she said. 'We are seeing the popular movements declared illegal and insurrectionary. Even when people are only defending their own homes and forests and fishing grounds, they are being criminalized.' According to Ethiopian-born economist Fantu Cheru:

> The World Bank and IMF are turning their attention toward a strategy against insurrections in the Third World. Environmental movements are one of the movements they are trying to stop. They are going beyond attempts to appease the environmental movements by means of co-optation, to interventions to stop popular organizations.

But Fantu Cheru and others find in the movements of the poor and the marginalized much reason for hope. Charles Abugre, a development activist from Ghana, is helping the poor to build cooperatives in isolated regions of Uganda, a country badly ravaged by war, debt and disease. He told the forum:

> If I were to present our situation from the viewpoint of the dominant

paradigm, in terms of trade statistics, commodity prices, the quantities of financial and natural resources, and so on, Africa would appear as a picture of misery. But to talk that way would be to ignore our most important resource: our people.

The World Bank model widens the gap between people and their land, between what people want to consume and what they can actually produce, between aspirations and reality. That model is imposed not just by economic means, but by political and military power. But there is a movement among the marginalized, in the wake of retreat of the state, of energetic, microcosmic groups creating their own alternatives. At this stage they are developing their capability. They are not yet linked, and they haven't yet found a rhetoric that interests foreign NGOs. It is the empowerment of these people, and not debates among the élites about economic models, that will resolve the issue of structural adjustment.

Notes

1. International NGO Forum for Ecodevelopment, September 1990, Washington DC.

2. Report on an international consultation in New Delhi, India, sponsored by the International Council for Adult Education, in the *1988–89 Annual Report of the Association of Development Agencies*, Kingston, Jamaica, 1989.

3. World Bank, *How the World Bank Works With Non-governmental Organizations*, Washingon DC, 1990.

4. Author interviews, June 1988, Washington, DC.

5. Joan Ross-Frankson, *1989–90 Annual Report of the Association of Development Agencies*, Kingston, Jamaica, 1990.

6. ADA, 'For Your Information', Kingston, Jamaica, 1990.

7. Judith Wedderburn, 'NGOs and the Debt', Consortium Graduate School of Social Sciences public seminar, UWI, Mona, Jamaica, July 1990.

17. Toward a New US Policy

> Which economic system prevails is not determined by which one is more efficient, but by who has the power to impose their system on others. The constituencies of our NGOs fear reprisals, because to confront the policies that hurt them means confronting the state, and that can result quickly in repression and military force. What has begun as aid and loans may soon lead to US troops on our shores.
>
> Joan French, Sistren, Jamaica

Chapters 12 through 15 provide a glimpse of the potential for new, creative solutions to Caribbean economic and social crises. Caribbean citizens deserve a chance to explore these alternatives and to define development in their own terms. Experience suggests that there is no single answer and that workable alternatives will require a combination of approaches.

The complexity of the region's economic problems and the rapidly changing political context call for flexibility and an open-minded attitude. Many Caribbean NGOs have such an approach toward contentious issues such as the role of markets, terms and priorities in external trade, the balance between planning and decentralization, various forms of ownership of productive resources, the tensions between urgent needs and long-term sustainability, and the creation of new democratic institutions.

The US effort to impose a single development dogma, one that has already failed, is blocking the opportunity for experimentation and a more potentially fruitful, multifaceted development process. Moreover, the bias and rigidity of the US approach is shortsighted and detrimental in the long run to interests of the US majority.

In response to economic challenges from Europe and Japan, the United States is attempting to turn the Americas into an economic fortress. The goal is a US-dominated hemisphere, with weakened trade unions, low social spending, deregulation of corporate activity, and protectionist walls against foreign capital in areas where the US competitive position is weak, and minimal barriers to US exporters and investors within the region.

The means to this goal include not only AID programs and structural adjustment conditionalities but also the CBI, the Enterprise for the Americas Initiative and other not-so-reciprocal free trade agreements that allow retention of regulations and quotas to limit exports to the US. The United States has also been pressing for new provisions in GATT that would favor US agribusiness and other corporations. These include the elimination of agricultural price supports worldwide, and rules to prevent Southern and other countries from regulating foreign investment and from developing technology to produce goods and services, such as computer hardware and software, that might compete with US products. US success in its current efforts would enable US-based capital to rove freely through the western hemisphere, taking advantage of lowered wages, cheap commodities, and the opportunity provided by privatization policies to acquire ownership of Latin American and Caribbean land, minerals, timber and enterprises.

US success would also mean an accelerated increase in poverty, displacement from rural lands, urban unemployment and social decay, and environmental degradation. This would soon mean fewer buyers for US goods, social upheavals containable only by military force costly to the US, and the destruction of rainforest and other environments essential to the health of the planet and all of its residents.

Removing the Barriers to Development

A more far-sighted US policy could benefit the Caribbean countries and all citizens of the hemisphere. Some policy revisions that could support instead of block workable alternatives include the following:

Eliminate the bias in AID programs against food production for Caribbean needs
As Chapter 4 has shown, AID's agriculture policy in the Caribbean primarily promotes production of traditional export crops in an unprocessed state. In contrast to AID policy statements, AID programs do little to support crop diversification and almost nothing to support agro-industry and intraregional food trade. To the limited extent that AID does back production of non-traditional crops, it does so in a way that reinforces dependency on unreliable foreign markets, and leaves the most lucrative aspects of the export trade, shipping and processing, in foreign hands.

AID's support of traditional export crop production through the plantation system and its modern variants reflects the agency's tolerance of exploitative, poverty-creating social and economic structures. Through these structures foreign corporations and, to a lesser extent, the Caribbean upper strata have reaped the benefits of cheap Caribbean resources and labor.

AID's program reveals the US preference for alliance with the region's established élite and its reluctance even to recognize the challenge to these classes that is arising from the poor and the NGOs that work with them. Chapters 12 and 13 cited many positive proposals and some successful Caribbean-initiated small-scale projects in food production, processing and trade; almost none has received support from AID.

End the promotion of very low-wage export industry
US policies and AID programs support the expansion of low-wage export assembly industries. Meanwhile, the United States ignores or covertly supports the suppression and manipulation of trade unions by many Caribbean governments and turns a blind eye toward unsafe working conditions and other labor rights abuses.

Policies to maintain low wages reflect the US goals of maintaining the Caribbean as a cheap labor haven close to US shores, and of encouraging US business involvement in the region as a complement to US political influence and military presence there. US policymakers rationalize this stance by arguing that low-wage, export-oriented industrialization will lead to self-sustaining economic growth. The argument for low-wage industry ignores the experience of Europe and the United States, where growth has been based in large part on the expansion of domestic markets made possible, until recently, by steadily increasing wages. Economic growth is even less likely to occur, in the Caribbean today, given the context of debt, deregulation, and lower levels of aid.

Stop requiring favored treatment of US companies and end tied aid

AID grant agreements require recipient countries to purchase specified types or quantities of US products. The use of this type of tied aid to promote US exports benefits the companies involved but hurts the development prospects of Caribbean countries if it locks them into greater dependence on product lines and technologies they cannot afford.

The US CBI legislation requires favored treatment of US-owned companies by Caribbean and Central American governments as a criterion of CBI eligibility. As a precondition for US aid funds, AID requires Caribbean governments to give access to US firms to economic information, special government services, and investment incentives. It calls for unrestricted removal of profits by US-owned companies and deregulation of other corporate practices that can damage Caribbean environments and economies.

US insistence that Caribbean governments privatize government-owned land, government shares in joint public/private enterprises, and other public resources enables private investors to obtain Caribbean resources at fire-sale prices. But the goal of expanding US investment opportunities and Caribbean markets for US exports is negated by the policies described above. Impoverished or displaced farmers and workers earning bare-subsistence level wages cannot afford to purchase US products.

Cease backing structural adjustment programs that stifle development

As Part III explains, these programs do more to drain Caribbean resources than to increase the region's productive capacity or to promote sustainable economic growth. Continued dependence on agro-exports saps the strength of farmers and the fertility of the soil without building the basis for more sustainable food systems or more reliable sources of income. Low factory wages may increase the short-term profits of the factory owners but do little to increase the productive capacity of the host countries or the purchasing power of their citizens. Export assembly factories that cost countries more than they contribute to their economies do not help to balance budgets or repay debts.

Structural adjustment policies are causing increased poverty and import dependency, and are contributing to the breakdown of traditional support systems. They require reductions in social services on which the productivity and well-being of the population depend, and which are especially badly needed to cope with the consequence of worsening poverty and social disintegration.

In this context, the US alliance with Caribbean governing elites opposed to far-reaching change will sooner or later earn the animosity of those who suffer most from the crisis. This has already occurred in Haiti. The temporary suspension of US aid to the post-Duvalier regimes did not cause Haitians to forget US support of the Duvalier dictatorships, nor has it disguised the continued backing by the United States of the status quo, in which wealthy Haitians and foreign corporations reap the benefits of exploiting Haiti's land and labor. In other parts of the Caribbean, US support of established elites and its failure to heed the voices of the poor will surely undermine US influence over time.

It is also inevitable that policies that widen the gap between rich and poor will result in discontent and political turmoil. Political freedoms do not flourish in an atmosphere of acute economic distress. The 1980s saw strikes against structural adjustment austerity in Guyana and the Dominican Republic. The considerable public sympathy in Trinidad and Tobago for the actions of the Black Muslim militants who held the government hostage stemmed largely from widespread anger against the Robinson government's adjustment policies and its harassment of dissidents.

What the United States and the multilaterals are imposing on the Caribbean is not 'real structural adjustment', according to Neville Duncan, since it leaves structures for exploitation and removal of resources from the region intact. 'Real structural adjustment — the kind that could help lay the basis for development — has to involve the redistribution of assets.' Only in this way can the poor become more productive and economic growth be made sustainable, Duncan says. His views are shared by thousands of development activists in the region who workd on a day-to-day basis with farmers, workers and the poor.

Allow Caribbean states to steer their own development course
By means of conditions attached to AID grants, by backing structural adjustment programs, and through behind-the-scenes arm-twisting, the United States is pressing Caribbean countries to accept a single, made-in-the-North development model that functions primarily in the interests of the already-wealthy and is clearly failing to promote development. Ending these policies would not guarantee development, but would allow scope for Caribbean self-determination with regard to development goals and decisions.

One way for the United States to encourage pluralism would be to negotiate with Caribbean regional institutions, with Caribbean governments as a group, and especially with Caribbean NGOs that represent the poor. Caribbean regional institutions, rather than AID officials and consultants from the North, should have responsibility for allocating funds and for planning and monitoring development programs within a framework of goals and guidelines developed by Caribbean organizations, such as those outlined in chapters 12 to 15, and with direct input from grassroots organizations.

A precondition for such an approach is the separation of US foreign assistance from the geopolitical and military priorities of the White House and the Pentagon. The Washington-based development advocacy group, The Development GAP, has called for the establishment of a development aid agency independent of the US Department of State and directly accountable to Congress. The Development GAP cites the congressionally-funded Interamerican Foundation and African Development Foundation as precedents for US aid institutions that are structurally separate from the US executive.[1]

Practical Support for Caribbean-Led Development

In addition to eliminating the policies that hinder Caribbean development and self-determination, the United States could adopt positive measures to promote Caribbean food security, self-reliance and democracy.

In so doing, it is essential that the United States and other donors heed the voices and recognize the organizations of the poor and disenfranchised. It is not up to the United States to decide which organizations really represent the Caribbean's poor majority. However, the US could allow space for the strengthening of democracy and for the growth of genuinely representative structures, and for an active role in decision-making by the poor, by ceasing to favor governments which suppress the poor and which persecute unions and NGOs that are not supporters of those governments.

One process of genuine consultation with the people of the Caribbean began in 1982, when The Development GAP convened a meeting in Jamaica with NGOs from the region to elicit analyses of, and alternatives to, the Caribbean Basin Initiative. This process culminated in 1987–89, when The Development GAP organized for the US Congress a series of three public forums in the Caribbean on the CBI, US–Caribbean economic relations and a Caribbean development agenda. The forum participants included representatives of a broad range of non-governmental and governmental institutions and achieved a consensus on many policy issues. Among the specific positive steps proposed at these consultations and in other forums by Caribbean scholars and development activists that the United States should take are:

Emergency economic aid
- Provide balance-of-payments assistance grants to countries facing severe foreign exchange shortages in accordance with the priorities and principles listed in chapters 12 through 15, and for the import of critical basic consumer goods and inputs for small and medium-scale industries, farms and cooperatives. The use of such funds should no longer be restricted to purchases from US sources, nor tied to structural adjustment conditionalities.
- Replenish the Multilateral Clearing Facility of CARICOM, a fund established to facilitate trade within the Caribbean.
- In cases of disaster and drastic food emergencies, and of material aid in general, provide funds to purchase and transport needed food and medical, construction and other supplies *from Caribbean sources* to the greatest extent possible.

Support for regional institutions and economic integration
- Channel all assistance through Caribbean regional organizations. When consultants or subcontractors are hired, hire consultants, cooperatives and other enterprises identified by Caribbean regional and non-government organizations.
- Support regional institutions, including NGO coalitions, credit associations, academic and other research bodies, the CDB, CARICOM, and others established on the initiative of Caribbean citizens and organizations.
- Provide assistance to such institutions in planning and implementing regionally initiated and coordinated development, in accordance with the priorities and principles outlined in chapters 12–15.
- Provide scholarships and aid for technical training, and support efforts by regional institutions to build their capacity to provide such training.

Trade and industry
- Enter into long-term arrangements that guarantee stable markets and prices for the region's exports. Such guarantees are essential during the period of diversification and transition from dependence on a few unprocessed commodity exports.
- Expand in Caribbean countries commodity stabilization funds which compensate Southern exporters for income losses resulting from declines in world market prices for these commodities.
- Provide credit and grants for trade of Caribbean products by Caribbean organizations and small- to medium-scale businesses within the greater Caribbean, the South, and other parts of the world.
- Restore US quotas for Caribbean sugar imports during the period of diversification toward alternative crops and alternative uses of sugar-cane products. Eliminate US government price setting that guarantees high sugar prices, at the cost of an estimated US$1 billion yearly to US consumers, to a few companies that produce cane and beet sugar in the United States. Provide transitional unemployment compensation for Caribbean seasonal laborers who would no longer work on US sugar plantations.
- Reward the use of locally made components in Caribbean industry. Current CBI and other trade policies make access to US markets conditional on the proportion of US-origin inputs, thus favoring the types of investments that have the least linkages to Caribbean economies.
- Offer tax incentives to US companies that reinvest a substantial portion of their earnings in Caribbean countries where they operate, and to those which transfer skills and technology according to guidelines set by regional institutions.
- Respect the rights of Caribbean workers by enforcing the provisions of the US Trade Act of 1974; do not provide aid to any enterprise or government that fails to extend and enforce basic workers' rights as defined in section 502 (a) (4) of that Act.[2]

Food and farming
- Support the implementation of the CARICOM Regional Food and Nutrition Strategy developed in 1983.
- Support for research and experimentation by Caribbean scholars and NGOs in developing agricultural production and processing technologies that are sustainable and appropriate to Caribbean conditions.
- Support the development of new crops for regional consumption and industrial uses, alternative uses for traditional crops, and linkages of agriculture with other economic sectors.
- Provide assistance for food trade within the greater Caribbean region, including credit, and aid to Caribbean organizations for planning, marketing, and transportation and storage facilities.
- Support Caribbean-owned, small- and medium-scale cooperative and community-based farming and food-processing enterprises to increase food security and provide rural employment.
- Encourage far-reaching land reform and redistribution, backed up with credit and appropriate technical assistance to cooperatives and small-scale farmers.

Tourism
- Support regionally planned expansion of tourism that is culturally and ecologically sensitive, makes maximum use of local resources and skills, and integrates the industry with other aspects of local economies.

Ecologically sound development
- Support the direct involvement of Caribbean farmers, fishers, communities and grassroots groups in managing and renewing the region's natural resources.
- Support research and practical activities by Caribbean organizations to promote sustainable and resource-conserving farming, forestry, aquaculture and industry.
- Support development of wind, geothermal, small-scale hydroelectric, solar, biogas and other renewable and non-destructive sources of energy.
- Support environmental education for farmers, workers, planners and development activists, and development of ecology curricula for Caribbean schools.
- Monitor and prevent both the dumping of toxic wastes from US sources and the export of chemicals banned in the US or in Caribbean countries.

Many of the US policy reforms listed above, and additional measures, have subsequently been elaborated in legislation by the House Subcommittee on Western Hemispheric Affairs in consultation with The Development GAP and Caribbean NGOs. They are contained in a bill, the Caribbean Regional Development Act, which has been approved twice by the US House of Representatives but which, as of early 1991, had been blocked by conservative members of the US Senate.

Reversing the Militarization of the Region

In the first half of this century, the United States occupied or invaded countries in the greater Caribbean region at least 17 times, in addition to engineering the overthrow of governments by proxy forces. Today, the high-profile US military presence in the Caribbean and Central America is, and is intended to be, a deterrent to countries that might seek a foreign policy of non-alignment, or adopt non-capitalist policies as part of their development strategies. A senior Eastern Caribbean government official expressed an attitude common in the region when he said, 'Of course, there are options we cannot consider because the Americans would not allow it.'

The US military straddles the Central American isthmus, with a communications center in Key West, Florida, and major footholds in Honduras and Panama. Its control of Caribbean water is centered in Puerto Rico, the site of the major air–naval complex based at Roosevelt Road and numerous communications installations and training sites. The inhabited Puerto Rican island of Vieques, two-thirds of which is owned by the US government, is the target of practice bombardment by the US navy. Other US installations in the Caribbean, including bases in Antigua and the US Virgin Islands, were expanded during the 1980s and the major base at Guantanamo, Cuba, remains in US hands.

The memory of the US-sponsored invasion of Cuba in 1961, the occupation of the Dominican Republic by 20,000 US troops in 1965, the October 1983 invasion of Grenada, and the continuing US backing of sabotage and slaughter by the contras in Nicaragua (even after the election of a US-backed president in 1990), and the 1989 US invasion of Panama remain ominous reminders of the US readiness to use armed force in the Americas to pre-empt policies or overturn governments believed by US officials to threaten the interests of the United States. Jamaicans who were active in the movement to resist harsher IMF austerity requirements in the 1970s note that the fear of direct US intervention was an intimidating factor that weakened the will of some Jamaicans to risk pursuing a more independent course.

The Grenada revolution was anathema to some Caribbean nationals, particularly conservative officials and economic élites, but the Bishop government's emphasis on Caribbean pride and sovereignty, political non-alignment and regional unity made it attractive to many others. The revolution stimulated the regional exchange of development skills and ideas, as Caribbean citizens came to Grenada to participate in the programs of the revolution. It inspired many to seek closer cooperation within the region and replication in their own nations of the revolutionary government's successful social programs.

These same characteristics of the revolution made the Bishop-led government seem threatening in the eyes of US officials. The alleged endangerment of US medical students and the blatantly false claim that Grenada's new airport was a Soviet military base in disguise were merely pretexts for the US invasion. The underlying purpose was to suppress an alternative that might spur other Caribbean and Central American states to slip out of the sphere of US dominance.

Memories of this and other US military interventions are kept fresh by the stationing of US troops in Honduras and Panama, the presence of US-trained special service units (SSUs) within Caribbean armies and police forces, and by the almost continuous military maneuvers in the Caribbean–Atlantic region, punctuated by annual war games coordinated from US command posts and bases in Panama and Puerto Rico.

The alleged communist threat is no longer an effective excuse for US military meddling in the affairs of sovereign states. While the US government continues to use this rationale for armed intervention, it has begun to make use of others, such as stopping drug traffic (in Panama and Peru) and protecting 'our' resources (such as Middle Eastern oil) and Caribbean sea lanes. Recognition by US citizens of the real threat to their own interests of such actions, and effective mobilization against them, is the best hope for preventing further US military intimidation and destruction.

Debt: The Case for Cancellation

The single most important step the North could take to promote Caribbean development would be to cancel the region's outstanding external debt. Debt reduction is an essential precondition of sustainable economic growth. Debt cancellation is also called for from an ethical standpoint because those being asked to sacrifice the most had no say in the decision to borrow, and got little if any benefit from the loans. Some governments made unwise decisions about the size of debt they took on and the uses to which loan funds were put, but they did so with encouragement, often pressure, from Northern governments and financial institutions. Furthermore, neither the poor nor the governments that accepted the loans are responsible for the sharp interest rate increases that have multiplied the amounts owed.

The US position: protecting the banks

The United States government, however, has consistently opposed proposals for comprehensive debt relief for indebted Southern countries. Some European governments, particularly France, decided in 1988 to write off loans to impoverished African debtors. The Canadian government announced in 1989 that it would cancel most of the debts owed to it by poor Caribbean countries. The United States refused to follow suit.

The recent US proposal for partial debt relief, known as the Brady Plan after Treasury Secretary Nicholas Brady, who announced it in March 1989, calls for a partial write-off of commercial bank debts. This step has already been taken by some US and many European and Japanese banks because they recognize that the debts are not collectable. Under Brady's plan, banks that did so would receive guarantees that their remaining debts would be repaid, if necessary with the aid of the multilateral lenders.

This, in effect, would give the taxpayers of the world, whose governments are ultimately responsible for covering IMF and World Bank loans, the burden of protecting and subsidizing commercial banks, and primarily those based in the United States. US taxpayers already cover part of the cost of failed commercial bank loans when the banks take tax deductions for their paper losses, in addition to subsidizing the bail-out and reorganization of US savings and loan institutions and commercial banks.

The Brady Plan and subsequent Bush administration pronouncements hinting at US-supported debt swaps in the Americas will not stop the downward spiral of debt and depression in Southern economies. Even if fully implemented they would not stop the net flow of funds from South to North.[4] This is especially true in the Caribbean and in Africa, where most of the foreign debt is owed to governments and multilateral lending agencies, not private banks. And the United States continues to oppose any debt reduction negotiations with groups of indebted countries, insisting instead on a case-by-case evaluation of which of the world's poor nations are 'deserving' of debt relief.

In addition, the Bush administration proposals include an ominous departure from the previous official US position. They have put the United States on record in favor of debt-for-equity swaps, in which lenders are given shares of debtor country resources, such as mining companies, public utilities and government-owned banks and pension funds, in exchange for the partial reduction of debt claims. This presses impoverished countries to trade foreign debt for foreign ownership and to relinquish even more of their diminishing ability to influence the distribution of wealth and resources within their own borders.

The IOUs from Caribbean and other indebted Southern nations held by commercial banks largely represent windfall gains from interest rate increases and debt refinancing aided by Northern governments and multilateral lenders. The banks did not do anything other than to risk relatively small amounts of capital to earn the vast sums they are owed on paper. It is reasonable that the profit-seeking financial corporations that made the risky loans, rather than US taxpayers, should accept the losses. Refusal by the United States to bail out the banks would also be consistent with the US official position that governments should not interfere in economies.

The multilateral lenders: saving the status quo
The multilateral funding institutions, despite the development assistance image they try to project, have been even more unwilling than most Northern governments and commercial banks to reduce or write off their uncollectable debts. This rigidity stems from several related factors. One is that the multilaterals see themselves as the final bastion of stability in an increasingly unstable and unpredictable international financial system. If they were to cease their refinancing of loans and their recycling of cash out of poor countries and back to the over-extended banks of the North, these mega-agencies fear, many Southern governments would have no choice but to stop paying their loans and declare defaults.

This could start a chain reaction that might result in the downfall of major private financial institutions and the partial loss of some large private fortunes. At the same time, such a turn of events would wipe out many of the paper claims held by individuals and institutions in the North on vast amounts of minerals, timber, land, labor and other resources in the South. Increasing numbers of Southern spokespeople argue that, despite the loss, at least temporarily, of international commercial credit that default would probably precipitate, such a stance would be more in the interests of Southern debtor nations and the majority of their citizens than the present, resource-draining system.

An alternative to outright and uncontrolled default on the one hand, and the current failing and destructive policies on the other, would be a managed reduction of bilateral, multilateral and commercial debts, in consultation with debtor country governments and NGOs representing the poor. Thus far, the World Bank and other major multilateral lenders have been adamantly opposed to such a process. To forgive a significant amount of the debt would put the reputation of the World Bank on the line. It would mean acknowledging the fallacy of the premise on which the Bank and its sister agencies stake their claim to authority over Southern economies: that maximizing the international flow of for-profit trade and investment is possible, is desirable for the greater good of all, and will ultimately result in development.

By setting a precedent, debt forgiveness could increase pressure for further cancellations and defaults. But a major reason for the continued existence of the multilaterals is precisely to prevent such a scenario and to keep capital flowing to and, at present, mainly out of the South. To accept a substantial loss on some World Bank loans might lead to a lowered credit rating and difficulty raising funds by selling bonds to private investors. This could force the Bank to turn to its member countries and ask them to pay out the significant amounts of money they have pledged to guarantee the Bank's payment of its obligations to its bondholders. Such a step would mean, in effect, that US and other taxpayers of the world, through their governments' contributions to the World Bank, would be protecting and subsidizing the fortunes of some of the world's wealthiest institutions and individuals — the shareholders of commercial banks and the World Bank's own bondholders.

The Bank wants to avoid actually calling for payment of the funds put up by its subscribing member countries. As many analysts and some members of Congress have pointed out, the US public would thus be covering the losses of the Bank and its sister agencies so that they could continue to carry out their main role and fundamental mandate — that of protecting global trade and the interests of private, for-profit bank, corporations and individuals with investments in the South. Such a choice would provoke intense controversy in the US at a time of fiscal crisis and austerity in the United States itself.

More of the world's citizens are coming to realize that the current system of allocating global resources according to criteria of profitability — the free market development model — is not only not leading to development, but is creating increased polarization of wealth, human misery, hunger and environmental devastation. Ultimately, and probably much sooner than most Bank and government officials realize, the role of the World Bank and similar institutions in perpetuating this cycle of destruction will be questioned and will have to be transformed.

In the meantime, there is nothing to prevent bilateral donors from cancelling or substantially reducing their loan claims on the world's most impoverished and debt-burdened nations. By writing off its loans to the hopelessly indebted countries in what it considers its own backyard, the US government could take a step that is both practically necessary and morally urgent. Even more constructive would be for the United States to take this action in concert with the governments of other donor countries, and to do so in consultation with the indebted Caribbean countries as a group. However, current US proposals for partial forgiveness, under the Enterprise for the Americas Initiative, of certain Latin American and Caribbean debts to the US government may well do more harm than good, since the write-offs would be made contingent on stringent structural adjustments with the IMF or World Bank and on new agreements with commercial lenders for repayment of sums that might otherwise not be repaid.

Exporting US Problems: A No-Win Policy

These same US policies that inhibit Caribbean development and block the exploration of alternative strategies are also self-defeating in terms of the United States' own long-term economic interests and foreign policy goals. One reason is that the objectives on which these policies are based are mutually contradictory. The AID criterion of enhancing business opportunities for US exporters and investors undermines the Agency's claimed objective of fostering self-sustaining economic growth in the Caribbean.

The use of AID grant conditionalities and CBI stipulations to promote US business interests is part of an effort to export the United States' own economic problems and solve them at poor countries' expense. The expansion and support of low-wage industries by means of subsidies from US and Caribbean governments is one response to the declining competitiveness of US manufactured goods in world markets.

The causes of this declining competitiveness include obsolete plants and technologies, poor management, the lack of coordination and planning of industrial research and development, the drain of military expenditures (the costs of which outweigh their contributions to the US economy), and the trend of increased use of capital for speculative rather than productive purposes. Instead of addressing these problems, the US government has chosen the least-cost, short-term option of encouraging US-based corporations to take advantage of low-wage Third World labor.

The response of US firms to Caribbean investment incentives has been far less enthusiastic than predicted by proponents of this strategy.[5] To the extent that US companies do respond to incentives to relocate their operations in the

Caribbean, US workers lose jobs, Caribbean countries gain little for nothing (since earnings are low and incentives costly), and the problem of declining US competitiveness is merely partially postponed, not solved.

The promotion of US exports through tied aid is also a response to a US economic problem, that of persistent balance of trade deficits. By subsidizing US exports in the short term through AID grants, trade credits and insurance, the United States government hopes to create or expand markets for US products that will not require subsidization once the economies of the South begin to grow. However, these policies are doing more to stifle than to enhance the prospects of such growth. Thus, in the longer term, such policies weaken the ability of Caribbean and other Third World countries to buy US products or participate in joint economic enterprises with the United States.

The pressure on Caribbean governments to meet debt service payments, and the US reluctance to recognize officially that most of these debts are not payable, is also in part a reaction to a US economic problem. High-risk loans by US banks and unwise use of loan funds by recipient governments have left US banks dangerously overextended.[6]

The goal of meeting basic human needs for food, shelter, education and health services has been largely eclipsed since the early 1980s in AID programs by the objectives of privatization, deregulation and US business promotion. Not only are these US priorities self-defeating as economic policies for the Caribbean. The US-backed effort to squeeze a surplus from overburdened economies for debt payments and exports also imperils the expressed US objectives of political stability and enhanced democracy in the region.

Ending the US policies that damage Caribbean development prospects would entail a major reorientation of current US foreign aid and trade priorities, but it would not necessarily require increases in foreign aid expenditures. The current amounts of US aid to Caribbean countries are almost negligible as a proportion of the US foreign assistance budget, but even this low level of funding could give significant support to the alternative development options outlined in chapters 12 to 15.

Substantial support for development of agro-industry, intraregional trade, appropriate import substitution, training and education, public services, and environmentally and culturally sensitive tourism could do a great deal more. Not only could Caribbean citizens have a better chance of carrying out genuine development, but US workers and consumers would benefit from trade and other exchanges with stable and thriving Caribbean societies.

Notes

1. *Aid for Just Development*, The Development GAP, Lynne Rienner, 1988, Boulder and London.

2. See the Caribbean Regional Development Act. Copies of this proposed US legislation are available from The Development Group for Alternative Policies, Suite 52, 1400 I Street NW, Washington DC 20005.

3. Ibid.

4. Sarah Bartlett, 'US Efforts to Aid Debtor Nations Bring "Profound Disappointment"', *New York Times*, 24, 25 and 26 July 1989; Carol Barton, 'A Critique of the New US Administration Plan for "Third World Debt"', Church Women United, New York, March 1989.

5. US investments in the Caribbean, as noted in Chapter 10, declined during the 1980s. In many cases it has been investors from Korea, Taiwan and other countries who have set up shop in Caribbean low-wage havens.

6. The United States' own dangerous fiscal crisis is an impediment to proposals that would reduce the debts of Southern countries by requiring the United States to cover US bank losses either directly, through US government compensation, or indirectly, through guarantees to the banks by the World Bank and IMF, for which the United States and other sponsors of the multilateral lenders are ultimately responsible.

18.   The Caribbean and the World

We are in the midst of a second industrial revolution, based on microchip electronics, information control, and biotechnology. The first industrial revolution was financed in large part by Caribbean sugar and the exploitation of slavery. The second is now partly financed by a massive outflow of capital in the form of debt financing. This second industrial revolution will result in social dislocations and political upheavals even greater than that of the first one. The entire world — not just the Third World — has to transform our economy. The new technologies can give us the potential to do so, but only if we wrest control of the system from the hands of the international élite.

David Abdullah,
Oil Workers Trade Union, Trinidad and Tobago

The Caribbean crisis, while unique in some features, reflects a similar intensification of social and economic pressures in most countries in Africa and Latin America and many countries in Asia. Most Caribbean countries share with the other nations of the global South characteristics which reflect their colonial past and constrain their development prospects. Among the most important of these common features are: rapid urbanization of predominantly rural societies; the breakdown of traditional social and economic structures; trade patterns based on exchanging unprocessed agricultural and mineral commodities for imported manufactured products and basic consumer goods; lack of control over export prices, resulting in balance of trade deficits and high levels of external debt.

But the single most important reality that underlies the poverty and dependency of the Caribbean is the lack of connection between the uses of the region's resources — land, water, minerals, and human knowledge and labor — and the real needs and desires of the region's people. Individuals and institutions outside the Caribbean determine what the region will produce, what it will sell at what price, and what it will import at what cost. This lack of congruence between the way resources are used and the needs of the population characterizes, to a greater or lesser degree, all the world's so-called underdeveloped countries — a better term is maldeveloped — and is the central reason for their continuing impoverishment.

Caribbean societies are almost entirely creations of colonialism. The majority of the populations were brought to the region from abroad, as slaves from Africa or indentured laborers from Asia, after the region's indigenous populations were almost entirely wiped out. (Indigenous people still live in Guyana, Surinam, Cayenne, Belize and, in smaller numbers, in Dominica and St Vincent.)[1] Social and economic structures, particularly the plantation system, were imposed from the outside and developed and modified to meet the needs of the colonizers. Thus, the gap between the needs of the population and the use of local resources to serve outside interests is even wider in the

Caribbean than in parts of Asia, Africa and Latin America where traditional societies, food systems and industries were distorted, but not entirely destroyed, by the colonial process.

Ominous Trends

The extreme openness of Caribbean economies (the unusually high dependence on imports and exports described in Chapter 2) makes them especially vulnerable to external political pressures and changing conditions they cannot control. The small size of most Caribbean countries means that those countries have little bargaining power in negotiations over trade, investment and lending. Unlike nations such as Brazil and Mexico, which owe huge sums to Northern-country banks, Caribbean nations could default without greatly harming the financial systems of the creditor countries. The divisions among Caribbean countries resulting from language differences and ties to the former colonial powers have made it even more difficult for the nations of the region to chart their own destinies.

Despite these distinctive features of the Caribbean region, the almost total separation between needs and resources seen in the Caribbean today portends the future of other, less totally colonized societies. The concentration of control over land and minerals, markets and trade in the hands of a minority, which has characterized the Caribbean since the colonial period, is becoming typical throughout much of the South. With the expansion of world trade, the globalization of investment and the penetration of the market economy into all regions of the earth, the world's remaining self-provisioning peasant societies are being subsumed into, and undermined by, the international cash economy. As agriculture is being commercialized and mechanized, and local staples displaced by export crops, farmers worldwide are being pushed off the land by legally sanctioned eviction or by force, or because they are unable to compete with large-scale growers or with cheaper, imported foods.

In this system, which is particularly far advanced in much of the Caribbean, it is profitability, or the lack of profit-making potential that determines what products are grown or manufactured, where they are produced, by whom and for what remuneration. Increasingly, access to cash, or the lack of cash, determines who will consume what is produced. Whether or not one needs food, and whether or not one is willing and able to work to grow it, is less and less the factor that determines whether one shall eat.

This discrepancy between those who produce and those who purchase, between those who need and those who consume, is reflected worldwide in an increasing disparity between living standards and patterns of consumption of the countries of the North and those of the South. The United States, with only 4 per cent of the world's population, consumes an estimated 25 per cent of the world's resources. Among these are more than US$4 billion yearly worth of products from the Caribbean.

The flow of wealth from South to North

Many citizens of the North believe that their relatively wealthy, industrialized nations are supporting many countries in the South through foreign assistance programs. The reality is the reverse. Since 1986, there has been a net transfer of wealth from the countries of the South to those of the North, US$43 billion in 1988, according to World Bank calculations. Much of this transfer has come about through the efforts of countries in the South to make payments on their massive foreign debts, which totaled more than US$1.2 trillion in 1990. In terms of debt service alone, the South has been paying yearly about two and a half times the total it receives from the North in the form of foreign aid.[2]

The global debt crisis reflects the concentration of control over world resources in the hands of a minority. In essence, Third World debt is nothing more than a claim by a relative handful of wealthy individuals and institutions in the industrialized countries over vast amounts of minerals, land and labor power in the countries of the South.

In an effort to pay their foreign debts — in order to be eligible for additional loans needed to stave off bankruptcy — governments of the South are squeezing every bit of available wealth from their already weak economies. The sources of wealth they are tapping and, increasingly, making available to foreign investors, are underground minerals, tropical forests, fertile lands, and the sweat of factory workers and farmers. Thus debt has become a powerful siphon, draining the economic lifeblood of Caribbean and other nations of the South.

The increasing gulf between the world's well-fed minority and the hungry majority is a threat to the well-being of all. The privation of farmers, workers and the unemployed in the South is causing increasing political instability that leads to insecurity in the North as well as the South and enhances the likelihood of war. And already, the results of environmental deterioration are affecting everyone on earth. For all these reasons, the efforts of people and organizations in the Caribbean to chart a new path to development that is more self-reliant, that places the needs of the impoverished majority over the comforts of local élites and the profits of foreign investors, and that is safe and sustainable in the long run is very much in the interest of citizens of the United States and of the entire world.

The Search for New Models

By 1990 in the United States, Western Europe and Japan, government and business spokespeople were celebrating the nearly worldwide triumph of the capitalist brand of democracy, equated with multi-party electoral contests, free trade, and the deregulation and dominance of the private sector. But even as the victory party continued, there was a deepening realization that the formal structures of representative democracy do not necessarily guarantee a democracy which is meaningful for the majority of citizens. The institutions of parliament and party have proven to be quite compatible with the concentration of power in the hands of the few.

The Stalinist version of the vanguard party and the bureaucratic socialist state have been more widely discredited. Yet the socialist ideal that places the needs of people in front of the rights of private property is far from dead. The placing of the collective good ahead of individual gain also resonates with the values of many traditional societies. At the same time, the democratic ideal of a society in which ordinary people have a say in the decisions that affect their lives, and civil liberties are honored, is also very much alive. And the badly abused precept of respect and care for the natural environment has become urgently compelling.

While the ideals of democracy, equality, the common good, and harmony with nature remain meaningful, the socio-economic systems and political ideologies to which they have been attached no longer provide ready-made answers. Caribbean and other Southern NGOs are striving to find solutions to the pressing problems of poverty and, in the process, to create new structures and methods for achieving social justice and sustainable development. It is clear that these goals cannot be achieved by means of a free market, trickle-down process. But neither can they be accomplished by a 'trickle-up' model that calls for small- and micro-enterprise promotion and the unleashing of entrepreneurialism in the informal economy. So long as Southern country economies continue to be drained, this approach would provide opportunities only for certain individuals or groups, owners of a small business, for example, while leaving the poor majority marginalized.

Sustainable development cannot be attained merely by means of a gradual, quantitative accretion of income-generating projects. The economic success of individual cooperatives or micro-enterprises cannot provide a formula for development in the context of the continuing and deepening impoverishment of the South as a whole. Only far-reaching and fundamental structural changes can reverse the net outflow of human and natural resources from impoverished populations and indebted nations.

The nature of such changes, and the path to equitable, sustainable and democratic development, cannot be charted entirely in advance. New structures and methods will be created through a process of practical experimentation and constant re-evaluation, and in relation to changing economic and political conditions. This process must permit a multiplicity of models; what works under one set of circumstances may fail in another. Among the issues to be explored through this dialectical dynamic are:

- the relation of local and grassroots organizations to national and regional institutions, and the relation of private organizations to the state, in the creation of workable democracy;
- the appropriate balance between individual initiative and community and national planning, and between centralized and decentralized economic structures;
- the role and scope of markets at the local, national, regional and international levels, and the pros and cons of various forms of managed

    trade, protection, price-setting and subsidies;
- the advantages and limitations of various forms of ownership — individual, cooperative and state — of land and other productive resources, and of forms of collective consumption of goods and services (such as communal refrigeration and laundry facilities as opposed to privately owned refrigerators and washing machines);
- the means of addressing immediate needs without endangering longer-term sustainability, and the development of ecologically sound and energy-conserving systems of production, transportation and waste management;
- new definitions and measures of development that take into account the holistic criteria outlined in chapters 14 and 15; and
- inequalities of gender, color, ethnicity and class within the movements for change, and the ways in which grappling with these deep-rooted and daunting problems is part of the broader development process.

The South within the North

As the international economy becomes integrated on a global scale, people in the North and the South find ourselves part of one world, albeit a world divided among competing capitalist power centers and characterized by immense and increasing extremes of poverty and wealth. In this world, even as resources continue to flow out of the South to support the economies of the North, other characteristics that once distinguished developed from underdeveloped societies are losing their meaning. Many manufacturing and some service industries are moving from Northern to Southern countries in search of cheap labor and resources, state subsidies, and freedom from taxation, worker safety standards and environmental regulations. This adds to chronic unemployment, falling real incomes, shrinking tax revenues, and government fiscal deficits in the North.

In the United States and Canada, government is seeking to create conditions and provide incentives to retain private investors. These incentives are similar to those used to attract the private sector in the South: decreased taxation of corporations and wealthy individuals, relaxed financial and environmental regulation of corporate activity, and sharp reductions in social spending in the context of government fiscal crisis. Unification of Europe under the free market banner is likely to accelerate the polarization of wealth and enlarge the underclass of people who lack secure access to employment, incomes, health care and shelter. Cracks are appearing in the glossy facade of Japanese industrial society as financial speculation and international competitive pressures heighten internal social stress and tarnish the myths of ethnic unity and class harmony.

These trends are fostering the growth of 'the South within the North'. The effects of privatization and deregulation (and, in the United States, of military spending and huge budget deficits) can be seen in decaying infrastructure, scarce, expensive and poor-quality health and education services, declining real incomes for the majority, and the continuation and increase of wasteful and hazardous processes in industry. In the United States during the past two decades, privatization (of, for example, child care, postal services, public housing and transportation) and deregulation policies have shredded the social safety net and eroded government programs for public welfare that were already less extensive than those in Western or Eastern Europe.

The polarization between the haves and have-nots is becoming greater and more stratified along lines of color and gender, especially in the United States. Symptoms of the trend toward marginalization of the majority within the debt-ridden and unstable US economy include surging social violence, rising numbers of people crippled by dependency on hard drugs, rising rates of increase in the spread of AIDS and other preventable diseases among the black and Hispanic populations, and substantially higher morbidity among non-whites than among whites from nearly all other major preventable diseases. (The mortality rate for black infants born in central Boston, a city known worldwide as a center of high-technology medicine, is three times that of white babies and, at 24 deaths per 1,000 live births, more than double the officially reported IMR of Jamaica.) Poverty is becoming 'feminized' as women head a growing proportion of households but earn only 65 per cent of the average male wage. Alienation and non-participation characterize the political process in the United States; the majority of the eligible electorate does not vote and only the wealthy or corrupt can afford to run for public offices of more than minor importance.

As farming worldwide is subsumed by agribusiness and agribusiness is increasingly international, farmers in the North and South are pitted against each other. All are under pressure to grow more, more quickly, for lower prices, and by methods that boost short-term productivity by depleting or poisoning soil and water resources. Farmers and others displaced from the Caribbean and other regions of the South by these trends, and by the broader economic crisis, flee to the North in search of means of survival. There they find themselves in competition with the unemployed for scarce and low-paying jobs.

Communities are disrupted and families strewn about the globe. Unable to envision an alternative or to bring about real change, many are entrapped in the pursuit of material symbols of pleasure and success promoted worldwide by the electronic media. Torn or alienated from our cultural roots and from the land which gives us life, we take refuge in the fantasy world of consumerism. But increasingly in the North, as in the South, what we consume or desire to consume has less and less relation to our own productive abilities or to the availability or existence of the resources necessary to fulfill our imagined desires. The lifestyles and patterns of consumption to which many aspire are so wasteful of resources and destructive of the environment that they cannot long be sustained even among the upper strata in the North, much less be reproduced in the South.

The failings of the formal institutions of representative democracy to cope with this crisis are glaringly apparent. The great majority of people, in the North as well as in the South, are effectively excluded from access to true information and from power or participation in the processes of decision-making that determine the conditions of their lives.

In this setting, change-oriented NGOs in the North and the South have the basis for a common agenda. A thoughtful participant in this process is Jean Christie, director of a Canadian NGO, InterPares. Among InterPares and its Canadian and Caribbean partner NGOs, says Christie:

> We are thinking beyond the aid relationship, to understanding the basis of interaction between people in our countries, and what people who have the capacity to influence governments at both ends should be doing to change those relationships. We are moving toward action on policy questions beyond aid, such as debt, trade, tourism, and migration.
>
> Yes, we can transfer responsibility for how money is spent over to Southern NGOs, but our relationship has to become a more profound one, based on a common analysis and common purpose. We are beginning to strategize together about how to dismantle the unequal, unjust, and exploitative structures that exist between our societies and within our societies, and how specifically we can put our resources to work on each side to do that.[3]

CARIPEDA coordinator Dr Adrian Fraser comments on this process from a Caribbean perspective:

> Although funding remains the bottom line at this stage, we are attempting to grow beyond a funding relationship with Northern NGOs, to develop confidence and trust in each other, and to develop structures that allow for real input. Some of the issues are practical ones of reporting and evaluation, and improving the information flow from agency to agency.
>
> Northern NGOs have to play more of a role in influencing policies in their countries; whatever happens in Washington and Wall Street affects us. We in the South have a role in feeding information and views on the impact of those policies, and not only on the impact on ourselves. Now Canada is going through a sort of structural adjustment, and we have been able to explain some of the symptoms and the impacts to be expected as a result of this adjustment on people in the North.[4]

As Caribbean NGOs themselves point out, there is as yet no consensus in the Caribbean or in any one nation about the details of a new development model for the region. There is, however, widespread agreement about the essential elements of a development alternative. Among the most important are:

Cooperation. No one Caribbean nation can achieve genuine development on its own. Planning and coordination within the Caribbean and among Caribbean countries and their Latin America neighbors is crucial. Equally important is cooperation and exchange, on a basis of greater equality than now exists, between Caribbean countries and their industrialized neighbors to the North.

Equality. Real progress requires greater equality in the distribution of land, wealth and power in Caribbean countries. Also essential are secure access to the physical necessities of life, relevant education, and time necessary for nurturing and for creative, social and spiritual life. Only in this context can the full productive and creative capabilities of Caribbean nations and individuals be realized.

Sustainability. Development success cannot be measured in the short term. Realistic criteria must take into account the needs of future as well as present generations, and the long-term health and life-sustaining capacity of lands, waters and the whole of the natural environment.

Democracy. If democracy is to reflect its definition as 'government by the people', its image and institutions must be reconstructed from the bottom up. Only through such a process can the majority of people, and not just local élites and foreign interests, participate effectively and constructively in the decisions that affect their lives and in shaping the destinies of their nations.

As Caribbean people and organizations continue to pursue these goals, people in the rest of the world, South and North, will have a great deal to learn from them.

Notes

1. The Arawak people nearly all died or were killed. The majority of the Carib (Karifuna) populations of the Eastern Caribbean were killed by war and disease or chose to take their own lives. Hundreds were taken by the British to the Atlantic Coast of Central America, where their descendants survive. Small populations of Carib and part-Carib people still live in St Vincent and in Dominica, where they hold land in common in a partially self-governing territory.
2. The 1989 *World Debt Tables*, published by the World Bank, report that debtor nations, most of them in Asia, Africa and Latin America but including five Eastern European countries, paid US$105.108 billion in debt service in 1987. The Bank's 1989 *World Development Report* gives a figure of US$41.531 billion as its estimate of the total official development assistance provided that year by the member nations of the Organization for Economic Cooperation and Development, which includes most Northern donor countries, to all nations.
3. Author interview, August 1990.
4. Ibid.

Index

About South End Press

South End Press is a nonprofit, collectively run book publisher with over 150 titles in print. Since our founding in 1977, we have tried to meet the needs of readers who are exploring, or are already committed to, the politics of radical social change.

Our goal is to publish books that encourage critical thinking and constructive action on the key political, cultural, social, economic, and ecological issues shaping life in the United States and in the world. In this way, we hope to give expression to a wide diversity of democratic social movements and to provide an alternative to the products of corporate publishing.

If you would like a free catalog of South End Press books or information about our membership program—which offers two free books and a 40% discount on all titles—please write us at South End Press, 116 Saint Botolph Street, Boston, MA 02115.

Other titles of interest from South End Press:

The U.S. Invasion of Panama: The Truth Behind
'Operation Just Cause'
Prepared by the Independent Commission of Inquiry on the U.S. Invasion of Panama

Freedom Under Fire: U.S. Civil Liberties in Times of War
Michael Linfield, with an introduction by Ramsey Clark

Walking to the Edge: Essays of Resistance
Margaret Randall

The Praetorian Guard: The U.S. in the
New International Security State
John Stockwell

The Caribbean: Survival, Struggle and Sovereignty
Catherine Sunshine